Israel–Palestine

Israel–Palestine
Federation or Apartheid?

SHLOMO SAND

Translated by Robin Mackay

polity

Originally published in Hebrew by Resling. This translation is based
on the French edition, published as *Deux peuples pour un État ?
Relire l'histoire du sionisme* by Éditions du Seuil in 2024.

Two poems by Mahmoud Darwish reproduced with kind permission of the
Mahmoud Darwish Foundation.

Polity Press
65 Bridge Street
Cambridge CB2 1UR, UK

Polity Press
111 River Street
Hoboken, NJ 07030, USA

ISBN-13: 978-1-5095-6439-2 – hardback
ISBN-13: 978-1-5095-6440-8 – paperback

A catalogue record for this book is available from the British Library.

Library of Congress Control Number: 2024933986

Typeset in 11 on 14pt Warnock Pro
by Cheshire Typesetting Ltd, Cuddington, Cheshire
Printed and bound in Great Britain by CPI Group (UK) Ltd, Croydon

The publisher has used its best endeavours to ensure that the URLs for external
websites referred to in this book are correct and active at the time of going to press.
However, the publisher has no responsibility for the websites and can make no
guarantee that a site will remain live or that the content is or will remain appropriate.

Every effort has been made to trace all copyright holders, but if any have been
overlooked the publisher will be pleased to include any necessary credits in any
subsequent reprint or edition.

For further information on Polity, visit our website:
politybooks.com

Contents

Preface

There is an apartheid state here. In a territory where two people are judged under two legal systems, that is an apartheid state.

Tamir Pardo, former head of Mossad
(the Israeli intelligence service), interview with
Associated Press, 6 September 2023[1]

Towards the end of 1967, shortly after returning from combat in Jerusalem, I became a political activist. From that point on I began to write 'Down with the occupation' on the walls of Tel Aviv. Since then and until quite recently – in other words, for half a century – I remained stubborn in my support for the idea of creating a Palestinian state alongside Israel, within the 1967 borders. The right to self-determination for the two peoples that, over the course of a most painful and violent process, have become established between the sea and the river Jordan – this has been my guiding principle. As a soldier and as a citizen, I had to apply my anticolonialist ideas in my everyday life: just as I had fought for Israel to become a state for all Israeli citizens (and not the state of all Jewish people in the world, who, as is known, don't live there), I have also wished wholeheartedly for the creation of an independent Palestinian republic alongside it.

With the passing years, Israel has continued to consolidate its hold on the occupied territories. Thousands of Israelis have set up home close to indigenous villages and Palestinian towns. They have acquired a great deal of land at low prices, and this has become the property of the new settlers, for whom a whole network of roads are exclusively reserved. Severe oppression and denial of the basic rights of the local population have engendered violent resistance, which in turn has fuelled ever harsher repression.

The outbreak in 1987 of the first Intifada, which led to the 1993 Oslo Accords, inspired new hopes for a potential end to the conflict. Many believed that Prime Minister Yitzhak Rabin would evacuate the settlements and return Israel to the 1967 borders, but the profound inequality of power between the two sides prevented them from reaching any sincere and balanced agreement; violence flared up again, while colonisation continued to expand.

The left-wing camp to which I had pledged allegiance continued to call for the evacuation of all territories occupied in 1967, hoping that the Israelis would see that, logically speaking, they simply could not expand their country at the expense of others while continuing to live in peace with them. We penned numerous articles, organised hundreds of demonstrations, and spoke at many meetings and public gatherings. None of it worked! The demographic balance has shifted; the Israeli presence in the West Bank – particularly in the vast belt around Al-Quds, which is officially annexed to Israel – was rapidly boosted by 875,000 new settlers. Four of the ministers of the actual government live in West Bank settlements, as do a number of senior state officials (the chief of the general staff, for example). In parallel, budget allocations to settlers have soared to unprecedented heights.

In 2023 there were mass protests against the new government's arbitrary antiliberal measures, but the protestors made no mention of Israel's presence in the occupied territories. Public calls to defend Israeli democracy have passed over in silence the fact that, for fifty-six years, millions of Palestinians have been living under a military regime, being deprived of civil, legal, and political rights. Worse still, Palestinians under occupation have to live side by side with colonisers in what is becoming ever more obviously an apartheid system. They are forbidden to live in the settlements; they are allowed only to work in them. They are forbidden to marry Jews and cannot apply for Israeli citizenship. Many Palestinian workers cross the old borders every day, to come and work in poor conditions in the Israeli economy, and must return to their homes before nightfall.

And then 7 October came upon Israel, with Hamas's brutal attack on areas next to Gaza. This horrible massacre bears certain similarities to the 1982 Sabra and Shatila massacre, which was carried out by Christian Phalangists while the Israeli Defence Forces under Ariel Sharon stood by, allowing the attack to take place. It was the same Ariel Sharon who, later, in 2005, evacuated the Gaza Strip and contributed to Hamas's rise to power, further exacerbating the discord within the Palestinian leadership.

The events of 7 October came as an utter shock to the Israeli public. True, Gaza was under siege and the quality of life remained insufferable, but the Israeli settlements were now long gone, uprooted by Sharon. In addition, unlike the West Bank, Gaza lacked the oppressive presence of a foreign army. So what was the source of this raging hatred that translated into such terrible war crimes?

It was convenient for many Israelis to explain the massacre in terms of the traditional hatred of Islam towards Jews, thus ignoring the long history of Muslim–Jewish relations since the Crusades and Salah ad-Din. Others rushed to argue that Jews anywhere in the world have always been and will always be hated for no reason, and that 7 October was some kind of an encapsulated Holocaust.

In 1956 Moshe Dayan, an Israeli chief of staff at the time, eulogised a fallen Israeli soldier who had been cruelly murdered by insurgents from Gaza. He said: 'Let us not cast the blame on the murderers today. Why should we declare their burning hatred for us? For eight years they have been sitting in the refugee camps in Gaza, and before their eyes we have been transforming the lands and the villages, where they and their fathers dwelt, into our estate.'² Not many Israeli leaders have dared to speak in such a manner.

Ahmed Yassin, the founder and spiritual leader of Hamas, was born in 1936 in Al-Jura, a village that once stood where the Israeli city of Ashkelon now stands. After his parents were expelled to Gaza in 1950, he grew up in Al-Shati, a refugee camp. Ismail Haniyeh, the head of Hamas's political bureau on 7 October, was born in the same camp in 1963. His parents were also expelled from Al-Jura – in 1950, after the place was emptied and then annexed to Ashkelon. Yahya Sinwar, the military leader of Hamas on 7 October, was born in 1962 in the Khan Yunis refugee camp. In 1950 his parents were expelled from Al-Majdal, which later became part of Ashkelon as well. These leaders' stories are not uncommon, nor are the stories of other leaders. More than 60 per cent of Gaza's current population of 2 million consists of descendants of refugees who were driven from their land and homes after 1948 and have lived in the camps ever since.

The 7 October massacre was in some ways an indirect repercussion of the Nakba, which occurred seventy-five years ago. The origins of the Palestinians' hatred and of the long, heart-breaking conflict lie in 1948 even more than in the occupation of 1967. Given these circumstances, can an exclusively Jewish state in the Middle East have any secure future? The only answer given by the Israeli government in response to the devastating blow was a war of revenge, without any clear political objectives and arguably just as cruel as the October 7 attack. A solution to the bloody conflict seems further away than ever.

At the time of writing this preface, the immediate consequences of the latest catastrophe are still unknown to me. The animosity between the two groups has only increased, and the occupation of the Palestinian people remains entrenched and unyielding. Meanwhile the world pays lip service to the idea that, at some point in the future, a Palestinian state may be recognised. What remains of the Israeli left continues to chant the hollow mantra 'two states for two peoples', with no real intention of making it happen. The Palestinian Authority, totally dependent upon Israeli power and without any real popular support, echoes the tragicomedy of these empty formulas and collaborates in this unbearable situation, while knowing perfectly well that Israel has no intention of recognising real Palestinian sovereignty.

It is this situation, in which hollow, abstract political discourse rubs shoulders with the reality of a binational situation, that prompted me to write this essay. I began writing it with a great deal of scepticism as to the possibility of ever seeing an egalitarian Israeli–Palestinian federation come about, and I am still wrestling with a great many theoretical doubts. My excursion into the dark corners of Zionism's ideological past did, however, present me with some surprises. When I began writing, I had no idea that the great thinkers of the pacifist currents in Zionism, and those who came into close contact with them, had rejected the notion of an exclusive Jewish state in a land predominantly populated by Arabs and had instead supported moves to construct a binational political entity. Across generations, from Ahad Ha'am, one of the founders of spiritual Zionism at the end of the nineteenth century, through Gershom Scholem, Martin Buber, and Hannah Arendt, to the famous writer A.B. Yehoshua, the intellectual elite worried

that the future of a little Jewish Sparta at war with a hostile
Middle East was by no means secure. They believed that only
egalitarian integration within the framework of a common
state would ensure that Israel becomes a safe haven for all of
its inhabitants.

I am highly sceptical as to whether what is in actuality a
binational existence can be embodied in a federal entity of the
same type as Switzerland, Belgium, Canada, or other similar
states. Recent developments and the growing symbiosis, on
both sides, between religion and radical nationalism are hardly
conducive to the emergence of compromise and political integration. It seems that the region is condemned to undergo a
number of catastrophes before reason, equality, and justice
find some way to take root in it. But, as Theodor Herzl, the
founder of the Zionist idea, once said, 'if you will it, it is no
dream'.

1

'Land of the Ancestors' or
Land of the Indigenous People

Identity is what we bequeath, not what we inherit, what we
invent, not what we remember.

Mahmoud Darwish, 'You, from now on, Are Not Yourself'[1]

People write on the gate of their house,
'No entry to strangers',
yet they themselves are strangers within it.

Yehuda Amichai, 'Four Resurrections on
Emek Rephaim Street'[2]

Vladimir Jabotinsky is remembered in the historio-
graphical and political tradition as the founding father
of the Zionist right. An original and uncompromising thinker, he never gave an inch to his many opponents in
the Jewish national movement. In 1923 he wrote (in Russian)
the essay 'The Iron Wall', which to this day is considered the
principal summary of his position on Palestine. Unlike most
Zionist leaders, who often hailed from the left, Jabotinsky
always refused to wrap his words in sanctimonious, hypocritical language. In his view, the arrival of Jews in Palestine
quite clearly announced a colonial undertaking, indisputably

comparable to other colonisations in history. 'My readers have a general idea of the history of colonisation in other countries', he writes. 'I suggest that they consider all the precedents with which they are acquainted, and see whether there is one solitary instance of any colonisation being carried on with the consent of the native population. There is no such precedent.'[3] By the admission of this future leader of the nationalist right, the Zionists were no different from the Spanish conquistadors of South America or the Puritan settlers in the North. Just as in other places natives fought with all their might against foreigners coming to colonise their lands, it is quite logical for the Arabs of Palestine to oppose foreign Zionist colonisation, and this opposition could be expected to continue.

For Jabotinsky, though, this did not mean that Zionism was immoral. In a follow-up article, he set out an argument that he saw as being decisive: from Morocco to Mesopotamia, the Arabs had vast areas of land at their disposal, whereas the Jews had not even the slightest of territories.

> The soil does not belong to those who possess land in excess but to those who do not possess any. It is an act of simple justice to alienate part of their land from those nations who are numbered among the great landowners of the world, in order to provide a place of refuge for a homeless, wandering people. And if such a big landowning nation resists, which is perfectly natural – it must be made to comply by compulsion.[4]

But Jabotinsky says quite explicitly that this in no way implies expulsion of the local residents: 'I consider it utterly impossible to eject the Arabs from Palestine.' Two peoples will live in Palestine, he proposes, but the wandering people will have to secure a position of military superiority – an 'iron wall' – in order to gain the upper hand over the indigenous people, which refuses to welcome the wanderers onto its territory.

Most Zionists were well aware that the Christian evangelical slogan 'Palestine is a land without a people for a people without a land' brandished by Israel Zangwill at the beginning of the twentieth century was erroneous and misleading. No less significant is the fact that, in his founding text, Jabotinsky did not appeal to 'historical rights' in order to claim the land, nor did he assert that it did not belong to the indigenous Arabs. In 1923 many educated Zionists knew full well that there had been no mass exodus of the local population in antiquity, not even a significant wave of emigration. The dominance of the age-old Christian belief in the exile of the people–race that had been cursed for having participated in the crucifixion of Jesus nonetheless left its mark upon a Jewish faith that, riddled with shame, came to see itself as condemned to exile (metaphysical rather than geographical) while awaiting the coming of the messiah. It should also be borne in mind that, throughout their long and painful religious history, Jews did not read the heroic, earthly Bible but the Talmud, a book about law that is not linked to any particular time or place and distances itself from the use of force.

From Israel Belkind, one of the very first to arrive in Palestine, in 1882, to David Ben-Gurion, who founded the State of Israel in 1948, there were many who thought it likely that the local peasants were descendants of ancient Hebrews, which would have made it absolutely unacceptable to deny their presence or to uproot them. Belkind was convinced throughout his life that the indigenous people of Palestine constituted 'a significant section of our people [. . .] bone of our bone and flesh of our flesh'.[5] As early as 1918, Ben-Gurion and Yitzhak Ben-Zvi, the future president of the State of Israel, strongly insisted:

> the peasants are not descended from the Arab invaders who conquered the Land of Israel (Eretz Israel) and Syria in the seventh century. The victorious Arabs did not exterminate the

rural population they found there. They only drove out the foreign Byzantine rulers; they did not attack the local population.[6]

The Ancestral Homeland

As we know, Jabotinsky's principal claim – 'I have no other country' – was not in itself sufficient to morally justify Zionist colonisation and its iron wall. Hence the increasing appeal to the myth of exile and return to 'the land of the ancestors' after two thousand years of wandering – until it became secular Zionist dogma, presented as authentic historical truth.

In the first half of the twentieth century nationalism was still at its height all across Europe. The Germans were convinced that they were the descendants of Teutonic tribes, just as the French were convinced that their ancestors were the Gauls who had fought against Julius Caesar's Roman legions, whose direct heirs the Italians believed themselves to be. The forming of a national consciousness has always involved the need for an 'origin' and a great deal of 'history'. So there is nothing exceptional about Zionists' ability to imagine a lengthy genealogy for themselves. They set about constructing a land of the ancestors on the basis of Bible stories transformed into historical facts, which would then become a compulsory subject taught in all Israeli schools. Academic historiography and archaeology were summoned to sculpt a consistent 'scientific' past out of snippets of legend, bits of ruins, and rocks that were not always identified. The journey from the exodus from Egypt in the second millennium BC to the return of the people to the land of its ancestors and the creation of the State of Israel in the twentieth century completed a mythological circle designed to establish the quasi-eternal existence of a specific and extraordinary Jewish nation that, from time immemorial right up to the present day, has been guaranteed, by divine edict, the right to settle the entire expanse of land between the sea and the river Jordan, and even beyond.

The French of today know full well that they are not really descendants of Gauls; the same goes for Italians vis-à-vis ancient Romans. Most Germans will cringe if you remind them that their forebears thought of themselves as Aryans. Fortunately for them, Americans have been less preoccupied with such biological dilemmas (so long as the skin is white, of course). But the majority of Israeli Jews who have chosen not to pay attention to the historical existence of at least five Judaised kingdoms outside the land of Canaan continue to hold on to the dogma of their common origin, and are even willing to fund DNA research designed to prove that they have a genetic link with King Solomon and his thousand wives. (Moreover, many Jews from Ethiopia are convinced that they are the descendants of the liaison between this same polygamous king and the beautiful Queen of Sheba, who later returned to Africa.)[7]

From the outset, colonisation was justified through arguments based on existential distress, discrimination, and historical rights to a land supposedly given to the chosen people (if not the accursed people). This idea of an imaginary ownership was favourably received in the western Christian world, which did a great deal to promote it, not least because it seemed to promise a reduction in the Jewish presence in Europe. Lord Balfour, who had little sympathy for Jews, banked on the fact that his November 1917 Declaration would on the one hand consolidate British hegemony in the Middle East and, on the other, make it possible to divert to Palestine some of the Jewish masses that had come knocking on England's door.

Contrary to what Zionist historiography teaches, the national myth under construction was not convincing to the majority of Jews and their descendants. Religious leaders, both Orthodox and Reform, were well aware that a collective influx to the Holy Land contradicted their principles of hope in the coming of the messiah. In their view, beyond the nationalism en vogue, 'the homeland' referred to the Scriptures, not to a physical piece of land.[8] As for laypeople, what they sought was a haven of tranquillity and security, far from the harsh realities of Eastern Europe. The hearts of distressed Jewish emigrants from those regions did not yearn for Zion: up until 1924, more than two million Jews had emigrated to the United States, while between 1882 and 1924 only around 65,000 landed in Palestine. Most of the latter were young nationalist idealists who, like Naftali Herz Imber – the author of 'Hatikvah' ('Hope' in Hebrew), the song that became the national anthem of the State of Israel – failed to put down roots in the East and soon joined the flow of westward immigration instead.

New restrictions on North American immigration along racial lines, restrictions aimed specifically at non-whites and non-Protestants, hit Jewish refugees from Central and Eastern Europe hard (were it not for this drastic limit on immigration, almost a million Jews might have escaped Nazi extermination). Between 1924 and 1936, in other words beginning with the American racial immigration laws and after the adoption of the racist Nuremberg Laws, almost a quarter of a million more Jews arrived in Palestine. More than 600,000 were present in 1948, when the State of Israel was created, most of them being Second World War refugees and survivors who had been refused asylum in western states. At that time, the Arab population of Palestine stood at 1.25 million.[9]

Jabotinsky knew perfectly well that the encounter between the Jewish settlers and the indigenous population could not possibly proceed calmly and peacefully. The former's acquisition of land sold by *effendis* (elite property owners) and the consequent expulsion of the *fellahin* (peasants) who had cultivated it for generations, along with a growing Jewish presence in the towns, aroused resentment and anger in the local population. Clashes occurred in Jerusalem as early as 1920, and then even more violently in Jaffa in 1921, where the death toll was forty-eight Arabs and forty-seven Jews. Deadly clashes with a religious dimension then took place in Hebron in 1929, where 133 Jews and 116 Arabs were killed. The year 1936 saw the outbreak of the great Arab Revolt – a revolt against British rule, but also against Jewish settlements. It lasted until 1939: almost five thousand Arabs, four hundred Jews, and two hundred British lost their lives. It was to mark the beginning of an ongoing confrontation that, despite periods of truce, continues to this day. Although it began as a clash between colonists and the indigenous people, the conflict subsequently took many other dimensions.

Gradually, in parallel with the imaginary, retrospective construction of a quasi-eternal Jewish people, the Jewish national movement succeeded in effectively founding an Israeli Jewish people – or a Hebrew people, according to the terminology in use before the founding of the State of Israel. Zionism developed an original local culture. The ancient Hebrew language, which Jews had not spoken for centuries, was revived, becoming both a vernacular and a poetic language. Zionism also founded municipal and national institutions, as well as a paramilitary force. It exploited the inspiring socialist myth, which it skilfully channelled into the national needs of colonisation. Within a short space of time, the pioneer immigrants had succeeded in laying the foundations of a new nation in the making, diverse but riven by antagonism and inequality – a nation that increasingly commanded a sense of patriotism.

Among the Arab population of Palestine, the emergence of a national consciousness took place more slowly. In my view, we cannot speak of a Palestinian nation in the full sense of the term, or even of a Palestinian people, before the 1950s. This, of course, should in no way diminish our moral judgement of the harm done to the local population, from expulsion from their land to mass expulsion from the country. The peasant's ties to the soil are certainly different from those of the patriot to the homeland, but they are no less intense. In order to fully understand the nature of the conflict, however, and the factors behind the success of Zionist colonisation, it is important, very obviously, to take into account the support provided by British colonialism and the fact that a specific, organised Palestinian nationalism emerged relatively late. With due caveats, it may be said that it came into being only after the Nakba – in Arabic, 'the Catastrophe', with reference to the forced exodus of 1948 – and it subsequently developed in decisive phases, in response to traumatic political situations such as the alienating dispersal into neighbouring Arab countries.[10]

Many Palestinian historians claim that a Palestinian people existed long before biblical times, and all the more – 'with scientific certainty' – before the beginning of the Zionist colonisation at the end of the nineteenth century. However, it is doubtful that the ploughman in Galilee thought of himself as a 'Palestinian' and would thereby have felt more solidarity with a farmer from near Jerusalem than with an Arabic-speaking peasant closer to him, in southern Lebanon. The same is true of other parts of the world: whether we look at colonists in North America or French who settle in Algeria, initial opposition to the colonisers is not nationalist in nature.

Let us recall that, throughout the period of the British Mandate (1920–48), all inhabitants and institutions in the United Kingdom called Arabs and Jews alike 'Palestinians'. The Jewish Agency bank was called the Anglo-Palestinian Bank, and the Tel Aviv philharmonic orchestra was known as the Palestine Symphony Orchestra. Jewish and Arab volunteers in the Spanish Civil War and in the British armed forces during the Second World War were called 'Palestinians'. One of the Arab newspapers published in Jaffa was called *Falastin*, but the English-language Zionist organ also went by the name of *The Palestine Post*.

It is quite natural, therefore, that, in the initial expressions of their nationalism, the nascent intellectual elites in Palestine in the first half of the twentieth century advertised themselves as

'Arab' rather than 'Palestinian'. The dominant discourse among these elites, and indeed among Zionists, placed the emphasis on the term 'Arab people'. In 1920, the Arab Executive Committee was founded to represent the Arabs of Palestine vis-à-vis the British, alongside the Supreme Muslim Council. The year 1936 saw the establishing of the High Arab Committee, which would lead the great revolt; the Independence Party (Istiqlal), a pan-Arab organisation, had been founded just shortly before.

Taqi a-Din al-Nabhani, a Muslim preacher from Jerusalem, was quite right when, in the early 1950s, he noted that the country's Arab inhabitants had 'adopted the name Palestine (and its derivatives) and use it as an Arab name, but refused to make it a designation of a distinct national identity or citizenship. When an Arab said he was "Palestinian", this was a mark of his bond to the country in which he lived; just as someone might say that they are "Damascene" or "Beiruti": in other words, it did not imply the existence of Palestinian citizenship or nationality in the same sense that, for example, "English" or "French" would imply.'[11]

Perhaps this absence of a specific Palestinian national consciousness explains, among other things, the weak mobilisation of the local population during the 1948 conflicts, as well as the absence of political movements for the creation of a Palestinian state in the territories that remained unconquered by Israel after the war and were annexed without resistance to the kingdoms of Jordan and Egypt.

Moreover, during the 1950s and up until the mid-1960s, the non-Zionist Israeli Communist Party commonly used the term 'Israeli Arabs'. The energetic nationalist movement El Ard ('The Land'), founded in Nazareth in 1958, initially rejected the idea of a specific Palestinian identity. In 1964, the year that saw the founding of the Palestine Liberation Organization (PLO), the first movement to seriously and systematically promote and disseminate a Palestinian national consciousness, the poet Mahmoud Darwish wrote 'Identity Card', a poem of national anger and protest against Israeli oppression, which opens with the exclamation 'I am an Arab'. This identification is hammered home in every verse of the poem, but without making any reference to a Palestinian identity.

From Hellenistic historiography onwards, the place has been known as *Palaestina* everywhere but in the Jewish religious tradition, of course. This name was incorporated into the Arabic language as early as the seventh century, but residents in the area who had farmed there for centuries had a recognised identity not as 'Palestinians' but as local Arabs, who in all probability were descendants of Jews who had converted to Christianity or Islam.

With the exception of Egypt, the formation of specific nations in the Middle East within the framework of the arbitrary borders drawn by colonialism was relatively slow and occurred later than many researchers tend to assume. This should come as no surprise: contrary to what traditional historiography teaches, it is not peoples that found states; on the contrary, it is states or national movements that create and shape peoples.

On the Nation

We have mentioned the terms 'nation' and 'nationalism', so it is worth pausing to briefly clarify their use in this book, whose aim is to reflect on ideas of binationalism. There is a great deal of confusion around central concepts in political history such as 'liberalism', 'democracy', and 'socialism'; and the same is true of 'nationalism'. Many historians continue to regard premodern monarchies and principalities as national entities – as if the England of King Edward I ('Longshanks') in the thirteenth century, or the France reigned over by Philip the Fair during the same period, were societies with a common national identity. These same historians like to present premodern revolts with a tribal or religious background as national insurrections. So Vercingetorix was a 'French' rebel, just as the Teutonic Arminius was 'German'. As for Judas Maccabaeus and Bar Kokhba, it goes without saying that they were heroes of the ancestral Jewish 'nation' – and so on and so forth . . . But in premodern societies – where the absolute majority of the population could neither read nor write, where there were no schools or printed books, where the peasantry spoke a different dialect in each region, and where the educated elite was extremely small, under the rule of feudal lords, and generally very religious – it is astonishingly lazy to speak of a national consciousness.

About forty years ago, for a variety of reasons, a number of researchers in history put forward the thesis that nations did not begin to form until the end of the eighteenth century. Major changes took place at that time: changes in the organisation and distribution of work; evolution in the modes of production and urbanisation, which required the development and extension of means of communication, given especially the spread of the printing press; creation of education systems that gradually opened up to the whole population . . . All of this, along with the advent of the principles of political equality and the idea of democracy, had the effect of transforming ancient monarchies into nation states in which the dominant collective consciousness ceased to be religious, traditional, local, or regional, gradually giving way to a national identity that would soon establish itself as hegemonic. Without embarking upon a detailed analysis here, let us simply put forward the hypothesis that the impact of nationalism stems (among other things) from the idea of democracy and from the democratic mindset. And I don't mean its liberal and pluralist characteristics, which have developed in many western democracies, but the simple populist principle that proclaims that the state belongs to all citizens, who wield sovereignty through their representatives.

In order to realise this vision of national identity and democracy, whether liberal or authoritarian, there had to be a maximal cultural and linguistic consensus between voters and their elected representatives, between citizens and leaders. For citizens to be convinced, almost instinctively, that the apparatus of power reflected their will and was working in favour of their fundamental interests, this apparatus had to speak their language as much as possible, making use of shared cultural expressions – in other words, it had to resemble them closely. It is only by doing so that the state can establish itself as the bedrock of nationalism; for the state is meant to ensure the security of the existence a people in a given territory, in the face of threats and dangers from other sovereign nations, with foreign mentalities and languages. The elected leader must therefore be 'of the people', but also patriotic. And so, whereas in the past the village fields were the peasant's homeland, now the great national homeland begins to appear on maps that hang in every schoolroom, often next to a portrait of the nation's leader.

But national mass culture was not created *ex nihilo*, nor did it emerge fully formed into a vacuum. It drew heavily upon cultures from the premodern past, partial and distorted collective memories, recent dialects, and declining religious beliefs that it kneaded and manipulated and to which it added a collective imaginary past. At the same time, with the help of school systems and state apparatuses, it shaped and sculpted a common memory and language. This process was sometimes relatively smooth, sometimes more like a steamroller (England being a good example of the former, France of the latter). In countries outside Europe, colonial oppression often played a major role in the birth of national cultures, as the struggles for liberation helped to drive the process forward.

After the unification of Italy in 1861, Massimo d'Azeglio, the former Piedmontese minister of foreign affairs, famously said: 'We have made Italy, now we must make Italians.' The process of nationalising the inhabitants of the Italian peninsula made slow progress, apparently only reaching completion with the advent of television after the Second World War. In other countries, on the other hand, the process of creating the nation state came up against various kinds of obstacles: these included strong linguistic traditions and widespread dialects, which in some places were formed on the threshold of modernity and held back the creation of states and of uniform national cultures.

In France, for example, the languages and cultural particularities of Occitania and Brittany were crushed under the steamroller of state centralism, while in Great Britain the Welsh, the Scots, and the Irish retained their premodern integrity, contributing to the existence of a hybrid multinational state. In Switzerland the confederal union of German, French, and Italian speakers has also resulted in a multi-identity state. The same is true of Belgium and Canada, which are considered binational or multinational states to this day. Despite friction and sometimes acute conflicts, these plurinational frameworks have survived and most of the population has accepted the linguistic division and the cultural plurality, taking care to preserve a specific relationship between citizens and their direct representatives in the democratic system.[12]

The dismantling of the premodern monarchies of Central and Eastern Europe gave rise to the creation of new nation states, with parallel multilingual political entities. Czechoslovakia, Yugoslavia, and even the Soviet Union constituted themselves as fragile federations, which struggled to survive under multinational bureaucratic state apparatuses until the communist regimes finally fell. One of the primary reasons for this fragility is that, as Hans Kohn demonstrated as early as the 1940s,[13] the dominant form of nationalism in Central and Eastern Europe has always been an ethnocentric nationalism rather than an inclusive and political one encompassing all citizens. Imaginary origins and 'blood ties' were the essential criteria for new collective identities in this region, in marked contrast to the inclusive civil and political identities that had emerged in western liberal states long since. Just as, in Poland or Hungary, a Jew could not be truly Polish or Hungarian, so a Slovak could not be primarily Czechoslovakian and a Croat did not really identify as a Yugoslav.

For most Britons, Canadians, Swiss, and Belgians, internal tensions, fracture lines, and alienation aside, some kind of common national consciousness has emerged. These nations are not just traditional liberal democracies based on the principle of 'one person, one vote'; they are also concordance democracies, as they not only recognise the civil rights of the individual but also incorporate a legal recognition of the collective rights of their various linguistic and cultural communities.[14]

Ethnocentrism

Zionism was born in regions where ethnic nationalism had flourished. Most of the thinkers, leaders, and activists of Jewish nationalism came from the lands between Vienna and Warsaw, or Odessa and Vilnius. They rejected out of hand the positions of the autonomist Bund party, which supported the formation in Eastern Europe of a Yiddish people with a language and culture that would be specific and open. The Zionists, on the contrary, claimed to speak on behalf of all Jewish believers and their secular descendants, across the whole world. No less significantly, most Zionists adhered not only to ancient Christian dogma but also to modern anti-Semitic discourse, seeing themselves as foreigners in Europe, 'orientals' whose origins in the East made them a 'Semitic race'.

The ethnocentric mindframe of Zionism was to have a considerable impact upon the development of its identity politics. This essentialist and exclusive attitude enabled the Zionist movement to keep Arab peasants on the sidelines rather than integrate them as members of 'socialist' kibbutzes, agricultural cooperatives, or workers' unions, supposedly vehicles of an inclusive and even internationalist ideology. In the future, the full weight of this rigid ethnocentrism would be felt in the prohibitions and discrimination against non-Jews who lived in the State of Israel and in the territories it would go on to conquer. Time and time again, one would invoke the biblical lines: 'Behold, a people who dwells apart / And shall not be reckoned among the nations' (Numbers 23: 9). This policy of ethnic purism has proved to be dominant in establishing relations with 'foreigners', including those who had no choice but to become Israeli citizens.

Surprisingly, however, this particularist ethnic conception contributed to the emergence of currents that were more open toward local Arabs. In reaction to the indifference of the Germans, Poles, Hungarians, and Ukrainians toward them, many Jews, feeling excluded, developed an imaginary sense of identity that was based on origin and race in equal measure, but that led to a strong sense of identification with 'Semites'. As noted earlier, some saw the local Arabs as distant cousins who had remained in the homeland and had not dispersed; others imagined themselves having blood ties to these very 'cousins'.[15]

Among the members of pacifist organisations such as Brit Shalom (the Peace Alliance), Kedmah-Mizraha (Eastward), and Ihud (the Union), alongside a whole lineage of figures that included Arthur Ruppin, Jacob Thon, Rabbi Binyamin, and Martin Buber, there were many who, as well as supporting a binational project and fighting the pompous policies of the Zionist establishment, continued to advocate a racial conception of Israel; this was by no means exceptional at the time. As we shall see later, strange as it may seem, this 'racism' sometimes played a significant role in providing an impetus for coexistence with the indigenous Arabs.

Unlike and in opposition to the arrogant orientalist attitude, which was dominant in Europe in the first half of the twentieth century and was shared by Theodor Herzl, Max Nordau, and Vladimir Jabotinsky, these 'Semitic' pacifists were sure that they could identify a great many spiritual and biological commonalities with the orient and draw from its legacy fruitful elements towards the development of a modern Jewish nationalism. The concept of race, then, fuelled not only the arrogant separatism that has left its mark upon the entire history of the conflict, but also visions of coexistence, integration, and even fusion with the other in the promised land.[16]

Many of those who, up until 1948, aspired to peace and partnership with the Arabs of Palestine, were driven by a desire to come together with them, something that seems astonishing today, in view of the new radical fusion between religion and nationalism on the part of Judaism and Islam alike. This may be linked to the fact that many of these pacifists were devoutly religious, rather than being atheists like Herzl, Jabotinsky and Ben-Gurion. We also know that, up until 1967, the Mizrahi party, which emerged out of the religious faction of the Zionist movement, took a rather moderate and cautious stance on taking possession of the 'Land of Israel' (this national–religious party even supported the plan for a Jewish state in Uganda in 1903). It is even less well known that not only Rabbi Binyamin, a strong supporter of federalism, but also eminent figures from Brit Shalom and Ihud including Hugo Bergmann, Ernst Simon, Martin Buber, and Leon Magnes were motivated by a strong religious ethic, which deeply influenced their liberal and pacifist vision of the world.

Binationalism?

The chapters that follow will show how binational and federative ideas in Palestine were largely the preserve of select, isolated intellectual groups. This is not to say that the central Zionist currents totally rejected binational, multinational, or federalist solutions. For as long as Jewish immigrants were in the minority in Palestine, the movement's leaders continued to tactically formulate various proposals for federative coexistence.[17] Stalling tactics of this kind appear almost constantly in the writings of Vladimir Jabotinsky, Chaim Weizmann, Yitzhak Ben-Zvi, Berl Katznelson, and David Ben-Gurion. They are always subject to a condition sine qua non – the achievement of a dominant Jewish majority as a prerequisite for any solution of statal coexistence – along with a staunch refusal to establish a political structure based on the democratic principle of 'one person, one vote', which would risk impeding Jewish colonisation. The Zionist leadership has engaged in frantic attacks against those who backed out from this consensus.

Ben-Gurion recounts the following anecdote from his past:

> One day I was invited to a meeting of this Brit Shalom; it was nineteen years ago, in 1925. There was a discussion between me and them [. . .] I told them that the Jews would not accept the binational formula, nor would the Arabs, because the main issue was *aliyah* (the 'ascent' of Jews into Palestine). Then they asked what 'binational state' means: does it mean like in Canada? In Canada there are two nations: the British are in the majority, the French in the minority. And they have national equality and the French language, a dominant French culture, but that's only for the French in Canada. They have no right to bring in French people from France or elsewhere. Nor do they claim any such right. Is that the kind of binational state we want?[18]

The question was, of course, purely rhetorical. Like most members of his party, Ben-Gurion had clearly understood that the Zionist colonisation project stood in fundamental contradiction to the idea of a common and egalitarian political structure shared with the indigenous inhabitants.

In 1918, Jabotinsky formulated the idea of a binational government, shared between the Jewish people returning to Eretz Israel (Greater Israel), which includes both banks of the river Jordan, and the local population. Did he sincerely believe that this was a real possibility? A liberal as well as a militarist, right up to the end of his life Jabotinsky supported cultural and linguistic autonomy for the Arabs and spoke out in favour of their equal civil and political rights while stating that he would not be opposed to the emigration of most of them.[19] And in 1925, in a private letter, he admitted: 'I am not a supporter of an Arab–Hebrew federation [...]. We are Europe: not only its disciples, but also the creators of European civilisation. What do we have to do with the "Orient"? In any case, everything Oriental is destined to be forgotten.'[20] Jabotinsky would be faced with quite a problem, however: his precious Enlightenment Europe barbarically expelled him and left him no choice but to emigrate to America or go and live in Palestine with the 'orientals'.

Beyond declarations of sympathy with multinational or binational ideas (and these did not prevent simultaneous discussions of the notion of transferring the local population), what was ultimately chosen was the option of creating a Jewish nation state free to integrate Jews at will, without paying heed to the point of view of the huge Arab population that lived there. Given that the Zionist movement, in all its components, has always sought to establish a Jewish majority, it has not really made a priority of encouraging binational or bicommunal relations based on the equality of the two peoples that had begun to emerge during the process of Zionist colonisation.

The Arab institutions and elites, on the other hand, apart from a few isolated outsiders, totally rejected the binational idea proposed to them by sincere Jewish pacifists. From their point of view, it was illogical to accept the Zionist colonisation they were undergoing as if it were natural or legitimate, or to enter into any negotiation over the right to national self-determination of the immigrant colonists who had just entered the country. It should therefore come as no surprise that, with the exception of communists loyal to Stalin, all these Arab bodies, elites, and leaders rejected the UN resolution of 29 November 1947 on the division of Palestine into two states that in any case did not take their rights sufficiently into account.

This UN resolution stipulated, *de iure* and *de facto*, a sovereign Arab state with a very small minority of Jews on 38 per cent of the territory of Palestine, and a sovereign Jewish state coextensive with 60 per cent of the same territory – but with a 45 per cent Arab minority. In other words, the Jewish state would comprise 598,000 Jews and 497,000 Arabs! (The Arab state, on the other hand, would comprise 725,000 Arabs and 10,000 Jews.) The UN resolution, although guided by the principle of separation, did not succeed in dividing the country between Arabs and Jews. If war had not been declared after the refusal of almost all Arab representatives to accept this arbitrary diktat, it is difficult to imagine what the fate of the Jewish state would have been, since, demographically speaking, despite massive immigration, it would swiftly have become a *de facto* binational state owing to the natural growth of the local population.

The cardinal problem in the *longue durée* history of this land lies in the fact that, despite its will and despite all its efforts, Zionism has never succeeded in establishing an effective separation between the two populations, which have continued to live side by side or, more exactly, one within the other. The 1948 war, which was followed by the expulsion and forced flight of a large proportion of Palestine's Arabs, might have led some to believe that the problem was solved with the creation of an almost homogeneous state of Jewish settlers, but 1967 changed all that. With the immediate annexation of the old city of Jerusalem and the resumption of colonisation throughout the West Bank, the demographic integration of the two populations has only increased, and today seems irreversible. While the idea of binationalism receded after 1948, the reality in which the majority of Palestinians find themselves today is increasingly akin to an apartheid regime and has had the effect of bringing this notion back into the public arena, both in Israel and in the United States, but also – unlike in the distant past – among a growing number of Palestinian intellectuals.

The account that follows will attempt to trace, from the beginning, the course of this idea in the history of Zionism, and also its non-Zionist fringes. I make no secret of my sympathy for the paradigm of a binational state designed to promote civil equality and based on a well-ordered democracy, but I remain highly sceptical of the possibility of seeing it put into practice in the near future. It is well known that the politicians who shape reality tend to opt for a rational and just solution only after having tried, for reasons of convenience and opportunism, all the worse alternatives.

The fact that the binational paradigm was once the aspiration of critical Jewish intellectuals but they never succeeded in bringing it to dominate the political landscape does not diminish its value, particularly in view of today's distressing reality. Although writers and artists cut off from political action tend towards the metaphysical, their analyses can often prove prophetic. The positions taken in favour of binationalism – from Ahad Ha'am to Judah Leon Magnes, according to whom the division of the country and the desire to create an exclusive Jewish state would lead to violent and insoluble conflict in the Middle East – have been proved entirely accurate. Whether the proposed alternatives could be realised is an important but separate issue, and this book will conclude with a critical examination of the possible solutions that are proposed today. Binationalism is not just wishful thinking but also the present reality of the region's inhabitants: today Israelis and

Palestinians live in conditions of flagrant inequality. This situation, in which 7.5 million Jewish Israelis, through a policy of expulsion, displacement, repression, imprisonment, and alienation, dominate a Palestinian–Arab people of 7.5 million, most of whom are deprived of civil rights and basic political freedoms, can only result in continued violence and terrorism. It is clear that such a situation cannot last forever, even if the balance of power has so far allowed it to continue. The dream of separation between the two peoples is dissipating and becoming increasingly unrealistic, and in its place there arises the foreboding of a tragic and brutal future, which infiltrates more and more hearts and minds.

Let us take a retrospective look and revitalise the hopes and dreams that nurtured the greatest minds of those who migrated to this piece of land or were born on it. Even if will alone is not enough to transform legend into reality, perhaps wills can still prevent tragedies.

2

'When a Slave Becomes a King'
A Hidden Question

They walk with the Arabs in hostility and cruelty, unjustly encroaching on them, shamefully beating them for no good reason, and even bragging about what they do, and there is no one to stand in the breach and call a halt to this dangerous and despicable impulse.

Ahad Ha'am, 'Truth from Eretz Israel'[1]

The lament of Arab women on the day that their families left Ja'uni-Rosh Pina to go and settle on the Horan east of the Jordan still rings in my ears today. The men rode on donkeys and the women followed them weeping bitterly, and the valley was filled with their lamentation. As they went they stopped to kiss the stones and the earth.

Yitzhak Epstein, 'A Hidden Question'[2]

Asher Hirsch Ginsberg, whom history remembers by his pseudonym Ahad Ha'am (One of the People), rallied to Zionism in the 1880s. While the Hungarian Theodor Herzl was still dreaming of being a perfect German and was inviting Jewish communities to convert collectively to Christianity, Ahad Ha'am, who was living in Ukraine, then part of the Russian empire, had fallen into deep spiritual distress. He was worried about the future of Jewish culture, which seemed dark and uncertain. Although he grew up in a Hasidic family and studied at a Talmudic school in his youth, he had severed ties with his faith and with traditional religious practices, but was reluctant to renounce what remained of his Jewish identity. In the wake of the violent pogroms that began in 1881, after the assassination of the tsar, and especially in view of the mass emigration of hundreds of thousands of Jews to the West that had begun shortly before, he feared that the drive towards secularisation, or its imposition, would eventually see the disintegration of what remained of the ancestral tradition. Moreover, he understood perfectly well that assimilation into modern culture would not lead to a general humanist universalism, but to absorption into some other concrete nationalism, which, because of the long Christian tradition, would be likely to remain strongly hostile towards Jews for many years to come.

The Lover of Others?

At the time, two great myths fascinated the intellectuals of Europe and fuelled their work: the socialist myth, with its many followers, and the national myth, which had claimed all others. The socialist myth celebrated the oppressed classes, predicting a radiant future for them; the national myth invented and mass-produced eternal peoples and nations. Unlike most intellectuals of Jewish origin, who tended to support Russian social democracy or else had participated in the creation of the large Yiddish political party that was the Bund, Ahad Ha'am chose to join the Lovers of Zion, a small movement that advocated the idea, shared by many young nationalists, of the quasi-eternal existence of a Jewish people. With the publication of the historical writings of Heinrich Graetz at the beginning of

the second half of the nineteenth century and the formalisa-
tion of the erroneous paradigm, borrowed from Christianity,
concerning the exile of the population of Judea, an intense
aspiration was born: to remain Jewish, one had to return to the
ancient homeland, Zion, which is Jerusalem.

The vision of the Jewish people as an 'ethnic', or even
'organic', people was a central theme in Ahad Ha'am's thinking.
Reading his work, it can sometimes be difficult to understand
what it is that he defines as secular Judaism, so intertwined is
it with religiosity. He constantly reverts to essentialist definitions, not far off the concept of a people–race that, through
marriages that were almost always endogamous for religious
reasons, has managed to avoid mixing or assimilating with
others. This fundamentally semi-biological conception, shared
by the majority of early Zionists and their successors, is apparent not only from a careful reading of his writings but also in
his biography: when his daughter Rachel married a Russian
writer of Christian origin, despite his son-in-law's conversion
to Reform Judaism, Ahad Ha'am refused to welcome him as
a member of the family and did not see his daughter or her
husband for almost ten years; he agreed to see his daughter
again only after she was divorced.[3]

What could unite and preserve a people that was disintegrat-
ing and being assimilated, if not opposition to mixed marriage
– a principle that would be rigorously adopted by the future
State of Israel? The answer that Ahad Ha'am contributed has
several aspects to it: the first was the founding of a Jewish
spiritual centre in Ottoman Palestine, the ancestral homeland
of the patriarchs. This spiritual centre would become a place
where an authentic everyday culture could be developed in
order to bring Judaism back to the supreme values communi-
cated in the messages of the prophets. The second aspect was
the revival of the ancient Hebrew language, which, because of
its sacred nature, had not been spoken for nearly 1,700 years.
In fact Ahad Ha'am, who spoke several languages, decided to

express his ideas almost exclusively in Hebrew, in writing. A prolific writer and publicist, he invented a new, refined style of writing, superior to anything that has been written in Hebrew even to this day. For him, the Hebrew language represented a homeland and a common denominator of all those who wished to preserve something of their Jewishness.

Impressed by the indefatigable activity of the Lovers of Zion, Ahad Ha'am continued to follow its pioneers closely. In 1891 he travelled to Palestine on behalf of the organisation, to see the land of dreams for himself. Upon his return, after a journey of eighty-eight days, he published a long essay entitled 'Truth from Eretz Israel', one of the very first accounts of the Zionist 'colonies' (the term that was used by the Zionists themselves at the time). The surprising and sad truth revealed in this text occasioned astonishment among Ahad Ha'am's admirers. It had taken him almost three months to decipher the secrets of the 'colonists' (as he called the pioneers), their modest achievements and their ridiculous failings, but the most severe criticisms he levelled at them concerned their behaviour towards the local population:

> From abroad, we are accustomed to believe that Eretz Israel is presently almost totally desolate, an uncultivated desert, and that anyone wishing to buy land there can come and buy all he wants. But in truth it is not so. In the entire land, it is hard to find tillable land that is not already tilled [. . .]. From abroad we are accustomed to believing that the Arabs are all desert savages, like donkeys, who neither see nor understand what goes on around them. But this is a big mistake. The Arab, like all children of Shem, has a sharp intellect and is very cunning. [. . .]. The Arabs, and especially those in the cities, understand our deeds and our desires in Eretz Israel, but they keep quiet and pretend not to understand, since they do not see our present activities as a threat to their future. [. . .] However, if the time comes when the life of our people in Eretz Israel develops

to the point of encroaching upon the native population, they will not easily yield their place.[4]

According to Ahad Ha'am, this is not an argument for curbing the flow of 'immigration' (he uses the word 'emigration', because *aliyah* has not yet become the obligatory term in Zionist parlance). However, the 'colonists' would have to be aware of the situation and must neither resort to convenient lies nor entertain illusions:

> They feel that the great multitude is not moved by love of Zion, and the plain truth will not suffice to captivate its heart, and thus they allow themselves to lie 'in the name of God' [. . .]. And thus our holy land became a new California.

Ahad Ha'am did not believe that a spiritual centre in Palestine would bring together Jews from all over the world and take them to its bosom. He was of the opinion that the material and economic prospects of the large majority of Jews would be far brighter in America and that they should emigrate there if they wanted to protect themselves against the waves of hostility towards them in Europe. But the vitality of a spiritual centre would serve to revive the moral tradition of Jewish secularism – and the relationship with the indigenous people there would be a mark of the ability to preserve the heritage of the ancient prophets:

> There is certainly one thing we could have learned from our past and present history: how careful we must be not to arouse the anger of other people against ourselves by reprehensible conduct. How much more, then, should we be careful, in our conduct toward a foreign people among whom we live once again, to walk together in love and respect, and needless to say in justice and righteousness. And what do our brethren in Eretz Israel do? Quite the opposite! They were slaves in their

land of exile, and they suddenly find themselves with unlimited freedom, the kind of wild freedom to be found only in a country like Turkey [here meaning the Ottoman empire, including Palestine]. This sudden change has engendered in them an impulse to despotism, as always happens when 'a slave becomes a king'.[5]

A Spiritual Centre?

We now live in a time when very few liberals, or even socialists, bother to take an interest in human rights in countries that have been dominated by colonial powers. Ahad Ha'am appears to have been an intellectual exceptional for his sensibility, and very specific in terms of his national or, to be more precise, 'infra-state' ideas. Unlike political Zionism, which began to take shape in 1897 through the meteoric activity of Theodor Herzl, Ahad Ha'am did not envision the creation of a Jewish nation state, which in his eyes would be no more than a poor cultural imitation of the European nation states of the time. He was disgusted by pompous European nationalisms, so full of supposed spiritual superiority and arrogance towards the rest of the world's peoples. Later he would reject outright the Eurocentric conception explicitly formulated by Herzl in his pamphlet *The Jewish State*, which declared: 'We should there form a portion of a rampart of Europe against Asia, an outpost of civilization as opposed to barbarism. We should as a neutral State remain in contact with all Europe, which would have to guarantee our existence.'[6]

Later, in 1902, Herzl, already a leader of the national movement, published *Altneuland* (*The Old New Land*), a utopian novel in which he described the Zionist colonisation of the country and presented the creation of a Jewish state as a benefit to the local population. In the novel Rashid Bey, an engineer who lives in Haifa and is the spokesman for the Arabs, full of admiration for the generous Zionists who have come to his country, exclaims enthusiastically: 'Would you call a man a robber who takes nothing from you, but brings you something instead? The Jews have enriched us. Why should we be angry with them? They dwell among us like brothers. Why should we not love them?'[7]

Ahad Ha'am's review of Herzl's novel was dripping with sarcasm: first of all, in this imaginary land dreamed up by the thinker of a Zionist state, the language is obviously German, not Hebrew, and in fact there is not the slightest trace of Jewish culture, only a mishmash of pseudo-liberal, artificial reproductions of European cultures – or, in Ahad Ha'am's own ironic words, 'an aping of others, with no national quality of its own'. It was in reality a national project for the collective assimilation of Jews, the individual assimilation of many of them, including Herzl himself, having been partly hampered by anti-Semitism. But it was the hypocrisy of the description of relations between Jews and Arabs in this visionary state that elicited the greatest sarcasm from the 'lover of Zion': 'How beautiful this idyll is! But it is a little hard to understand how the new (Zionist) society has managed to find enough land for the millions of sons of Israel who have returned from exile, if all the soil is still worked by the Arabs, in other words, if they still have most of the good land in Eretz Israel, and nothing has been taken from them.'[8]

Ahad Ha'am abhorred hypocrisy, which for him was something even more morally reprehensible than injustice; he therefore had serious reservations about Herzl's writings and ideas. For Ahad Ha'am, unlike for Herzl, the true homeland was not some strip of land; it was above all secularised Jewish culture, whose ethical standards, carried and reproduced within it, justified its preservation and further development. He had made up his mind early on: 'To our misfortune, we are not a literary people, and yet we are the people of the book [. . .]. But the people of the book is the slave of the book, a people whose soul has blossomed from the heart, and has entirely penetrated into what is written.'⁹ In order to escape the book, a spiritual centre would have to be founded in Eretz Israel on the basis of ancient religious and historical ties; this centre would be the guardian of the ethical image and a guiding light for peoples. In particular, this spiritual home would have to avoid becoming a small territory locked into its system of government and driven by political hostility towards foreigners; such hostility would recall the hideous Judeophobia by which Jews in the advanced countries of Europe were pursued and harassed. According to Ahad Ha'am, if Eretz Israel should not become a refuge for Zionist land speculators, who claim to have arrived in an empty country, neither should it welcome to its bosom all those fanatical believers for whom ancient holy stones are more precious than life itself. At the end of 'Truth from Eretz Israel' he gives a memorably scathing description of the strictly observant Jews who crowd around the stones of the Wailing Wall.

Ahad Ha'am spent his entire life battling against political Zionists and their followers – his polemical exchange with Max Nordau offers striking evidence of how the Zionist idea developed. In 1913 he wrote the following to Moshe Smilansky, a celebrated writer and one of the best-known leaders of the acquisition of land in Palestine:

> The psychology of the Zionist public is understandable [. . .] They do not like to remember, and they get angry at those who remind them, that there is another people in Eretz Israel, who are already established there, and have absolutely no intention of leaving their home. In the future, when this illusion has been uprooted [. . .] everyone will understand the weight and importance of this question, and how much we must work to get as close as possible to a solution.¹⁰

In 1921, before emigrating permanently from London to Mandatory Palestine, Ahad Ha'am published a collection of his

best essays – throughout his life he had never had the patience
to write long works full of complex terminology – and added
a new preface, which may be considered a kind of spiritual
testament.

This came after Lord Balfour's famous Declaration to Lord
Rothschild in which Balfour confirmed British support for the
establishment of a home for the Jewish people in Palestine – a
text that Ahad Ha'am approved of and translated into Hebrew
himself. It also came after the conquest of the region by British
troops. Ahad Ha'am's unrelenting polemicism continues in
the preface; referring to the historical declaration delivered by
the British foreign secretary, he points out that many Zionists
are doing their utmost to distort its meaning. They constantly
present the Declaration as if it said 'the re-establishment of
Palestine as the national home of the Jewish people', which
would mean 'helping to reconstruct Eretz Israel as the national
home of the Jewish people'. Zionist activists and writers, he
insists, are sowing illusions among the Jewish masses, telling
them that 'the end of exile is near, and soon Eretz Israel will be
a Jewish state'. He repeats that this is a vulgar deception, which
will lead to a never-ending historical conflict with the indigenous people. According to Ahad Ha'am, we must learn – and
teach – that the return of a part of the Jewish people to their
ancient homeland does not stand in conflict with the status of
the Arab people who live in their homeland.

According to Ahad Ha'am, the Jews' historical right to their
ancient land in no way invalidates the right of the country's
present-day inhabitants; they have a right too, because they
have lived and worked there for generations. This land is
their collective home, and they have the right to develop their
nationhood according to their capacities and needs. This situation therefore meant that Eretz Israel was a common space
for different peoples, a space in which each should work to
build their national homeland; at the same time, such a situation made it impossible for the 'national homeland' of either

people to be complete and sovereign in the full sense of the term.

> When you build your house on land that is already inhabited, in a place where there are already other houses and other inhabitants, you are the only master up to the door of your house. Inside it, you may arrange your affairs as you wish, but as soon as you go beyond your door, outside, all the inhabitants of the place live in common, and the general direction must be set in accordance with the interests of all. Similarly, in the 'national homelands' of different peoples who live on the same territory, each one is within its rights to claim national freedom, but only for its internal affairs, while the management of the country's affairs must be common for all and conducted by all the 'owners' together, if the relationship between them and their cultural situation allows it – or, if not, by a guardian who will ensure that no one's rights are infringed.[11]

Unlike Herzl, Ahad Ha'am does not speak of the individual rights of an Arab minority in a large sovereign Jewish state that extends over the whole of Eretz Israel. He proposes, quite explicitly, a reconciliatory binational arrangement that would take account of the collective needs of the two populations that live side by side, if not in each other's midst. He constantly emphasises that in fact neither the intervention of the British nor any legal measure could allocate the country exclusively to Jews. Conflicts will inevitably arise between the two peoples; actually they have already begun. This is why, in his view, it is absolutely necessary to appoint a guardian – the British Mandate – as a provisional guarantor that could enable the coexistence of two 'national homelands'. He does not hesitate to remind his readers that, twenty-nine years earlier, during his trip to Eretz Israel, he had foreseen the inevitable conflict that resulted from the blindness of Zionist colonisers towards the original inhabitants of the area.

Ahad Ha'am died in 1927, in Tel Aviv, the new Jewish town adjacent to Jaffa, the largest city in Palestine at the time. Still driven by his vision of coexistence with the natives, although illness and old age slowed him down, he had felt obliged to begin learning Arabic. To do so, he turned to the writings of Maimonides, whom he had always considered to be the greatest of Jewish philosophers. Most of Maimonides's texts were written in Arabic, with Hebrew characters. An inveterate advocate of the 'ethnic' conception of the Jewish people, Ahad Ha'am expressed a secret hope: 'Once we have become, within this land, a cultural force with a Judaic spirit, it is possible that the Arabs will meld with us; after all, they are the ancestral inhabitants of the country, and some of them may be descendants of our people.'[12]

Ignoring the Other

Another of Ahad Ha'am's activities as an intellectual was his founding, in Odessa in 1896, of the prestigious Hebrew-language magazine *Ha-Shiloah*, financed by the wealthy tea-growing Wissotzky family. The editorial board included the poet Hayim Nahman Bialik and the historian Yossef Klausner, and the editors were Yossef Haim Brenner, Shmuel Yossef Agnon, and a number of other well-known writers. In 1907 the magazine published a long article by Yitzhak Epstein entitled 'A Hidden Question'. This text appears to be, to a large extent, in direct continuity with the ideas of Ahad Ha'am, who had been replaced by Bialik as director of the journal.[13]

Epstein was born in 1862 near Minsk, which was a part of the Russian empire. He began his studies at a Talmudic school before graduating with flying colours from a secular secondary school. He applied to university to study agriculture, but was turned down because of the *numerus clausus* imposed on Jews.

He joined the Lovers of Zion and arrived in Palestine in 1886, to work as a farmer – in other words to fertilise the 'virgin' land of Baron Rothschild's colonies. He quickly moved into teaching and became one of the most prominent and gifted revivers of the Hebrew language. Thanks to him, the Hebrew lexicon was enriched with fundamental concepts that are still a structural part of Israeli expression in writing – for example 'sensibility', 'consciousness', 'activity', 'phenomenon'. Working in Rosh Pina and later in Metoula, he acquired a reputation as a charismatic teacher, attracting students from all over the country. He insisted that Arabic should also be taught at his school, and in Metoula he successfully integrated the children of Arab workers in his classes. He himself learnt the local Arabic language from a private teacher and developed the original Hebrew spoken accent for himself, borrowing from the Arabic guttural accent.

There is therefore nothing surprising in the content of Epstein's speech, delivered on the fringes of the Zionist Congress in Basel in 1905 and published two years later, in the form of an essay in *Ha-Shiloah*. The guiding principle is laid down from the outset:

> We pay close attention to all the affairs of our land, we discuss and debate everything, we praise and curse everything, but we forget one small detail: that there is in our beloved land an entire people that has been attached to it for hundreds of years and has never considered leaving it.[14]

Here Epstein adds an insistent comment: 'It may be assumed that a large part of the population is made up of our people and its refugees who assimilated with other peoples during periods of persecution and destruction.'[15]

As indicated in my first chapter, the hypothesis that among the *fellahin* (peasants) there were many descendants of the subjects of the ancient kingdom of Judah, who had not been uprooted from the country, given that there had never been a mass exile, was widespread among many Zionists at the time. In the same year when Epstein gave his speech on the fringes of the Basel Congress, Ber Borochov, a leading theorist of the Zionist left, published a book entitled *The Question of Zion and Territory*, a series of articles in which he developed 'the very likely hypothesis that the peasants in Eretz Israel are the direct descendants of the remnants of the Jewish and Canaanite agricultural community, with a slight mixture of Arab blood; bearing in mind that the proud Arab conquerors scarcely mixed with the mass of the people in the conquered countries'.[16]

This does not mean that Epstein was a Marxist, like Borochov. He saw himself as a spiritual Zionist, a disciple in the image of Ahad Ha'am. However, he did have a fundamentally 'materialist' starting point:

> The time has come to dismiss the discredited idea, spread among Zionists, that there is in Eretz Israel uncultivated land as a result of lack of working hands and the indifference of the inhabitants. There are no empty fields; to the contrary, every *fellah* tries to enlarge his plot from the land of the adjoining cistern [. . .]. And thus, when we come to occupy the land, the question at once arises: what will the *fellahin* do after we buy their fields? We buy the lands, for the most part, from the owners of large estates; these owners, or their predecessors, acquired their land by deceit and exploitation and lease it to the *fellahin*.[17]

Until 1858, in the Ottoman empire, land belonged to a clan (*muşah*), in other words to an entire village community. During the subsequent process of 'modernisation through privatisation', the title to the land passed into the hands of the clan chiefs. Knowing that this process entailed a significant tax obligation, the wealthy landowners (*effendis*) persuaded the poor farmers to hand over official ownership to them. Besides, many of these peasants feared that passing on their names to the authorities would make it compulsory for them to enlist in the Ottoman army. Moreover, the change in formal title had no major impact upon them, since they continued to cultivate their land as before. But the arrival of Zionist settlers changed the situation completely. The rich landowners sold their land at a high price to the new immigrants, while the peasants found themselves obliged to give up what constituted their vital resources.[18]

Epstein gives a detailed account of the deep ties between peasants and their land, and deplores this process of eviction. His point of view is founded on a notion of universal morality, but he does not stop at this: he considers himself more of a realist than most Zionists. His fears, like those expressed by Ahad Ha'am, relate above all to the future of the beloved homeland:

> Will those evicted really hold their peace and calmly accept what was done to them? Will they not in the end rise up to take back with their fists what was taken from them by the power of gold?[19]

According to Epstein, in 1905 the number of Arabs exceeded half a million, while the Jews were fewer than 80,000. This balance of power could lead to a dangerous conflict.

> We must not ignore its rights [. . .]. We must not provoke the sleeping lion! We must not count on the ash that covers the glowing ember; let one spark escape, and the conflagration will be uncontrollable.[20]

Epstein does not counsel the pioneers to leave Eretz Israel because of these dangers, but in the second part of his essay he presents an alternative to the land policy of Zionism:

> We come to our land to take possession of what is not already
> possessed by others, to find what others have not found [. . .].
> Regarding settlement, we will try first of all to acquire all the
> land that is not being cultivated because it requires improve-
> ment that is more or less difficult and expensive.[21]

Intensive agriculture and a developed, modern irrigation
policy, he argues, would open up options for colonisation that
would not affect local farmers severely. Further cultivated land
could also be acquired, provided that the *fellahin* can still work
there – together, shoulder to shoulder with the Jewish settlers
– and that they are not deprived of their vital resources. 'These
two peoples, the Hebrew and the Arab, can supply each other's deficiency, because what we can give to the Arabs they
can get from no other people.' Epstein goes on to emphasise
that,

> while we try to establish our nation, we will also support the
> revival of the inhabitants and will reinforce their national feel-
> ing in the best sense of the term. [. . .] It must be admitted
> that up to now we had the 'wrong address'; in order to acquire
> our land, we turned to all the powers that had some link to it,
> we negotiated with all the in-laws but forgot about the groom
> himself: we ignored the true masters of the land.[22]

Over and above differences in levels of historical development and the fact that the natives lag far behind the material
achievements of the West, the encounter between the two
peoples concerned not only the villages but also the new towns
under construction at the time. Hospitals, schools, kindergar-
tens, libraries, refectories, and leisure facilities, Epstein argued,
must be open to Arab inhabitants not in order to Judaise them,
but in order to secure an alliance with them. Just as Arabs
integrate into the Hebrew language and culture, Jewish immigrants must learn to use the Arab language and culture. In

this way ignorance of the other would give way to in-depth understanding of their experience.

How many Zionists shared this way of thinking at the beginning of the twentieth century? We will never know. Most of the pioneers worked hard as farmers, did not publish articles, and did not give lectures.[23] The fact that half of them left the country to go elsewhere is apparently not to be explained by ideological disagreement with the Zionist enterprise, but rather by hardship and material destitution. Nonetheless, Epstein's position was not entirely marginal.

At the beginning of 1907, Yehoshua Radler-Feldmann, a young intellectual from Galicia, published in Hebrew an article entitled 'The Arab Burden', a kind of original manifesto, brief and biblical in style, in which he called for unity with the Arabs, since the two peoples had racial Semitic and mental traits in common:[24]

> There is no difference or distinction between the Hebrew and the Arab: you have come to revive the land and its inhabitants: you have not come to take from others but to add to them: offer them a share of all the wealth of your spirit: open your school to them, so that their sons and daughters may come, and there they will be taught your language and their language.[25]

Radler-Feldmann, a lifelong believer who observed religious commandments, was aware that there was a greater theological proximity between Judaism and Islam than between Judaism and Christianity. In his view, Muhammad, not Jesus, was to be considered the last of the great prophets. Radler-Feldmann arrived in the country the same year his article was published, and worked as a farm labourer while continuing to write and speak in public; he was preceded by his reputation as an original and impassioned religious thinker. He became close to Arthur Ruppin and began to collaborate with him, despite many disagreements. Soon he would gain notoriety under the peculiar pseudonym Rabbi Binyamin.[26]

It is hardly surprising that these two figures, Epstein and Rabbi Binyamin, joined the Brit Shalom association in 1925 and remained faithful to the idea of binational coexistence throughout their lives. In addition to their fundamental humanism, their ethnocentric conception of nationality predisposed them to wanting to live and integrate with the indigenous population. They saw Arabs and Jews as immanent parts of a great 'Semitic ethnos' that had splintered in the distant past but was destined to unite again in the present. Many members of the organisation Brit Shalom entertained this very same idea.

3

Alliance of Peace
against the 'Iron Wall'

It seems clear to me that the Arabs living in Eretz Israel today
are the descendants of those same Arabs who were in Eretz
Israel two thousand years ago and were then called Jews. The
race has not changed [. . .]. We shall eventually reach some
kind of cultural understanding with the Arabs, one that will be
better than our understanding with Europe.

Arthur Ruppin, speech at the
Jewish Agency Executive, May 1936

Zionist nationalism went the way of most Central and Eastern
European nationalisms. But whatever the present or the future
was to hold, my participation, for almost twenty years, in the
Zionist movement enriched my life in many ways. It gave me a
better understanding of the pitfalls and self-deceptions.

Hans Kohn, *Living in a World Revolution*[1]

The founding in 1925 of the organisation Brit Shalom
(Peace Alliance) and the composition of its member-
ship remain, both, an enigma in the history of Zionism.
Arthur Ruppin was the founder and the chairman; Hans
Kohn was the secretary, while he worked simultaneously as

a propagandist for Keren Hayesod (the Foundation Fund); Radler-Feldmann (Rabbi Binyamin) was the editor of its magazine, *Sheifoteinu* (*Our Aspirations*). These were three personalities with radically different outlooks and motivations.

A wide range of opinions could be found among the other members of the organisation, too. Hugo Bergmann, Gershom Scholem, Shlomo Dov Goitein, Nathan Hofshi, Yitzhak Epstein, Jacob Thon, Haim Margaliot-Kalvarisky, Moshe Smilansky, Mordekhay Avi-Shaul, Siegfried Lehmann, Gerda Luft, Joseph Luria, Samuel Sambursky, David Werner Senator, and the sixty or so other registered members had diverse sensibilities, and sometimes even belonged to different political parties. Some defined themselves as socialists, others leaned towards a liberal economy and rejected all forms of collectivism. But all regarded themselves as Zionists with an ethical stance: one could come to the new land to live with its inhabitants, but certainly not to replace them. Most members of Brit Shalom could also be defined as intellectuals in the full sense of the word who, like the intellectuals involved in the Dreyfus Affair, felt obliged to enter the public arena collectively and noisily in order to prevent an injustice, and indeed a miscarriage of justice.[2]

Some members of the group participated in the founding of the Hebrew University in Jerusalem and were among its first lecturers; others held senior positions in national bodies or worked as journalists and essayists. The public support provided by the philosopher Martin Buber, then living in Germany, by Leon Magnes, founder of the University of Jerusalem, and a little later by Albert Einstein gave the group additional intellectual prestige.[3]

The organisation aimed to create a 'state for two nations, in which two nations live together in a land of complete equality of rights, in the form of two elements which, in equal measure, embody the destiny of the country, regardless of which of the two outnumbers the other' and states in its declaration of intent:

> In Eretz Israel, Brit Shalom strives to create a solid and healthy society for the Jews, which will contain the largest possible number of Jews, regardless of whether or not this means that Jews obtain a majority over the rest of the country's inhabitants, bearing in mind that the question of majority in the country must in no way be linked to any privilege in terms of rights.[4]

The Beginnings of the Alliance

The first meeting of Brit Shalom took place in Arthur Ruppin's spacious home in the Merhavia district of Jerusalem, probably after a lecture given by Josef Horovitz, a renowned orientalist from Frankfurt University who was visiting Palestine at the time. Ruppin, who was immediately elected president of the new association, was a well known public figure and was already described as the 'father of Zionist settlement'. As soon as he arrived in Palestine in 1908, Ruppin had become head of the Palestinian office of the Jewish Agency, and it may be said that, alongside Theodor Herzl and David Ben-Gurion, he was one of the figures who contributed most to the realisation of the Zionist enterprise. Ruppin was instrumental in developing the model of the group, which would soon become the kibbutz; it was also he who acquired the best land in the Jezreel Valley, the Strait of Haifa, the Hula Valley, and many other places besides. Ruppin was among those who contributed to the creation of the Bank Hapoalim (the Workers' Bank), the Mekorot Company, and other economic enterprises that directly or indirectly aided in the conquest of the land.

It is interesting to note that Ruppin adopted as his historical model and guiding example the colonisation carried out in West Prussia, where he was born. This colonisation, which took place in the nineteenth century, during the Second German Reich, with the aim of pushing back the Poles and changing the composition of the local population, was so successful that it served as a model for other colonial ventures. But from 1921 onwards, after thirteen years of energetic activity in Palestine, Ruppin began to exhibit the first signs of the weariness caused by his intensive involvement in colonisation: in his personal diary he expressed a desire to return to his scientific activities. He resigned from his prestigious post in 1924, and after that dedicated himself to research and writing.

As a young man, Ruppin had seen himself as a future intellectual or scientist, not as a politician or national investment entrepreneur. He studied law and obtained a doctorate in economics; he then became interested in eugenics, in other words 'racial hygiene'. In 1903 he published a treatise entitled *Darwinismus und Sozialwissenschaft* (*Darwinism and Social Science*), which won him a prestigious prize. After this he was invited to Berlin to work at the Office of Jewish Statistics. In 1904 he published a book entitled *Die Juden der Gegenwart* (*The Jews of Today*), in which he set out his basic position on Judaism: 'The structure of Judaism, once so solid, is crumbling away before our very eyes. Conversion and intermarriage are weakening Jewish ranks everywhere.'[5] For Ruppin, the real solution – a eugenic solution – lay in the Zionist idea, and particularly in the writings of Max Nordau, Herzl's second-in-command.[6]

Did Ruppin recant his racial determinist approach to Jewish issues when he founded Brit Shalom in 1925? Absolutely not. In fact his contact and continued relationships with people of high culture, members or close sympathisers of Brit Shalom, afforded him the opportunity to resume in earnest his 'scientific' work, which he had missed so much. The fact that the Hebrew University on Mount Scopus was founded in the same year was by no means a coincidence (through his position, in 1914 Ruppin had been able to preempt the land upon which the university was to be built). Nor is it surprising that in 1926, although he was fifty years old and had no serious professional credentials in the field, he obtained a post as a researcher and teacher in 'the sociology of the Jewish people'. We can only guess what this 'sociology' consisted in. Ruppin certainly quotes Werner Sombart, but the brand of biology that refers to 'people–races' attracted him far more than the writings of Émile Durkheim or Max Weber. In 1927, this sociologist from Jerusalem took part in a major conference on eugenics in Berlin.

At the end of 1930, he published in Hebrew and German, under the title *Soziologie der Juden*, the fruit of his four years' work at the Hebrew University. The title of each chapter of the book announces its content: 'The Racial Composition of the Jews in Eretz Israel', 'History of the Jewish Race outside Eretz Israel', and so on. At the end of the first volume, photographs of 'Jewish' portraits confirm the diversity of the races presented in the book. In 1933, shortly after Hitler came to power, the Jerusalem sociologist travelled to Berlin to debate with Hans F. K. Günther, his theoretical mentor and the father of the Nazi racial doctrine, the many points of convergence between them.

Ruppin was no longer a member of Brit Shalom when he met Günther. Indeed, the organisation was no longer really active. Ruppin had in fact begun to distance himself from it from 1929, following the bloody riots in Hebron. He still attended meetings from time to time, however. The question therefore arises: on the one hand, how could the most radical race theorist of the Zionist movement, someone who had wondered about the possibility of a reduction in the Semitic composition of contemporary Jewish blood, support, be it only for a few years, the principle of a federal state? And, on the other hand, did his open racism not disturb fellow scholars in this highly ethical organisation, of which he was a founder member?[7]

In fact Ruppin viewed Brit Shalom as a discussion circle and a research group rather than as a movement with political objectives. Moreover, aside from his pragmatic motivations, we may assume that he sincerely believed that the inhabitants of Palestine at the time really were the biological descendants of ancient Hebrews, and hence concluded that it would be easy enough to integrate them and live together in the distant future. This is why, in his view, some sort of modus vivendi had to be sought with the Arabs, who made up the vast majority of the population in Palestine, since the idea of a mass transfer was unrealistic.[8] Both the establishment of the revisionist Zionist movement, with its ideas about the creation of a military legion, and the notion of an 'iron wall' dreamed up by Jabotinsky, with its heavy load of pessimistic logic, were of genuine concern to Ruppin. He also sensed the beginnings of an Arab national consciousness among the urban elites in Jaffa and Haifa, and feared a conflict that might spread and ultimately hinder or even destroy the Zionist enterprise. In 1925 he wrote in his diary:

> The Arab question worries me. [...] I want the Jews to live on an equal footing with the Arabs, and I note with alarm the gulf that is opening up between the two peoples, the growing hostility on the Arab side, and the chauvinistic attitude and lack of understanding on the part of many Jews towards the Arabs. Together with a few people who feel the same way as I do, I have founded a club with the aim of improving relations, but for the moment I cannot see clearly the path ahead.[9]

The theoretical racism of the association's founder did not disturb the members of Brit Shalom. As we saw in chapter 1, most of them had ethnicist and even 'volkist' approaches to the concept of the nation in general and of the Jewish people in particular: this ancient organic people was supposedly Semitic, and therefore biologically related to the indigenous Arab population. All in all, Ruppin's positions were by no means exceptional within the Zionist movement; they were just more systematic, more outspoken, and more detailed. Friction with other members of Brit Shalom arose only when his misgivings about the Arabs directly influenced his guiding political strategy. He had come to the conclusion that there was an insoluble contradiction between the pursuit of the Zionist settlement and the demand for a federal state. He clearly opted for the first solution, thus distancing himself, albeit with numerous twists and turns, from the companions with whom he had founded the Peace Alliance.

Several other eminent members of Brit Shalom had, like Ruppin, experienced the frictions and symbioses between German and East European cultures (they included Poles from Poznan and Galicia, Czechs from Bohemia and Moravia, and even a Russian from Königsberg, then in East Prussia). The nationalist effervescence that had begun to emerge in these culturally and linguistically diverse regions had certainly fuelled the ethnocentric conception of the nation as an organic body of common blood and origin. But it had also led to the expression of a new sensitivity towards others and of an openness to binational or multinational ideas, as happened with many members of Brit Shalom. It is no coincidence that Otto Bauer and Karl Renner, two avant-garde thinkers of the national phenomenon at the beginning of the twentieth century, hailed from the Austro-Hungarian empire. Both advocated a principle of autonomy for linguistic and cultural minorities, and even supported federal solutions within a multinational structure.[10]

But if members of Brit Shalom such as Rabbi Binyamin, Hugo Bergmann, Hans Kohn, and Martin Buber hailed, like Ruppin, from the eastern fringes of German culture, others, for instance Gershom Scholem, Shlomo Dov Goitein, David Werner Senator, and Ernst Simon (who joined a little later) were natives of Berlin or Bavaria; mentally they remained *Yekim* ('pure Germans'). Although up until 1933 only about two thousand Jews had emigrated from Germany to Palestine, the strongest support for Brit Shalom in Europe came mainly from German Jewish intellectuals, not from East European ones.

Not all members of Brit Shalom were intellectuals in the full sense of the term, however; some were successful men and women of action. Ruppin was joined by famous settlement leaders and 'redeemers of the land': Jacob Thon, his former secretary at the Eretz Israel Office and one of the leaders of Hahsharat Hayishuv (a land-acquisition association), joined him straight away. Others would follow: Moshe Smilansky, also a writer, but someone who was involved in land purchase in the Negev and who chaired the farmers' union, and Haim Margaliot-Kalvarisky, a promoter of colonisation in Galilee, where he built many settlements. The 'colonisers', although favourable to the principle of binationalism, were considered to be the moderate and hesitant fringe of Brit Shalom and began to leave the organisation in 1929, around the same time as Ruppin.

The reasons that prompted leading figures at the heart of the Zionist consensus to join a pacifist organisation, which was desperately seeking channels for dialogue with the Arabs, are anticipated in the questions that Smilansky and Kalvarisky were asking themselves a few years before the creation of Brit Shalom. Even before the First World War, Smilansky had this to say: 'After thirty years, we who were close to the Arabs by race and blood remained strangers to them [. . .]. In the thirty years that we have lived in the country, they have not ignored us, but we have ignored them. They haven't turned their backs on us, it's we who have turned away.'[11] Kalvarisky wrote an emotional account of his experience which bears out this observation:

'The question of the Arabs first appeared to me in all its seriousness immediately after the first purchase of land I made here. I had to dispossess the Arab residents of their land for the purpose of settling our brothers. [. . .] I realized how tied the Bedouin is to his land.'

He had been dispossessing Arabs for twenty-five years, Kalvarisky said. It was not easy work, especially for a man like him, who did not see the Arabs as a flock of sheep but rather as human beings with hearts and souls. He had to turn them off the land because the Jewish public demanded it of him, Kalvarisky said, but he always tried to ensure that the people did not leave empty-handed and that the land-speculating *effendis* with whom he did business did not rob the simple folk of their money.[12]

The 'Extremist' Faction

The most radical and vocal faction of Brit Shalom, which wanted to turn the organisation into a local equivalent of the Fabian Society of the British left, included more authentic intellectuals. Some contributed to the creation of the Israeli intellectual sphere and, more marginally, to the political and ideological formation of a fringe of the intellectual elite.

Hugo Bergmann, a young philosopher born in Prague, a schoolfriend of Franz Kafka, had arrived in Jerusalem in 1920. He was appointed director of the National Jewish University Library, before becoming a lecturer at the Hebrew University, where he ended up as its first rector. He was one of the spokespersons for the radical faction. Even before his arrival in Jerusalem, he had written in 1911:

The system of land acquisition for the Jews has undoubtedly had the effect of creating enemies for us in the ranks of the Arabs. The land that is now in Jewish hands was acquired at the expense of the Arabs. The sellers were rarely small farmers. The *fellah* is attached to his land and does not wish to part with it. More often than not, we bought the land from

the big landowners, the *effendis* [. . .] but if the employees and
owners of the land are Jews, who totally expropriate the Arabs,
the question arises: are we going to dispossess half a million
people?[13]

Bergmann, like others, took an ethnocentric approach to the
nation; from time to time he spoke of 'two races in binational
Palestine' or of 'one race united again'. However, his conception of redemption and his deep religious moralism set him in
opposition to the dominant brand of Zionism and prompted
him to rebel against a policy that isolated Zionists by expelling
or discriminating against Arabs. Bergmann was close to Buber,
and was an enthusiastic advocate for a renaissance of Jewish
theology that could establish the region as a spiritual centre,
thus powerfully advancing the culture of the prophets that had
fallen into oblivion. But according to him the first condition
for the realisation of Zionism was to obtain the agreement of
the Arabs, which sooner or later would be sure to come so long
as the Zionist movement pursued a prudent and wise policy.
In the meantime, the Arab refusal to negotiate seemed to him
understandable and quite natural. Any natives anywhere in the
world would oppose an invasion of foreigners into their country. Therefore Bergmann held that, in spite of the Arab refusal
and although Jews were a demographic minority, Zionism
must support democratic principles and accept the establishment of a parliament or legislative council for all residents of
the country.

At the time, the Zionist leaders were strongly opposed to
the implementation of democracy, which they feared would
backfire on them; hence they categorically rejected Arab
demands for a parliamentary representation of the entire
population of Mandatory Palestine. Bergmann and his friends
Scholem, Kohn, Weltsch, Rabbi Binyamin, and others took the
opposite view. As democrats, they approved of the principle
of a parliament based on 'one person, one vote' – a stance

that earned them the ire of the moderates in Brit Shalom. The radical faction also renounced the central Zionist ambition to become a majority in the country no matter what, a long-held defining aspiration of the movement. According to Bergmann and his friends, in a best-case scenario, Jews could aspire to represent 40 per cent of the population of the country, and would therefore not constitute a permanent and real threat to the existing majority of Arabs. They argued that the efforts to obtain a majority at all costs – efforts promoted by all the Zionist leaders except Chaim Weizmann, who at one point raised doubts – stemmed from a dangerous principle, which fuelled growing hostility among the natives as the Jewish community developed.

In 1928 Rabbi Binyamin described the majority requirement as an 'unfortunate principle' and wrote:

> I wonder whether the fathers of Zionism were aware of this new principle, and whether they called it by its name. The love of Zion needs no majority [. . .] and political Zionism, in its ardent form, could not be satisfied with a majority. It had planned to bring in millions, great masses, in a short space of time. And I began to be fearful of the majority principle – who were its progenitors, and where did they come from, these desecrating progenitors. The parents of this principle [. . .] are despair and doubt.[14]

The abandonment of the idea of achieving a Jewish majority in Palestine at all costs further widened the gap between Brit Shalom and other Zionist currents, but the legacy of Ahad Ha'am still beat in the hearts of most of the association's members and guided their strategy.

Rabbi Binyamin, who regularly spoke out, supported Herzl and expressed reservations about Ahad Ha'am. As a messianic volkist, he dismissed any Jewish presence in Europe and America and came out strongly in favour of the maximal immigration of Jewish 'Semites' into Palestine, even as he rejected the idea of absolute sovereignty and domination over another people. Although he disagreed with the most secular faction of Brit Shalom, he continued to emphasise that '[t]he Prussian and the Bavarian have united in Germany in a federal state, just as the Ashkenazi Jew and the Sephardic Jew have united in the same community, so the Hebrew and the Arab will unite to build a single state, a densely populated state [. . .] which will not be the plaything of some other people'.[15]

In 1929, Hugo Bergmann, an active member of Brit Shalom, published an incisive programmatic article in which he set out the specific nature of the organisation in relation to all the other Zionist movements:

The antagonism between the political vision of the members of Brit Shalom and that of its opponents owes not only to our position in relation to the Arabs of Eretz Israel; it is far more profound and fundamental: our political position derives from a Judaic world view. We want Eretz Israel to be our country, in the sense that the ethical–political concepts of Judaism will stamp their seal upon the way of life of its inhabitants, and that we will put into practice the law that has lived in our hearts for two thousand years, whereas those who oppose us see things differently. When they speak of Eretz Israel, of our country, they mean 'our country' and above all not 'their country'. This vision of the world, borrowed from Europe in its hour of decline, is based upon the concept of a state that is the property of a single people. Just as it was once thought that the owner of the state could impose his religion upon all of its inhabitants, so it is now thought in some European countries that the existence of the state requires the granting of privileges to one people among all those who reside in the state. This people is the 'state people', while the other peoples are merely inhabitants, guests in this state. While in theory every individual enjoys the same rights, even if they belong to a minority people, it is still the case that the state remains the property of a single people, the dominant people. This injustice is justified by the sacred chauvinism of the state [...] We have proclaimed the Brit Shalom slogan: 'Eretz Israel, a binational country.' This must form the basis of our political education both among ourselves and among them. It must also be embodied in the political field, everywhere, and in all the circumstances in which we live together with them, and together form political institutions.[16]

The rejection of the Balfour Declaration by Bergmann and his friends also earned them Ruppin's ire. The radicals described the declaration as an imperialist show of force that discriminated against the natives. Great Britain, they argued, had taken a country that did not belong to it and handed it to the Jews, whom it had refused to welcome upon its own territory. They called for the declaration to be amended and replaced by another, which would take into account the rights of the local population, renounce the claim to Jewish owner-ship of the state, and contribute to binational reconciliation.

Gershom Scholem, well on his way to becoming an impor-tant scholar of mysticism, fully identified with the analysis of imperialism made by his friends from the radical faction.[17] In 1931 he published a virulent article in which he spared no words in criticising the service rendered by the Zionist move-ment to British power:

Zionism finds itself in the dangerous position of becoming a passing episode in the history of our people [...] The force to which Zionism allied itself in these victories [of the First World War] was an apparent and energetic force. Zionism neglected to ally itself with the hidden, oppressed force that will rise up and reveal itself tomorrow; can a renaissance movement be found on their fringes, or more precisely under the aegis and in the shadow of the victors of the war? Many socialists in our camp do not want to hear these questions and become angry when you speak of the imperialism to which we are committed by our alliance with the Balfour Declaration. [. . .] Zionism is not in heaven, which is why it cannot unite fire and water: either it will be drowned in the waters of imperialism, or it will burn in the fire of the awakening revolution in the East.[18]

Scholem's barb about the socialists is aimed primarily at Ben-Gurion and his partners on the Zionist left, who claimed to support the liberation of all the peoples of the world under occupation, with the notable exception of those living in Palestine. Scholem despised bourgeois liberal hypocrisy, just as in his youth he had felt only contempt for the charades of the Zionist left.

After the First World War – which had horrified him along with most members of Brit Shalom, because of its cruelty and because he saw its results as a source of future dangers – Scholem had expressed the hope that a new type of culture, less materialistic and less militaristic, would emerge from the East and that spiritual Zionism would form an integral part of this new movement. Only a pacifist national awakening, without brutality or colonial domination, could successfully build in Palestine a Jewish home capable of longevity and independent of the fickle whims of the great powers.

Scholem had his reservations about the messianic tendencies of the Zionist movement, although he recognised their role as a mystical stimulus ultimately conducive to the salvation of Judaism. Like his friend Bergmann, he was not at all impressed by extremist secularism and was wary of a potentially explosive future mix of religious tradition, faith, and nationalist impulses. Along with the other radicals in Brit Shalom, he was convinced that only a binational solution could save the Zionist enterprise from degenerating into pseudo-religious chauvinism. In the aftermath of the 1929 clashes, when the enquiry committee asked him to speak about Judaism's relationship with the Wailing Wall, he declined, arguing that belief in God should not be mixed with politics. Like the other members of Brit Shalom, he blamed both sides of the conflict for the outbreak of violence.[19]

While his brother Werner Scholem, a Marxist anti-Zionist, and his dear friend Walter Benjamin, a non-conformist and non-Zionist, were still alive, Scholem remained sharply critical of the Zionist establishment, even after the disbanding of Brit Shalom. He always saw himself as being closest to a communitarian anarchism, a credo he greatly preferred to organised political socialism. However, the tragic deaths of Benjamin and his brother in 1940, followed by the massacre of millions of Jews, saw him drawing closer to Zionist institutions and abandoning the idea of binationalism.[20]

Hans Kohn and the End of the Alliance

Hans Kohn, the secretary of Brit Shalom, was the most prominent figure in the radical group and became the principal target for its detractors. Like Bergmann, Kohn was originally from Prague. He had fought in the Second World War, had been taken prisoner by the Russians, and had experienced the horrors of war at first hand. These ordeals made him a committed pacifist and antimilitarist. Following the war and a lengthy period of captivity, he completed his law studies and lived for a time in England and France, then decided to emigrate to Palestine in 1925 after joining the War Resisters' International. He had already encountered Zionism in his youth when, along with Hugo Bergmann, he was a member of the Bar Kokhba student circle. He had also worked in the propaganda department of the Israeli fundraising organisation Keren Hayesod in London.

Like Bergmann, Kohn admired Ahad Ha'am and Martin Buber; from the beginning of his intellectual journey he saw cultural Zionism, not political Zionism, as the solution to the distress of Jews in the modern era. He recognised the existence of a Jewish ethics – and not just a religion – and viewed its aspiration for a homeland in the East as perfectly legitimate. This organic, rooted people lived in time and not in a space, being likely to serve as the model for a pan-human, generous, and open nationality. From the outset of his theoretical work, Kohn exhibited a clear preference for pluralistic expressions of nationality over the rigid cultural uniformity characteristic of standard nation states, his assumption being that various minorities would always exist alongside a dominant majority. In his eyes, Switzerland represented the ideal type of state, and very early on he began to envision an Arab–Jewish binational structure in the Middle East. His belief was that, if one day the Arab world ultimately accepted a Jewish–Zionist presence in its midst, that would be on condition that it did not demand exclusive ownership over the entire country. As early as 1921, he wrote to his friend Robert Weltsch: 'Palestine cannot be a Jewish nation state. It cannot be Jewish in the same way in which England is English, not only because that is not a step forward, but also because it is a concrete impossibility. Palestine must be binational, not Eretz Israel.'[21]

In 1922 Kohn wrote his first book, full of weighty messianism, on the meaning of Jewish nationality. The response was modest.[22] His *History of Nationalism in the East*, published in German in 1928 and in English in 1929, elicited slightly more interest.[23] He continued to work simultaneously at Keren Hayesod, devoting his spare time to politically engaged journalism. When Brit Shalom was set up and he became its secretary along with Rabbi Binyamin, he published articles in *Sheifoteinu*, the association's press organ. His opinions, which became increasingly radical, aroused the growing hostility of both moderates and right-wing critics.

Kohn's vision of a binational future for Palestine stemmed partly from his life in Prague and partly from the direct influence of Mahatma Gandhi's decentralising message about the

Indian national movement. In the very first issue of *Sheifoteinu*, Kohn outlined a desirable future for Jews and Arabs:

> The centre of gravity for the expression of political will must be found in communities. It will develop from the bottom up; the intervention of supreme bodies will be limited to cases of absolute necessity. [. . .] The majority of localities already have national aspects about them, almost without exception in the case of villages, and to some extent in the case of towns. [. . .] It will be necessary to group these localities into large units of districts and cantons. [. . .] In these districts, cooperation between the two nations will be made possible on a larger scale than in the towns. [. . .] There will, however, be general bodies representative of the autonomy of the two peoples, larger than the district authorities, and which will cover the whole country. [. . .] This type of autonomous national body may be based on two foundations: (1) on a territorial basis where, in a given territory, there is a concentration of a population belonging almost entirely to the same nationality, (2) on a personal basis [. . .] in large towns where there is a mixture of populations [. . .] Two main areas of management will be conceded to the central authority: the economy and constitutional development.[24]

In addition, two languages, Arabic and Hebrew, were to be given official status, and there were to be two independent education systems. Within this binational framework there would be no state religion, and the holy sites would be regarded as extraterritorial.

Kohn remained committed to his binational utopia and tried to convince all the members of Brit Shalom to adopt his programme, so that they could form an activist group with clearly defined political objectives. Initially he was convinced that the Zionist movement, under Weizmann's leadership, would move towards open and reconciliatory nationhood, but the bloody crisis of 1929 shattered any remaining hopes of this.

Kohn witnessed at first hand the murder of an Arab in the street where he lived, under the indifferent gazes of passers-by, and found it extremely difficult to recover from this experience. At the beginning of the 1929 riots he had hoped that the terrible violence would prompt Zionist leaders to explore new strategic avenues and, in particular, to abandon the ambition for a Jewish majority in the future state. He was all the more disappointed to witness instead a hardening of attitudes towards the Arabs:

> We pretend to be innocent victims. Of course, the Arabs attacked us in August [1929]. Since they have no armies, they could not obey the rules of war. They perpetrated all the barbaric acts that are characteristic of a colonial revolt. But we are obliged to look into the deeper cause of this revolt. We have been in Palestine for twelve years [since the start of the British occupation] without having even once made a serious attempt at seeking through negotiations the consent of the indigenous people. We have been relying exclusively upon Great Britain's military might. We have set ourselves goals which by their very nature had to lead to conflict.[25]

In 1929, Kohn resigned from his position at Keren Hayesod, and from then on made a living, with great difficulty, by writing articles for the German press and giving lectures abroad. At the same time his application for a post at the Hebrew University was rejected. Unlike Ruppin, who had immediately been appointed to a senior post in Jewish sociology, Kohn, in keeping with his pacifist convictions, had applied for the new chair in political science, a post devoted to international peace. Leon Magnes, the all-powerful chancellor of the new university, tried to support his application, but there was too much disagreement among the management about the political stance taken by the most 'extremist' member of Brit Shalom.

In September 1930 Kohn sent his letter of resignation to the Brit Shalom secretariat, asking for it not to be made public. Throughout that year he had clashed with Ruppin's remaining supporters in the organisation, whom he regarded as apologists for the propaganda of the Zionist establishment – an establishment that, for its part, accused him of deceitful ideological manipulation. Towards the end of 1929 Kohn wrote to one of his friends: 'I was concerned not with the Arabs but with the Jews, their Jewishness and the confirmation of their humane [values]. It has, alas, become increasingly clear to me that, in this respect, the Zionist Organization has failed utterly.'[26] A few months later he made the following confession to his friend Robert Weltsch:

It is likely that by using aggressive means, it will be possible to establish here a [Jewish] majority. But what will be here then? Nothing. A small Jewish state. What do I have to do with that? What does anyone have to do with it? [. . .] For this small state [. . .] will always be armed to the teeth against the irredentism from within and the 'enemies' all around. Aware of its weakness, it will always remain a hotbed of exaggerated nationalism.[27]

In a letter to another friend, he pursues this line of thinking:

And even if we become the majority, we shall not obtain peace, because the Arabs, even if they become a minority, will continue to seek union with their Arab neighbours, and the Jewish people will be obliged to be an armed people. [. . .] It is impossible to claim that these are warnings about the distant future, as Ruppin likes to assert, and that we should limit ourselves to worrying about the next twenty to thirty years. This is an easy self-deception, because the disastrous results are already in place, and everyone will have to account for what their actions today will lead to tomorrow. In the future, everyone will say, astonished: This isn't what we wanted.[28]

This prediction is also an admission of great sorrow; the sorrow of a consistent pacifist and humanist who foresaw that the nation he wished for and over many years participated in building would be transformed forever into a militarised fortress. He felt powerless and became overwhelmed by despair. Since he was unemployed, he had time to write further texts, which were published between 1930 and 1932: *Nationalism and Imperialism in the Hither East*, and *Nationalism in the Soviet Union*. But, since he was married and had a child, his savings began to dwindle, and he turned to Magnes for help. The university chancellor once again tried to get him on board, and this time even managed to win over his opponents, but at the last minute Kohn changed his mind and asked Magnes to help him join an academic institution in Great Britain or the United States. With the help of his friend, he eventually landed a post at Smith College in Massachusetts and left Palestine in 1934, never again to set foot in the land of his youthful dreams.

Kohn taught for a decade at Smith, where his research output was prolific. He published several new essays before the publication in 1944 of his most famous work, *The Idea of Nationalism*, which saw him recognised as the most important mid-twentieth-century theorist and pathfinder on the national question. The breadth of his erudition and the richness of his ideas impressed readers. Zionism appears in his writings only in a relatively limited form, but the twenty-five years during which he identified as a Zionist undoubtedly contributed to the development of the most important paradigm for which he is known today. The dissent between Czechs and Germans in Prague, which shaped the structures of his thinking in his youth, served as a guiding thread; as for the Zionist essentialist conception of the Jews as a people–race, it would prove to be a relatively discreet but by no means marginal ingredient in the genesis of his historical analyses.

As was pointed out at the beginning of this book, according to Kohn, two types of nationalism developed during the process of modernisation and of emergence of the masses into the political arena. On the one hand, there were various forms of civil nationalism, inclusive and assimilative, generally typical of the liberal western countries: the United States, Great Britain, France, and Holland. On the other hand, there were various forms of ethnic nationalism, exclusive, repressive, insular, and invariably invoking a mythological past. This ethnic nationalism had increasingly taken hold in the countries of Central and Eastern Europe. Kohn described the first type of nationalism as a rational, self-confident construction that invites all citizens, regardless of origin, to identify with the state. The second type of nationalism, on the other hand, is fundamentally romantic and suspicious. It sees the other and the different as a hostile stranger who poses a threat to national unity. There are intermediate cases, of course, and national sensibilities are always changing, but the dichotomy between these two forms remains a cornerstone for understanding the various forms of collective identity around the world.

Kohn later realised that the idea of Zionist binationalism that he and his friends in Brit Shalom had promoted was doomed to failure from the start. Switzerland, Canada, Great Britain, Belgium, and even Spain may be home to successful binational or plurinational constructions, but the prospect of such an arrangement becoming a reality in countries with a solidly ethnocentric national character is far more problematic and complicated, and perhaps non-existent. For example Czechoslovakia, Yugoslavia, and even Romania and Hungary – states that are culturally and linguistically plurinational – have always behaved like mononational states in which national minorities are regarded as temporary guests, to be tolerated until the next crisis comes along. As for the Zionism to which Hans Kohn, Hugo Bergmann, Robert Weltsch, Gershom Scholem, and others were so attached, wasn't it immanently linked to the essentialist and closed-minded nationalism so characteristic of Central and Eastern Europe? Kohn refused to give an unambiguous response to this question, even though his painful divorce from Zionism provided a kind of answer by itself. Ultimately he would come to see the Jewish presence in the American melting pot, with its civil nationality, as a preferable alternative to Zionism.[29]

This may explain the reticence of the Jewish community in Palestine vis-à-vis Brit Shalom. Throughout the period when Jews were a tiny minority, many in the Zionist movement had 'flirted' with binational or federal ideas; nonetheless, the leaders of the movement were quite aware that they were not allowed to promote the image of the 'chosen people' locked in with another, as a minority, within the framework of a binational state. And so they rejected this 'alliance of bizarre intellectuals', who always refused to ignore the fact that an Arab majority existed in Palestine, a majority that the process of colonisation would end up gradually expelling from its own land. This is why Brit Shalom's Zionism seemed to them to be more than dubious and even suspect and harmful.[30]

In 1934, a year after the association disbanded, Natan Hofshi, one of the best-known and most inquisitive pacifists (and vegans), who had been an active member of Brit Shalom from the outset, looked back on its sad fate and tried to give a brief and partial explanation for its failure:

This organisation, upon putting forward its proposals for a solution to the Jewish–Arab question, was met with provocative articles, inflammatory speeches, professional dismissals, threats, calls for boycotts, and slanderous accusation of treachery. [. . .] The 'Yishuv' (the Jewish proto-state in Mandatory Palestine), divided into a multitude of parties, was united in its hatred of and its war upon Brit Shalom [. . .]. War was declared against those who had betrayed the idea of the 'nation'.[31]

4

Martin Buber, Hannah Arendt, and the Undivided Territory

A bi-national socio-political entity [. . .] with complete equality of rights between the two partners, disregarding the changing numerical relationship between them, and with joint sovereignty founded on these principles – such an entity would provide both peoples with all that they truly need.

Martin Buber, 'Two Peoples in Palestine', June 1947[1]

The magnificence of this people once lay in its belief in God – that is, in the way its trust and love of God far outweighed its fear of God. And now this people believes only in itself! What's going to become of this?

Hannah Arendt, Letter to Gershom Scholem, 24 July 1963[2]

'I heard from Buber himself that one day, thirty years ago, when he was the editor of the Viennese Zionist newspaper *Die Welt*, he went to Dr Herzl to tell him that he wanted to resign as editor of the movement's organ of expression. Herzl asked him why. He replied: to found the opposition.'[3] This anecdote was reported by Gershom Scholem, no doubt with some exaggeration. But Martin Buber, the greatest of Zionist philosophers, was indeed a rebel throughout his life, disrupting and upsetting institutions of all kinds. Unlike Elisha ben Abuyah, who was a Talmudic heretic, he did not quite tip over into the heresy of Jewish nationalism that was in the process of crystallising, but he was undoubtedly an extraordinary charismatic figure, a thinker who processed religion in the deepest layers of the soul, and an anarchist who did not care for the decrees of orthodoxy: he no longer set foot in the synagogue. He was also, with every fibre of his being, a nationalist Jew, but one who consistently opposed the creation of a separate Jewish state.

To say that all the members of Brit Shalom were sons of Martin Buber would obviously be an exaggeration: Arthur Ruppin and Gershom Scholem both tended to distance themselves from Buber and his philosophy of life. However, the most radical members of the association, particularly those who were part of the Bar Kochba Circle in Prague and had attended his lectures there – for example Hugo Bergmann, Hans Kohn, and Robert Weltsch – had become pure Buberians and remained so for most of their lives. The philosopher, who was still living in Germany in the 1920s (in fact he remained there until 1938), supported Brit Shalom's activities from afar and enthusiastically disseminated its political views. This is why, to this very day, the protest group is still identified with this non-conformist thinker.

Kohn, one of Buber's earliest admirers, published a biography of the philosopher in 1930. It is the only biography to have been approved by Buber himself, and contains a moderately critical review of a part of his life and writings.[4] Many essays and hundreds of articles have since been devoted to Buber, whose profound thought has not yet been fully deciphered. It is true that he is not easily categorised, as his writing style sometimes verges upon poetic abstraction. It must also be said that, while some of the contradictions that emerge in his thought can be resolved, others remain obscure even with repeated rereadings. But we shall concentrate here primarily on his views on the nation, rather than on the deep waters of his existential philosophy.

From Volkism to 'I and Thou'

In three eloquent speeches to the young people of the Bar Kochba Circle in Prague, Buber had already revealed himself to be both a vitalist and a volkist thinker, rejecting the 'dry' rationalism of the nineteenth century. Following in the footsteps of German romanticism, Kierkegaard, Nietzsche, and probably indirectly Bergson, he thrilled and galvanised his listeners with invocations of a very specific form of *élan vital*, a potential energy that, according to him, was harboured within Jewish identity. For centuries, Buber suggested, Jewish law (*Halakha*) had strangled Jewish vitality, until Hasidism, which swept over Central Europe like a storm, had temporarily reinvigorated it; but neither Rabbinic orthodoxy nor liberal reformism would be able to truly reawaken and renew this ancient people, which today was decaying in a modern materialistic dung heap. According to Buber, Ahad Ha'am was correct in pointing out that Judaism is not just a religion or a church and that its spiritual centre in Eretz Israel is a valid idea but is insufficient in itself.[5] According to Buber, each people has its own character, and the uniqueness of the Jewish people lies in the unity of action, precept, and future.

However, Buber was not content with this invocation of an original great spirituality passed down from generation to generation. An organic and racial approach, typical of many contemporary Zionists, was already perceptible in the articles he penned long before his Prague lectures. In these writings the Jewish people was an ancient tribe, certainly united by particular spiritual beliefs but also – and no less – by blood ties. Pyramidal ethno-national features characterise Jews:

origin means more than a mere connection with things past; it has planted something within us that does not leave us at any hour of our life, that determines every tone and every hue in our life, all that we do and all that befalls us: blood, the deepest, most potent stratum of our being.[6]

Buber had an extraordinary rhetorical talent; his young listeners eagerly embraced his irrational, volkist messages, and some of these ideas would stay with them for the rest of their lives.

To some extent, Buber fell short of espousing a problematic biological determinism and romanticism thanks to three cardinal moments in his thought and experience: historical reality, which had shaken him to the core, like his entire generation; religious existentialism, which constantly deepened his understanding of God and the world; and the ways in which he understood social reality.

The First World War had transformed the Jewish volkist into a German one. Like most intellectuals of his time, Jewish and non-Jewish alike, Buber was deeply moved by the clash of giants in 'the defence of the fatherland'. Max Weber, Sigmund Freud, Thomas Mann, Rudyard Kipling, Émile Durkheim, and Henri Bergson (to name but a few!) were all carried away, like most intellectuals, by the patriotic wave that swept through Europe. Buber experienced the war as a renewal and redeployment of collective energies and emotions in a Europe weakened by decline and degeneration. He went so far as to compare it to the ancient revolt of the Maccabees, seeing it as a war destined to engender a new alliance between the ancient Jewish tribe and 'the German nation of salvation' in the heroic struggle against Russian despotism. Gustav Landauer, a militant anarchist and antimilitarist, tried to calm his friend's irrational patriotic fervour, but to no avail: Buber's enthusiasm could not be curbed.[7] The philosopher would repent and apologise for the rest of his life for the militaristic positions he had adopted during the war and to which he had lent a mystical tone. Towards the end of the war one can perceive a break and a significant change of direction in his thought, both philosophical and politico-social.

From 1918 onwards, Buber set about formulating his philosophy of dialogue, which reached full maturity in his famous work *I and Thou*. This text, which was not published until 1923, immediately established him as one of the most eminent and original philosophers of his time. 'Through the *thou* a man becomes *I*',[8] Buber asserts trenchantly, and on this key position he constructs a very specific anthropology, which places empathy, proximity, and identification with others at the centre of what it is to be human: according to Buber, it is these sentiments that define what makes humans 'human'. Direct dialogue, without intermediaries, is the foundation of the bond between humans, of the approach to truth. To a great extent it is also an invitation to dialogue with God, the eternal *Thou*.[9] Any existentialism that does not address a human's relationship with the other and the dialogue that shapes it is meaningless, he proclaims.

What is more, alongside the 'I and thou' there is also an 'I and it'. The 'it' is the other, which for me is no more than an object of utilitarian usage. So these relationships of alienation and estrangement exist alongside 'I and Thou' relationships and are illustrative of the deterioration of modern society, which has become less and less humane and more and more profit-centred. It is a society that is neither a community nor a congregation but only a haphazard assemblage of alienated persons who move side by side, in mutual ignorance and fear. Buber states that, while it is true that the human being cannot exist without the 'it', the person who lives only with the 'it' is not a human being.

By 1908 Buber had moved closer to Landauer's anarcho-socialist movement, although for a long time he remained relatively indifferent to Landauer's vision of the utopian commune. At the end of the war, after the execution of his friend, who had been minister of education under the Bavarian Socialist Republic, Buber embraced an explicitly anti-statist ideology.[10] This declining, conflicted world needed to be transformed, but not through the state apparatus, as Marxists imagined. According to Buber, the response to the distress of alienation and exploitation in modern capitalist society would come not from party politics but from the rapid reconstruction of human communities, which economic modernisation has pushed to the point of disintegration and continues to despoil.

Here Buber, who originally drew upon the Hasidic tradition, refers to the work of Ferdinand Tönnies, adopting the German sociologist's fundamental distinction between *Gemeinschaft* and *Gesellschaft*, that is, between community and society, as a starting point in defining *havruta* (fraternity) as the highest social ideal. Society is a union based upon interests, whereas *havruta* is an 'association for life'. The path to a change of social regime, Buber insisted, is not to be found in a revolutionary upsurge but in a work of labour on hearts that must involve, as of now, the implementation of practices of living together, since these alone are capable of forming the basis of a future civilisation. *Havruta* largely represents a social instantiation of, and a complement to, Buber's existentialist 'I and Thou' problematic. This explains why, in the context of his support for colonisation in the land of Zion, Buber was an early supporter of the kibbutz movement in Palestine.[11]

Unlike all other Zionists, however, Buber did not believe that Jews had a historical right to the Land of Israel. In fact he totally rejected politico-legal claims to collective historical rights over a given territory, noting that 'every chapter in world history which is used as an authority for justifying a given right was preceded by another chapter, which in turn can support a different right'.[12] It was rather through the ancestral religious link to the Holy Land, which had never been a matter of nationality, and through current ways of working and constructing this beloved land that a claim to it could be staked and granted.

The profound aspiration to bring together once again a people that is not like other peoples, to create a small state that differs from all other small states, and especially to take one's place in a territory that should not become an object of permanent quarrels and divisions will grant Zionists a new kind of right to the Holy Land. But this will happen only on condition that Judaism, reborn in this new form, instils 'a meaning for all mankind' into its work. In other words, Buber suggested that national deliverance will constitute only one part, one phase, of the salvation of all humanity. Only an ethical approach of this sort could justify the Zionist colonisation of the Middle East. The rebirth of the Jewish people in Zion must be the beginning of the salvation of all peoples. At this point Buber had left behind the synthetism characteristic of his original thinking, explicitly replacing it with a myth held together by a universal morality.[13]

Towards Binationalism

We now need to understand how Buber arrived at his vision of coexistence, and why he persisted with and held on to this position for most of his life. In his view, binationalism could serve as a model and measure of the moral dimension of Zionism – and equally as a demonstration that it was not an aggressive, colonial movement. Yet in 1918 he was still hesitant and worried. He wrote to his young friend Hugo Bergmann:

> We must face the fact that most leading Zionists (and prob-ably also most of those who are led) today are thoroughly unrestrained nationalists (following the European example), imperialists, even unconscious mercantilists and idolators of success. They speak about rebirth and mean enterprise. If we do not succeed to erect an authoritative [Zionist] opposition,

the soul of the movement will be corrupted, maybe for ever. I for my part am determined to commit myself totally to this cause, even if this should affect my personal plans.[14]

Buber supported the peace agreements and the League of Nations that had been set up after the First World War, although he was aware that they were really imperialism dressed up as humanitarian intervention. He also emphasised that Zionists must pay attention to any national expression that comes from the Arab side and at the same time be on their guard in the face of the nationalism stirred up on both sides: 'It depends on us whether we shall appear before the awakening East as hateful agents and spies or, rather, as beloved pioneers and teachers.'[15]

Buber's conception of nationality is probably helpful for understanding his vision of coexistence in Palestine. When it comes to the emergence of a national consciousness in history, he largely lays it out in terms of the difference between *Gemeinschaft* and *Gesellschaft*. In his view, nationhood came into being with the French Revolution and its wars of expansion, but its actual origin lies in the destruction, during the modern age, of the insular community life that had offered the individual security in the past. The new human, isolated and unsheltered,

> reached out for a community-structure which was just putting in an appearance, for nationality. The individual felt himself warmly and firmly received into a unit he thought indestructible because it was 'natural', sprung from and bound to the soil. He found protection in the naturally evolved shelter of the nation, [and the] group-egoism of the individual emerged in its modern form.[16]

Modern nationalism is not in itself a negative thing, Buber argues, since it can serve as a reason to rise up against tyranny or a foreign conqueror. It becomes harmful when the nation is seen as an end in itself, when it rejects supranational moral obligations and treats the people as an idol before which we must kneel. Judaism was a community of believers before it became a nation, so Buber argued that its national movement is distinctive and differs from other national movements. However, Jews have not longed for Palestine as a nation but as a community of believers, and in the absence of this metaphysical dimension Zionism would be nothing more than a collective assimilation into modernity. What is more, national sovereignty becomes deceptive and arbitrary if it does not retain a sense that it is subject to the world sovereign. The presence of God imposes a limit upon a people's arrogant and arbitrary sovereignty over itself. Dialogue with God is the condition for welcoming others as your equals. 'God is king' in both biblical and modern times, and this theological conception is a guarantee that nationalism will be articulated with a higher morality.[17]

Writing in the first half of the twentieth century, Martin Buber was unaware of the destructive possibilities that were to emerge later out of the relationship between religious belief and radical nationalism, in Judaism as well as in Islam and Christianity. The example of an aggressive expression of nationalism he had before his eyes was Germany during and after the First World War, and this nationalism was centred upon volkist secularism, not upon a symbiosis with Christian religiosity. In this respect, both the Jewish orthodoxy of the time and Jewish reformism were predominantly anti-nationalist or non-nationalist. Moreover, as we saw earlier, the religious wing of Zionism (the Mizrahi) was then among the most moderate political movements. There was no Gush Emunim (Bloc of the Faithful), the group Kach (Thus) formed by Rabbi Meir Kahane and his disciples had not yet appeared, no Hamas (Fervour) existed yet, and there were no Guardians of the Islamic Revolution in Iran, no extremist currents such as American evangelism or Italy's new extreme right. All these movements, which combine a nationalist and a religious radicalism, emerged and gained momentum only in the last quarter of the twentieth century.[18] Buber could scarcely have imagined that someone like Zvi Yehuda Kook, the master of a Talmudic school and Israel's Chief Rabbi, would compare tanks to phylacteries and would regard the Jewish appropriation of every clod of earth in Eretz Israel as a necessary condition for the coming of heavenly salvation. In the 1920s and 1930s, it was still possible for Buber to think that voracious nationalism could be held back by the moderating influence of an almighty divine sovereign.

Acknowledging the presence of neighbours and taking them into account at all times appeared to Buber as another brake on nationalism. He was well aware that the colonisation of the Land of Zion involved a degree of injustice: 'Let us imagine that we were were the ones who lived in Eretz Israel and others came to us: then we would understand what that means.' Therefore Zionism had to aspire to mitigate this injustice as far as possible, to develop sincere solidarity with the Arabs and, unassumingly, to improve the material situation of both populations: 'Our aim is to combine the requisite independence with the possible coexistence – in other words to achieve what is called a binational state.'[19]

In 1938, at the very last moment, Buber fled Germany and arrived in Palestine, which he had already visited several times. Thanks to his symbolic and academic capital, he immediately obtained a post at the Hebrew University, although, in order to shelter 'sensitive minds', the chair he was offered was neither in philosophy nor at the Institute of Jewish Sciences, but in a new discipline dubbed 'sociology of culture'.[20] Naturally, it did not take him long to break free of the academic constraints that had been placed upon him and, likewise, he decided to take an active part in local intellectual politics.

His first opportunity to express his point of view publicly came in the wake of Mahatma Gandhi's critique of Zionism.

For all his empathy and solidarity with the suffering of Jews in Europe, Gandhi formally asserted that Palestine belonged to the Arabs, just as England belonged to the English and France to the French. The Zionists' ardent religious link to Jerusalem, he stated, did not give them the right to colonise a land that was already inhabited, and certainly not with the help of foreign bayonets, as was the case especially during the final phase of the Arab Revolt of the 1930s, which was harshly put down by the British with support from Jewish settlers.

Buber responded to Gandhi, whom he admired, in a long and somewhat convoluted letter in which he justified the Zionist enterprise with arguments of a historical, religious, and political nature. One can sense in this letter that it was not easy for Buber to advocate colonisation in Palestine. He invoked the mythical argument that the Jews had been driven out of their country two thousand years ago and the Arabs conquered it later and settled there by force of arms. Was this colonisation more legitimate than that of the Zionists in the modern era? – asks the Zionist philosopher, adding:

Ask the soil what the Arabs have done for her [sc. Palestine] in 1,300 years and what we have done for her in 50! Would her answer not be weighty testimony in a just discussion as to whom this land 'belongs'.[21]

For a moment, the German patriot of the First World War suddenly seems to rear his head again, now in the guise of a typical Jewish colonialist. But Buber immediately reconsiders and seeks to balance his rampant 'orientalism' with a proclamation of his political identity: 'I belong to a group of people who, from the time when Britain conquered Palestine, have not ceased to strive for the concluding of genuine peace between Jew and Arab.'[22]

He is apparently referring here to his constant support for Brit Shalom during the 1920s. In April 1939, the new immigrant had played an active part in the creation of a fragile political body called the League for Jewish–Arab Rapprochement and Cooperation, which set itself the goal of establishing a framework for living together in spite of the worsening conflict. Within this framework, Buber sought to promote three objectives: abolishing the slogan *Avoda Ivrit* ('Hebrew Labour') used by the Zionist left; abandoning the call for unlimited Jewish emigration; and renouncing the demand for a Jewish majority.[23] This is why Buber was one of the first to join the Ihud association, founded by Leon Magnes in 1942. Despite Magnes's sudden death in 1948, the organisation continued to exist after the creation of the State of Israel, and Buber would remain loyal to it for the rest of his life.

After the 1948 Arab–Israeli War, the philosopher continued to fight for the rights of the Arabs who remained in the State of Israel, also calling for Israel to accept the return to its territory of some of the refugees who had been expelled or had fled. He opposed the Israeli government's massive confiscation of land and the extravagance of the military administration. With some regret, he ultimately abandoned the binational idea, replacing it with a federal vision of the Middle East.

In 1965, at the age of eighty-seven, weak and exhausted, Buber made the following point in what turned out to be his last article:

> The situation here may rather be compared to that of Switzerland. The basis on which a federative union can be established is, by necessity, so that for each of the two partners the full national autonomy is preserved.[24]

Hannah Arendt and Anti-Semitism

Can biographical or theoretical parallels be drawn between Martin Buber and Hannah Arendt? Both grew up and were educated on the eastern fringes of German culture, Buber in Lviv and Arendt in Königsberg. Both were forced to leave Germany by the advent of Nazism (and both married non-Jews). Both were strongly influenced by the social thought of anarchist thinkers: Gustave Landauer in Buber's case, Bernard Lazare in Arendt's. Both revered the communitarian socialism of the kibbutz enterprise. But, although German culture was their common cradle, their philosophical and religious vision as well as their relationship with Zionism developed in totally different ways. As young people, both were attracted by Kierkegaard's existentialism, but, where Buber was inclined to look for the mystery behind what existed, Arendt, for whom the sacred and mystery were not part of lived experience, sought relentlessly to decipher the political stakes behind every social relationship and hardly paid any attention to the theological dimension. Be that as it may, there is an essential point of convergence, political and moral, at the heart of their respective conceptions of Jewish nationality: both sincerely supported the principle of creating a binational state in Palestine.

While Martin Buber, like Ahad Ha'am, embraced the Zionist idea out of a sense that Jewish identity was in disarray, Hannah Arendt, much like Theodor Herzl, was attracted to it (although she never fully embraced it) because of the upsurge in anti-Semitism. When it comes to her move towards Zionism, it is in fact with the French anarchist Bernard Lazare that Arendt should be compared. Lazare, who was totally overshadowed by the Israeli culture of memory, was the first Dreyfusard, before Émile Zola, and it was thanks to his commitment that the military trial of Dreyfus became a high-profile public affair, which ended with the release of the accused. Despite a certain anti-Jewish tone in his early writings, Lazare also became the first French Zionist, perhaps even the first western one, and as such was received as a hero at the Second Zionist Congress. However, he was quick to criticise severely the opportunism of Herzl's movement, which in his view was courting the most conservative forces: the emperor of Germany, the tsar of Russia, and the Ottoman sultan, Abdul Hamid II – indeed, Herzl went so far as to help the latter absolve himself of responsibility for the massacre of the Armenians. Lazare, on the other hand, believed that only solidarity with other oppressed peoples could justify the national struggle of the Jews – which is why he chose in the end, not without sadness, to be ostracised by the Zionist movement.[25]

Arendt admired this modern figure who had fallen into oblivion and on many occasions returned to his thinking, on the one hand as a source of encouragement and identification with the pariahs of the world, and on the other as an argument for the harsh criticism of those parvenus who aim only to climb the social ladder.[26] Her idealistic vision of the sociopolitical future was fuelled by Lazare's anticentralising anarchism, and up until the end of her life she supported federalist positions and even expressed sympathy for the idea of creating self-managing councils (not on the Soviet model, of course!). To the very end, Arendt identified with the lower classes and with pariahs, while at the same time expressing her aversion to the rabble – this constant object of manipulation for parvenu leaders.

It would appear that this basic political conception, which dominates the whole of Arendt's thinking, comes from a semi-anarchist dimension interwoven with liberal principles: only the participation and autonomy of the greatest number in the public arena – from the Athenian democracy to the student revolts of the twentieth century – can make politics a truly political praxis. By contrast, state totalitarianism consists precisely in the attempt to erase the political and to destroy any concern for the general interest and for public life, coupled with intervening unrestrainedly in private life. Human rights, which are undermined by totalitarianism, are certainly not political freedoms, but they are their condition.

Lazare, who died in 1903 and therefore lived most of his life in the second half of the nineteenth century, would have preferred national Jews to organise themselves as an independent fighting force wherever and whenever Judeophobia reared its ugly head. A territorial solution confining them to a small corner of the Middle East seemed to him less attractive and less logical. As for Arendt, in the 1930s she began to see Palestine as a priority refuge for persecuted Jews, without ever completely abandoning Lazare's idea of a political option for Jews to defend themselves autonomously within Europe.

In her biography of Rahel Varnhagen, a Jewish woman who hosted a salon during the period of the Enlightenment and romanticism, Arendt explored the problems of the Jewish presence in European history, and in particular the great difficulties and frustrations that Jews had to endure in the process of assimilation: 'In a society on the whole hostile to the Jews [. . .] it is possible to assimilate only by assimilating to anti-Semitism also.'[27] Amid the turmoil of 1934, a year after she fled Germany, Arendt published her first article on Judaism. As a stateless refugee, she began working in France for Zionist associations and decided to write about Jewish issues in the magazine *Jüdische Rundschau*, edited by Robert Weltsch, a member of Brit Shalom. On Palestine, she had the following to say:

> Palestine is not at the centre of our national aspirations because 2,000 years ago some people lived there from whom in some sense or other we are supposed to be descended, but because for 2,000 years the craziest of peoples took pleasure in preserving the past in the present, because for them 'the ruins of Jerusalem are, you could say, rooted in the heart of time' (Herder).[28]

During her last years in Europe Arendt became increasingly 'Jewish', but her second husband, Heinrich Blücher, who for a time remained a Marxist despite his hatred for Stalin, along with her sceptical universalist friend, Walter Benjamin, helped to restrain her uncontrolled enthusiasm for making the desert in Palestine bloom with 'collective villages'. In her first essay on anti-Semitism, written in France, she was highly critical of the 'assimilationist' philosophy of anti-Zionists on the one hand and, on the other, of essentialist Zionists – who, just like anti-Semites, saw the Jew as an eternally foreign element in the world's civilisations, from which they sought to keep him apart.

Arendt makes a very clear distinction between Christian Judeophobia and modern anti-Semitism, but she makes the bizarre and even shocking claim – presumably echoing the prejudices of the pre-Dreyfus Lazare – that, up until the nineteenth century, Jews were just as responsible as Christians for the rift between themselves and their hostile environment. Her first attempt at historicising anti-Semitism, although highly sophisticated, was vitiated by numerous weaknesses and errors, some of which would be rectified in the first part of her famous book *The Origins of Totalitarianism*, published in 1951.[29] There she formulates the problematic idea that 'anti-Semitism grew in proportion as traditional nationalism declined', or again, the dubious assertion that 'fifty years of antisemitic history stand as evidence against the identification of antisemitism with nationalism'.[30] What stands out most in Arendt's writings on Jews and Judeophobia, however, is the relative silence on the special situation of the *Ostjuden*, the Jews of the Yiddish people of Central Europe, and their mass exodus to the American continent, which radically altered the contours of the Jewish presence in the world.

When Arendt arrived in the United States with her husband, Heinrich Blücher (the majority of refugees fleeing Nazism had been refused permission to emigrate to South America or Palestine), she continued to write on Jewish subjects, while remaining very much engaged in general political philosophy. She imagined setting up a Jewish army to join the forces that fought against Nazism. The stateless refugee couple received considerable help from Jewish institutions: she was recruited as director of the Schocken publishing house even as she continued to concern herself with the fate of Jews in the Middle East. Arendt had already visited Palestine in 1935, but her first visit to Israel took place in 1955. She returned in 1961, on the occasion of the Eichmann trial, and her last visit took place after the Six-Day War of 1967. She continued to maintain a rather contradictory dialogue with Zionism and with Israel, whose attitude towards the Arabs she harshly criticised, although this did not prevent her later on from expressing her esteem for the Jewish Defense League in the United States, going into ecstasies about the power of the Israeli army, and expressing her admiration for Moshe Dayan.[31]

A Jewish Nation State?

In the early 1940s Arendt began to express doubts as to whether Zionism was an appropriate response to anti-Semitism, let alone a serious riposte to Nazi persecution. Indeed, she suggested that, if Field Marshal Montgomery had not blocked General Rommel, the latter would have continued his march eastwards and arrived in Palestine.[32] Besides, the Zionist colonisation of the Middle East gave rise to a new anti-Semitism, she claimed, and created problems for the entire Arab world. Arendt did not hesitate to describe Zionism as a 'transportation enterprise' – for Jews, but also for anti-Semitism.

In 1944, the Conference of American Zionists, which met in Atlantic City, adopted a motion calling for the creation of a free and democratic Jewish community across the whole territory of Zion, neither divided nor reduced in size. This demand was subsequently endorsed by the World Zionist Organization. Arendt reacted with a virulent and sarcastic article. In her view, as Zionism had grown stronger, it had become increasingly extremist. At the famous Biltmore conference in New York in 1942, it was decided that 'the Jewish minority had granted minority rights to the Arab majority. This time the Arabs were simply not mentioned in the resolution, which obviously leaves them the choice between voluntary emigration or second class citizenship.'[33]

Arendt came to the conclusion that the Zionist movement, both at the Biltmore conference and in Atlantic City, had revealed its true face and had in fact abandoned any search for peaceful coexistence with the local inhabitants. She added that 'it is simply preposterous to believe that further partition of so small a territory [. . .] could resolve the conflict of two peoples'.[34] The transfer of all Arabs out of Palestine would not change the situation either: faced with a hostile Arab world, the future Jewish state would have to rely constantly on the help of the great powers to defend itself against a threatening environment. Arendt was categorical on this point:

> Since theirs was a national movement, the Zionists could think only in national terms, seemingly unaware of the fact that imperialism was a nation-destroying force, and therefore, for a small people, it was near suicide to attempt to become its ally or its agent. [. . .] [A]n alliance between a lion and a lamb can have disastrous consequences for the lamb.[35]

Arendt disapproved of the partition plan adopted in 1947, strongly fearing, among other things, military confrontation and the casualties that would result. For this reason, she argued in favour of an international supervisory council that for a given period would enforce the fundamental rights of both peoples. She was particularly worried that, '[i]f the *Yishuv* went down, it would drag along in its fall the collective settlements, the kibbutzim – which constitute perhaps the most promising of all social experiments made in the twentieth century, as well as the most magnificent part of the Jewish homeland'.[36]

Beyond outright hostilities, she had almost given up hope of preserving even a grain of Jewish–Arab friendship. According to her, the attacks carried out in Haifa at the end of 1947 by the Irgun (an armed organisation of the Zionist right), followed by the massacre in the village of Deir Yassin in April 1948, had created a panic that caused many Arab inhabitants to flee, and had driven a further wedge between the two populations.

Up until this point, Arendt had hesitated to support binationalism and had distanced herself from its supporters. But from this phase of her work until the stabilisation of the State of Israel in the 1950s, she saw the federal framework as the fundamental basis for the continued presence of Jews in the Middle East:

> The partition of so small a country could at best mean the petrifaction of the conflict, which would result in arrested development for both peoples; at worst it would signify a temporary stage during which both parties would prepare for further war. The alternative proposition of a federated state, also recently endorsed by Dr Magnes, is much more realistic; despite the fact that it establishes a common government for two different peoples, it avoids the troublesome majority–minority constellation, which is insoluble by definition. A federated structure, moreover, would have to rest on Jewish–Arab community councils, which would mean that the Jewish–Arab conflict would be resolved on the lowest and most promising level of proximity and neighbourliness.[37]

Arendt did not think that a permanent federal solution could be imposed by force, but she was convinced that '[t]he independence of Palestine can be achieved only on a solid basis of Jewish–Arab cooperation'.[38] The only alternative to peaceful coexistence would be the creation of a Jewish state that lived permanently with arms at the ready, invoking the Masada myth, and looking very much like a modern Sparta.

Shortly before his death in 1948, Leon Magnes, who had become a close friend of Arendt's, asked her to write an essay on the conflict. His untimely death prompted her to dedicate the essay to his memory. The essay, 'Peace or Armistice in the Middle East', published in 1950, is permeated by a pessimistic and rather depressive tone. Arendt briefly reviews the history of offers of compromise made by humanist and pacifist Zionists: Ahad Ha'am and Yitzhak Epstein, Brit Shalom and Hashomer Hatzair, and finally Martin Buber and Leon Magnes; she expresses her fears for the future: the powerlessness of the vast majority of the parties to the conflict and their unwillingness to opt for the path of compromise will lead to war and more distressed refugees. Palestine can only live within an egalitarian federal framework, otherwise one people will always dominate the other.

During the UN vote on the plan for the partition of Palestine in 1947, Arendt, like Magnes and Buber, was tempted to support the minority resolution put forward by three non-western states: Gandhi's India, Tito's Yugoslavia and the Shah's Iran. This resolution called for the creation of a federation or confederation with Jerusalem as its capital. As mentioned earlier, the partition plan finally adopted provided for the inclusion of 497,000 Arabs in the Jewish state, alongside 598,000 Jews – in other words, it was to be a Jewish state with more than 45 per cent non-Jewish inhabitants. All agreed that no Arab could possibly approve of such a plan; alas, it was only natural that it should lead to armed confrontation – an outcome that, according to Arendt, only a federalist plan might have avoided, notwithstanding all the difficulties involved in implementing it.

At the same time, she advocated a confederative union of the Middle East, although she doubted the feasibility of such a project in the short term. She believed that the alternative to progress towards a federation would be a widespread balkanisation of the region, with nationalisms running riot, cynically exploited by the great powers. This would leave the Jewish state all the more isolated, and the isolation would degrade the notion of Jews as 'the chosen people'; this notion would 'degenerate into hopeless vulgarity'.[39]

With regard to Israel, the pessimistic conclusion reached by Arendt was to be of great importance in the development of her ideas:

> National sovereignty, which so long had been the very symbol of free national development, has become the greatest danger to national survival for small nations. In view of the international situation and the geographical location of Palestine, it is not likely that the Jewish and Arab peoples will be exempt from this rule.[40]

This prognosis has proved to be incorrect. It is true that, immediately after the war, the Arab state planned in Palestine was carved up simultaneously by the Jewish state and by monarchist Jordan; however, after the transfer of a part of the Arab population in 1948, Israel managed to survive, become stronger, and put down roots with the help of the major powers, American Jews, and German compensation. As Arendt feared, the Jewish state has indeed taken the form of a kind of enclosed ghetto surrounded by a hostile environment, or, we might say, a heavily armed but prosperous 'Spartan state'.

By the time of her death in 1975, Arendt had witnessed Israel's involvement in three more wars – the Sinai campaign in 1956, the war of 1967, and the war of 1973 – as well as violent infiltrations and numerous reprisals. Since then, the long war in Lebanon that began in 1982, the two bloody Intifadas in 1987–9 and 2000–2, the ongoing missile battles with Hamas in Gaza in the twenty-first century, and the fear of a nuclear confrontation with Iran have set the tone for a situation that seems likely to be long-lasting, if not permanent.

5

Theopolitics and the Pacifist Ihud Association

It is up to us to give up once and for all the idea of a 'Jewish Palestine' in the sense of a Jewish country that will supplant Arab Palestine [. . .] Zionism did not exist at the beginning of Judaism, and if it does not agree with Judaism from a moral point of view, woe betide Zionism!

Letter from Leon Magnes to Felix Warburg,
13 September 1929

This historical right [of Jews over the country] is a metaphysical category [. . .] so it is not binding for the Arabs, but for ourselves. It is a category internal to Judaism.

Ernst Simon, 'Against the Sadducees', 1931[1]

Brit Shalom officially disbanded in 1933. A few former members continued to express critical views publicly, but in a strictly personal capacity. In 1936, shortly before the outbreak of the great Arab Revolt, a new organisation called Kedmah-Mizraha was founded. Several former members of Brit Shalom – Haim Margaliot-Kalvarisky, Moshe Smilansky, Jacob Thon, and Rabbi Binyamin – were members of the founding assembly of the new group, which nevertheless did not see itself as a continuation of Brit Shalom and did not explicitly call for the constitution of a binational state. The new organisation confined itself to formulating various federalist ideas in rather equivocal terms. Its demands included a call for the recognition of the culture of the peoples of the East and for a Jewish–Arab rapprochement, in coordination with Zionist institutions and in the spirit of unconditional loyalty to 'the great return to Zion'.[2] Politically, the new organisation was rather heterogeneous: almost every colour of the political spectrum was represented. The presence of traditional Sephardic Jews was one of its trademarks.

Kedmah-Mizraha disbanded in 1939, before the outbreak of the Second World War. It was replaced by a fragile new organisation that took the form of a coalition and never really got off the ground. This one became known as the League for Jewish–Arab Rapprochement and Cooperation. Unlike Kedmah-Mizraha, the League declared itself cautiously in favour of a binational political structure. It was joined in this by several movements: Hashomer Hatzair (The Young Guard), Hakibboutz Ha'artzi (a kibbutzim organisation linked to Hashomer Hatzair), Poale Zion Smol (Left Workers' Party of Zion), and the New Aliyah Party (made up of liberal immigrants from Germany and Austria).[3]

Until the adoption in 1942 of the Biltmore programme, which provided for the creation of a sovereign Jewish state in which Arabs would have minority status, binational ideas were acceptable, but only cautiously and in moderation, and obviously without abandoning the demand for a Jewish majority or cutting oneself off from the Zionist mainstream – to avoid being assimilated with the former 'extremists' of Brit Shalom. Realising that the enlarged League brought together a number of political organisations, another group, intended to be more coherent, was created at the same time on Leon Magnes's initiative, in immediate reaction to the Biltmore programme.

The Unquiet American

One day, when asked which American Zionist leader he held in highest esteem, David Ben-Gurion replied without hesitation: 'Magnes'. When asked why he would choose such an obvious political opponent, the head of state replied: 'But he came to the Palestine, the others did not.'[4] Here Ben-Gurion uncovered a truth that Zionists had generally found difficult to admit or to formulate. In the West, from the banks of the Rhine to the beaches of the Pacific in California, very few Jews, including well-known Zionist leaders and activists, had actually emigrated to Palestine or, later, to Israel. From this perspective, Leon Magnes was an original Zionist, and one endowed with an extraordinary personality.

Magnes was born in 1877 in Oakland, California. His mother was born in New York, his father had arrived from the Polish city of Lodz at a very young age. Magnes very soon became a Reform rabbi, before going to Germany to complete his doctorate in theology and Semitic languages at the universities of Berlin and Heidelberg. At a time when the rabbinate, both Reform and Orthodox, was firmly opposed to Zionism, Magnes persisted in his nationalist ideas, distancing himself from those around him and becoming increasingly attached to Zionist ideology. He also moved away from Reform Judaism, founding a conservative religious studies circle.

In Germany, Magnes became both a Zionist activist and a committed pacifist. Although as an individual he had supported the creation of an armed Jewish self-defence organisation after the pogroms in the Russian empire, from 1898 onwards he opposed the colonialist confrontation between the United States and Spain. The outbreak of the First World War and its development hit him hard, and he publicly protested against his country's entry into the war. Magnes sympathised with the American socialist pacifists; for a time he was even an admirer of Vladimir Lenin, who called for an immediate end to the fighting. For the same reasons he became interested in the American Quakers, and later on became an enthusiastic supporter of Mahatma Gandhi. He deemed the Versailles Conference and subsequent diplomatic sessions hypocritical imperialist forums whose object was the cynical division of spoils. He also regarded the Balfour Declaration as a politically violent manipulation engineered by Great Britain; it could not be considered the proper historical terrain for an enterprise as laudable as Zionism.[5]

Magnes's public status within American Judaism continued to grow. He was appointed secretary of the Zionist Organization of America while his reputation as a charismatic rabbi and talented orator preceded him; but suddenly he chose to take another turn. In 1907 he made his first visit to Palestine, then returned in 1912, before settling permanently in Jerusalem in 1922, to the astonishment of his friends and family. By so doing, he marked his difference from most American Zionists, who, according to a well-known joke, spent their time collecting funds from other Zionists in order to send East European Jews to the Holy Land. This is not to say that Magnes saw the gathering of Jews in Palestine as a global solution to Jewish distress. Almost as soon as he had formulated his Zionist stance, he turned to Ahad Ha'am, notwithstanding the latter's atheism and secular vision, entering into correspondence with him and expressing his admiration on numerous occasions. The new Jerusalem must be a beacon for the Jews of the whole world without their having to physically go there, Magnes insisted. Jews have succeeded over the centuries in preserving their identity, and Jewish culture can be developed and preserved in modern times with the help of this close spiritual link with Zion.

According to Magnes, if Jerusalem was to be a cultural and emotional centre for the Jews of the world, then the Hebrew University had to lie at the heart of this centre. This great temple of knowledge would be able to enrich Jewish culture with universal thought and to answer the questionings entertained by Jews amid the turmoil of the twentieth century. Plans to found a university had already been formulated at the first Zionist Congress in Basel. The foundation stone was laid in 1918 on Mount Scopus, and the opening ceremony of the new establishment took place in 1925. The board of governors, which included Ahad Ha'am, Hayim Nahman Bialik, and Albert Einstein, immediately elected Magnes as chancellor. He galvanised the creation of the first research institutes (the teaching cycles had not yet been set up), and proved to be an outstanding academic leader.[6]

Magnes succeeded in attracting renowned speakers and in raising substantial funds in the United States, his relations with the American government enhancing his prestige. Unlike the Zionist leadership – in particular Chaim Weizmann, who wanted to turn the university into a megaphone for national ideology – Magnes threw all his weight behind the preservation of complete academic autonomy. The only consensus reached from the outset was to make Hebrew the common language, as far as this was possible. Magnes executed the functions of an unbending and all-powerful chancellor for ten years. By 1935, when the university was on a firm footing, his role was scaled down, but he continued to represent the institution as its president until his death in 1948. In his memoirs, Gershom Scholem, who knew Magnes well as an academic leader and admired him, albeit not without certain criticisms, described him as 'an American radical and people's tribune on the one hand, and a no less American boss on the other'.[7]

From the outset Magnes had made no secret of his reservations about the ways in which Palestine had been settled by the Jewish community and the nature of its relations with the indigenous population. But, given that in the early 1920s a great many spokespeople of the Zionist establishment were making accommodating and noncommittal pacifist noises, this did not yet mark Magnes out as a 'marginal extremist'. His ideas on binationalism were not explicitly formulated at the time, and his correspondence with Weizmann bears witness to a dialogue that was by no means confrontational. He held fast to the idea that the Land of Zion should be an international territory at peace and should not fall into the hands of the dominant powers. At this stage, Jews represented less than 20 per cent of the country's population, while indigenous Arabs made up the other 80 per cent. Multinationality, a rather abstract concept, was hardly in vogue, but was beginning to be spoken of; Magnes continued to advocate it, and attention came to focus on him as a result.[8]

When Arthur Ruppin founded Brit Shalom in 1925, the very year in which the university was founded, Magnes did not join, despite his close proximity to its spirit of conciliation with the Arabs and with the pacifism of the organisation's members. With his American cultural background, Magnes remained relatively distant from the ethnocentric identity politics of the majority of members, particularly Ruppin. He had grown up in an open national context, both civilian and statal, and the close correlation between nation and 'racial' origin, fairly widespread at the time, seemed less natural to him than to some members of the Alliance.[9] It is also possible that he felt a certain antipathy towards Ruppin, despite having endorsed his appointment to the university, and doubted the pacifist sincerity of the 'saviour of the soil'. It is also likely that Magnes's status and his intense activity in running the university prevented him from committing himself openly to a group with such an explicit ideological platform. He did, however, establish close relations with some members of Brit Shalom – Hugo Bergmann and Hans Kohn in particular – and Beatrice Magnes, his wife, did join the organisation.

In 1929, amid violent clashes between Arabs and Jews, particularly in Hebron and Safed, Magnes, increasingly troubled, began to publicly express his pacifist convictions. A few months after the riots, at the opening address of the academic year in

November 1929, he openly formulated his political vision, in a speech that met with hisses from the audience:

> As you know, I think that we need to find ways out, and that not each one of us is paying enough attention to our living and working together, to the level of social relations, to the cultural, general, and political level, and more generally to peace and understanding. If the Jewish National Home has the bayonets of some empire as its only point of support, our whole enterprise is not worthwhile [. . .]. It is one of the great cultural tasks before the Jewish people to try to enter the Promised Land not by means of conquest, like Joshua, but through peaceful and cultural means, through hard work, sacrifice, and love, and with a decision not to do anything that cannot be justified before the world conscience.[10]

In this remarkable speech Magnes was unsparing in his criticism of the leaders of the Arab population: according to him, figures of feeble conviction who had either fanned the flames or remained silent during the murderous explosion of violence. But in this wave of violence he also saw a direct result of the immigration of Jews en masse, and said that he was ready to accept the idea of a temporary limitation upon this immigration. He therefore called upon the British to pardon the murderers in order to silence the voices of Arab agitators and demagogues. At the same time he moved towards the conclusion that the creation of a national state and the struggle for a Jewish majority would not prevent future wars, but would, on the contrary, make them a certainty. After this speech, Magnes would be *persona non grata* in the eyes of many Zionist leaders, and there were numerous complaints that someone so political should hold the post of rector at the Hebrew University. Groups of right-wing students and lecturers demonstrated on several occasions to demand his resignation (Benzion Netanyahu's voice was perhaps one of the loudest among the protestors).[11]

Like Ahad Ha'am, Magnes did not pen voluminous or complex books or essays, nor was he a systematic thinker. He did, however, publish a host of texts and articles and send many letters. He was also in the habit of debating with himself in a diary, which makes for fascinating reading. At the end of 1929, he wrote:

> You claim [. . .] that there has been, in each of us, not only a Jeremiah, but also a Joshua; be that as it may, the dominant current in our tradition was that of Jeremiah and his kind. I feel that I am one of Jeremiah's people, heir to the slave of God, heir to that same tradition which, during the period of political subjugation, strove to raise existence to a spiritual level, and to preach the rejection of physical force.[12]

According to Magnes, ever since his time as a Reform Zionist rabbi, he had not seen nationality as an end in itself, but as a phase in the evolution of humanity, preparatory to a deeper and wider universalism. As a peace-loving American in perpetual search of divine grace, it now seemed to him that Jewish nationality, because of the difficulties encountered in its colonisation enterprise, was following in the footsteps of Joshua, the biblical figure who led the military conquest of the land of Canaan. Magnes's prophetic conception of justice and his deep thirst for salvation, but also his periodic doubts about the foundations of his faith, drove him to become more involved in the public arena, both in Palestine and in the United States. He also increasingly sought contact with foreign public figures and diplomats.

The Prophetic Chancellor

All eyes were on the president of the university, who had begun his speech. He had been a Reform rabbi in his youth and had been forced to leave his post because he was a Zionist. Although he retained some of the mannerisms of the Reform rabbinate, which are considered ridiculous in this country, his height, style, and dignity led even the cynics in the hall to listen to what he had to say.[13]

In this passage from his novel *Shira*, the writer Shmuel Yossef Agnon, castigating the academics of Jerusalem, highlights the singular personality of Magnes. And indeed, in the early 1930s, many people did find unbearable the public admonitions of the university chancellor and his sharp criticism of Zionist policy.

At the end of 1929, Magnes published his theological–political reflections under the title *Like All Nations?*, a book in which he raised a cardinal question. 'Is our nationalism like that of all Gentiles: idol-worshiping backed up by power and violence? Or is it a spiritual nationalism?' In the introduction he specifies that, while the three principles of 'immigration (*aliyah*)', 'settlement on the land', and 'Hebrew life and culture' must be guaranteed, he is 'willing to yield the Jewish State, and the Jewish majority' and to accept 'a legislative assembly together with a democratic political system'.[14] From this point on, Magnes would entirely renounce the idea of exclusive Jewish sovereignty as a necessary condition for an agreement and, until his death, would remain an advocate of federation as the basis for achieving justice and a lasting, non-confrontational coexistence between Jews and Arabs in Palestine. If there is a Jewish conscience, he writes, it 'must recognise, and better one hour before, and better voluntarily than under compulsion, that the inhabitants of this country, Arabs and Jews, have not only the right but also the obligation to participate effectively and equitably in the governance of their common homeland'.[15]

The federal structure of Magnes's native country directly influenced his political ideas on the problematic future of the Middle East. He was guided by basic principles, drawn as much from the founding fathers of American liberalism as from the biblical prophets, and this symbiosis between a specifically Jewish theology and a conception of human and civil rights shaped his demands for national coexistence, which would remain the essential paradigm of all the positions he took on the Jewish–Arab conflict.[16] In *Like All Nations?* he advocates

> the creation of two assemblies: a lower legislative assembly, elected by all inhabitants, in which there will obviously be an Arab majority, and an upper house, which will be elected or appointed on the basis of equality between the three nations: one third Jewish, one third Arab, and one third English. This is similar to the Constitution of the United States, where the Senate is made up of two representatives from each State of the Union, large or small, and regardless of the number of inhabitants. This expresses the equal rights of all the Member States of the Union, while the Legislative Assembly represents all the inhabitants as individuals.[17]

At this point the university chancellor decided to enter the political fray to promote his ideas. As a first step he met St John Philby, a former senior British diplomat who had been involved in the creation of Mandatory Palestine before converting to Islam and had later become an adviser to Ibn Saud, the king of Saudi Arabia. Philby proposed a plan for a compromise between the High Muslim Council and the Zionist movement. The plan was meant to bring the two communities closer together around a project of creating democratic parliamentary institutions, while allowing for a British veto. It was clear that, under this plan, Jews would give up their claim to become the majority in Palestine. Magnes, representing no one but himself, accepted the proposal in principle, despite the reservations of Zionist authorities, thereby deepening his alienation and further distancing himself from the establishment.[18]

But Magnes's break with the Zionist leadership was not yet complete. Chaim Weizmann considered him a traitor and

Vladimir Jabotinsky described him as a comical and harmful character, yet David Ben-Gurion agreed to meet him and dissociated himself from some of the violent attacks made against him. Magnes, for his part, did not give up all hope of pursuing contact with Arab figures; in the early 1930s he strove to foster dialogue by every possible means.[19] When Lord Passfield – Sidney Webb, first Baron Passfield, member of the Labour Party and minister of colonies – published his White Paper in 1930, Magnes was inclined to express his support for it, despite the opposition of all the leaders of the Yishuv. The Passfield White Paper contained the proposal that the sale of land to Jews be possible only if it did not have negative effects on the local peasants. In addition, the immigration of Jews would be limited in accordance with the capacity of the local economy to integrate them. Another point that aroused great irritation was the proposal to create a common legislative council for all inhabitants. Magnes, on the other hand, welcomed the idea of electing a council, which he felt should include around 40 per cent Jews; and he more or less accepted all of the provisions of the White Paper.

On the eve of the Arab Revolt of 1936, Magnes joined forces with Moshe Smilansky, chairman of the farmers' union, Pinhas Rutenberg, director of the electricity company, Gad Frumkin, judge at the High Court of Justice, and Moshe Novomeysky, director of the Dead Sea phosphate company, to form what would come to be known as 'the group of five'. Their aim was to prevent clashes between the two communities and to find channels for dialogue with Arab leaders, however isolated and marginal they might be. However, against a backdrop of growing tension, the failure of the five produced dark despair among all pacifists about what was to come.

It is important to remember that in the first waves of emigration, during the 1880s and up until 1924, just over 100,000 Jews arrived in Palestine. For the ten years or so between the end of 1924, when the United States shut its doors to Jewish immigration from Eastern Europe, and the beginning of 1936, when the Nuremberg Laws were enacted in Nazi Germany, around 250,000 immigrants in distress came to Palestine. This immigration, although not ideological, was to have a decisive impact upon the escalation of the conflict. Its effects were felt in the daily lives of the Arab inhabitants (who numbered more than 900,000 at the time) and contributed to an increase in incidents and to the outbreak of the first serious revolt in Palestine. The year 1936 saw the start of the insurrection, during which the High Arab Committee was set up, a general strike was proclaimed, and acts of sabotage were carried out. All political parties, with the exception of communists, were represented on the High Arab Committee, which made these formal demands: an absolute ban on the sale of land to Zionists; a halt to Jewish immigration to Palestine; and the creation of an autonomous government, representative of all its inhabitants. During this long and bitter revolt, nearly five thousand Arabs, four hundred Jews, and two hundred English people were killed.

The end of confrontations, which came just a few months before the outbreak of the Second World War, opened up a few timid attempts to resume dialogue with representatives of the Arab community. In the summer of 1939, Haim Kalvarisky founded the League for Jewish–Arab Rapprochement and Cooperation, mentioned earlier, and members of various parties joined it. Magnes, who had not been involved in the founding of the League, became a member, and many of his close friends, for instance Ernst Simon, Martin Buber, Robert Weltsch, and Rabbi Binyamin, participated in its activities. The affiliation of Hashomer Hatzair movement, of Alia Hadatha (New Immigration), a party made up of German emigrants, and of Poale Zion Smol, as well as their union with another, smaller league created earlier by Israel and Mania Shohat yielded an alliance whose ideological and political heterogeneity made it impossible to pursue any effective initiatives. All participants approved the principle of binationalism, but they remained divided as to its implementation. Some emphasised the common Semitic destiny of Jews and Arabs, while others dreamt of a binational socialist republic, albeit one with a Jewish majority, of course.

Martin Buber, who had arrived in Palestine in 1938, after escaping from Germany, felt it was urgent to create a more unified organisation, which would make three provocative demands: to abolish the slogan 'Hebrew labour' and relinquish the aspiration to produce exclusively by Jewish labour; to abandon the demand for unlimited immigration; and to give up on the demand for a Jewish majority.[20]

This was in effect a declaration of war on the Zionist Organization, and one that the more politicised members of the League were not really prepared to accept. In the summer of 1942 the paradoxical alliance between politicians and intellectuals shifted, after the official affiliation of Hashomer Hatzair: from now on the torch of binationalism would be carried by another organisation.

The Ihud Association

In 1942 Magnes, in partnership with Martin Buber and Ernst Simon, founded Ihud (the Union). At that point he became less of a pacifist and lent his full support to total war until Hitler was defeated. The name of the new organisation was borrowed from American politics: it was a reference to Abraham Lincoln's famous call for the union of the divided American states. Henrietta Szold, Haim Margaliot-Kalvarisky, and Moshe Smilansky were appointed to the presidency of Ihud. To a certain extent, its creation was a reaction against the Biltmore programme, adopted in May 1942, which demanded the creation of a Jewish state across the entire western half of Eretz Israel, and which was approved in November of the same year

by the Zionist Executive Committee. According to the supporters of Ihud, this programme would inevitably and indefinitely
plunge the two communities of Palestine into incessant armed
confrontation. The members of Ihud saw the painful events of
1936–9 as a warning sign of a long process of conflict that the
generations would lament. They were convinced that the sine
qua non for a reconciliation between the local population and
the colonised population was the establishment of a modus
vivendi that both would deem acceptable, if only temporarily. They saw themselves as minimalist Zionists in search of
demographic equality and of a dual partnership dedicated to
the collective self-determination of the two communities.

In a letter addressed personally to Morris Lazaron, one of
the American leaders of Reform Judaism, Magnes wrote in
1942: 'It is true that Jewish nationalism tends to confuse people,
not because it is secular and not religious, but because it is
a sadly chauvinistic, narrow-minded, terrorist nationalism in
the purest style of Eastern European nationalism.'[21] The comparison with Eastern Europe perhaps attests to the continuity
of Magnes's relations with Hans Kohn. Morris Lazaron then
published the letter, which provoked a wave of indignation
against Magnes and earned him a barrage of insults from all
the Zionist leaders of the time. His attempts to rectify the
situation failed, and the supporters of Ihud felt more isolated
than ever. Some time later, Ben-Gurion declared: 'I believe Dr
Magnes detests Zionism. And yet, as a person, he has a stature
by comparison with which many Zionists are lacking in positive personal qualities.'[22]

Buber and Ernst Simon remained faithful to the principles
of Ihud and, like Magnes, totally rejected Ben-Gurion's policy
of founding a specifically Jewish state. The two of them took
charge of editing *Problems of the Time*, the organisation's
monthly magazine, which had some five hundred subscribers,
and tried to instil in its pages an atmosphere of reconciliation and understanding among all those opposed to exclusive

Jewish sovereignty; but they proved rather hesitant when faced with the various alternatives. The numerous reports of Nazi massacres of Jews mitigated their ostensible pacifism somewhat, but did not deter them from seeking a compromise with the indigenous inhabitants of Palestine. They continued with all their might to play their role as politically engaged intellectuals, and persisted in infusing this role with moral and universalist values.

For the members of Ihud, the Allied victory was an important source of encouragement for the continuation of their struggle. They opposed the terrorist acts of Irgun Zvai Leumi and of Lehi (aka the Stern Gang) and denounced the creation of the Jewish Resistance Movement, an umbrella name for all groups involved in armed struggle. However, the wave of refugees from Europe knocking on Palestine's doors was to shift their attitude to immigration. Ihud moved closer to the Zionist consensus and strongly criticised the indecisiveness of British policy. When the Anglo-American Commission on Palestine was set up in 1946, Ihud saw an opportunity to set out its position in favour of the creation of a binational structure that could, in certain circumstances, welcome refugees and uprooted people.

In their testimony to this committee, Magnes and Buber insisted on the need to create a body made up of representatives of both the Arab League and the Jewish Agency, as well as of British figures, in order to decide upon the rate of immigration until demographic equality was achieved (at the time, the number of Arabs was twice that of Jews). The process was bound to meet with Arab opposition, but so long as Zionism was not intent on creating an exclusive Jewish state, such opposition seemed unlikely to degenerate into armed opposition.[23]

Magnes and Buber highlighted to the Commission the advantages of a binational state arrived at through a gradual process:

1. There is no chance of peace in a mononational state where one people dominates another.
2. Only a binational system can defend the languages, institutions, and cultures of both peoples.
3. There is no point in focusing on the numerical weight of the each people if we are to build a progressive and self-assured federal union.

In the event, the report of the Anglo-American Committee of Inquiry ruled out the creation of exclusive Jewish or Arab states, a gesture that many interpreted as indirect support for the idea of a federation. However, the British prime minister's demand that immigration permits for 100,000 refugees be made conditional upon the abolition of private militias, including the Haganah, dampened the general enthusiasm that had taken hold among Ihud members and sympathisers.

After an escalation in terrorist acts carried out by Jews that culminated in the bombing of the King David Hotel in Jerusalem, a despondent mood set in. The assassination of Fawzi Al Husseini, leader of New Palestine, a small Arab group that advocated binationalism, added to the general disillusionment. Yet, in spite of all this, Magnes, Buber, and Simon did not give up but continued their fight. The fear of a general conflagration between the two communities gave them no rest, and their conception of Jewish faith and ethics gave them the strength to continue to oppose the hegemonic Zionist positions.

On 14 May 1947, the United Nations decided to set up a special commission of enquiry (SCOP) into the problems of Palestine. The UNSCOP was to examine the conditions for resolving the Jewish–Arab conflict, the principle being that representatives of the major powers should not interfere in the process. Ihud delegated Magnes as a witness, and he, of course, endeavoured to highlight the advantages of a binational solution. He saw the achievement of numerical equality within the framework of a mutual agreement as a fair objective and condition for creating a new political structure. Simon, speaking on behalf of the League for Jewish–Arab Rapprochement and Cooperation, also expressed his support for a federation.[24] Ben-Gurion, who was also called to testify before the commission, rejected the binational solution out of hand; he saw total Jewish sovereignty as the only possible solution to the conflict.

As we have already seen, at the end of August 1947 the majority of members of the commission had decided to divide Palestine into two states: one under Jewish sovereignty (with 45 per cent Arabs, in other words a demographically *de facto* binational state), the other under Arab sovereignty. The UN General Assembly adopted the Commission's recommendation by a majority vote on 27 November 1947. The creation of the State of Israel was proclaimed on 14 May 1948, and war broke out the very next day.

Leon Magnes died in New York a few months later. Shortly before his death he had met with the president of the United States, Harry Truman, and had tried to convince the Americans to impose economic sanctions on both sides in order to put an end to the bloodshed. The bold dream of a binational federation, to which this 'troubled American' had aspired, was shattered by his untimely death.

Ihud survived as a minor fringe group until the mid-1960s and Buber's death. The indefatigable Rabbi Binyamin continued to edit its journal *Ner* (*The Candle*); the group's struggle was no longer based on the idea of binationalism, but on support for a Middle Eastern federation, for the equality of Arab citizens, and for the abolition of the draconian regime of military administration imposed upon them.

Last of the Mohicans

Ernst Simon was probably the only member of the Ihud leadership to remain a militant Brit Shalom activist until the group's dissolution. He had arrived in Palestine in 1928 and had joined the Alliance immediately. Bergmann and Scholem had abandoned the arena of public struggle; Kohn, demoralised, had emigrated to the United States; but Simon continued his work for binationalism throughout the 1930s. He also joined the League for Jewish–Arab Rapprochement and Cooperation and was one of the founders of Ihud. A philosopher and a teacher, an admirer of Buber and someone close to Magnes, he opposed all aggressive and brutal nationalism until the end of his life (he died in 1988) and continually took part in various peace movements.

Simon's participation in the First World War, during which he was wounded on the horrific battlefield of Verdun, was a strong influence on his political career: it made a believer and an intractable pacifist out of him.[25] His sensitivity to Judeophobia, his religiosity, and his pacifist universalism led him to adopt a Zionist point of view after the war. Having obtained a doctorate in philosophy at Heidelberg, he joined the moderate Ha-Mizrahi movement and, while still in Germany, began to take an interest in the idea of binationalism. In 1928 he decided to emigrate to the Land of Zion, where he immediately joined Brit Shalom. He held on to a position of refusal to achieve a Jewish majority and to create a Jewish state at all costs. In his view, such Zionist aims were a threat to the indigenous majority and would lead to endless conflict, endangering the very presence of Jews in the Middle East.

As a teacher (he worked for several years in a secondary school), he was alarmed by the content of the textbooks used in Hebrew schools. The total absence of reference to the Arab inhabitants and, in the worst cases, their portrayal as 'desert savages' inclined only to aggression and crime distorted the national consciousness in a dangerous way, driving a wedge between the two communities. Nor did references to the country as 'the land of the ancestors', and hence as the exclusive heritage of Jews, contribute to a desirable coexistence.

Messianic nationalism, which looks upon the other with contempt, prepares the ground for future acts of hostility. The cynicism, the indifference, and the cult of strength that were spreading among Hebrew youths frightened him and reminded him of processes that occurred among German youths in the 1930s.

Invited in 1941 by the educationalist Siegfried Lehman, the founder and director of the Ben-Shemen youth village, to give a lecture to the village's pupils, Simon began by emphasising that the Arabs had a natural right to remain in the country and to participate in shaping its future configuration – a remark that met with harsh objections from the spokesmen of the Zionist establishment. A grenade was thrown at his home, and on another occasion students burst in during one of his lectures (he was teaching at the Hebrew University at the time) and physically assaulted him.

Simon was a religious man. He regularly attended prayer at a traditionalist liberal synagogue in Jerusalem, where he also delivered sermons on more than one occasion. For a time he was a member of the New Aliyah Party and did not consider himself to be a man of the left, although he valued Marxism as an antinationalist ideology and endeavoured to educate his followers in fraternity among peoples. For this reason, his relations with the representatives of Hashomer Hatzair were amicable and promising.

The statement made at the United Nations by Andrei Gromyko, the Soviet foreign minister, on 14 May 1947, came as a surprise and gave Simon, along with all the members of Ihud, a breath of fresh hope. For a time, the organisation's difficult situation was forgotten, as was the usual Stalinist anti-Zionism in vogue in Moscow. For the first time in its history, the Soviet Union had recognised a new people in Palestine – and, above all, Gromyko had proposed the creation of a binational state as a first step towards resolving the conflict.

6

The Left and
'Fraternity between Peoples'

A plan for a communitarian federalism based on the idea of
equal participation by two national communities in the running of the state [. . .] each with a dual role: managing internal
national affairs, and participating collectively in the running of
state affairs.

> Binational Solution for Eretz-Israel, drafted by the
> Hashomer Hatzair Workers' Party, March 1946

Palestine is a binational country, but Arabs and Jews do not
live in separate territories; the two populations are for the most
part mixed with each other. [. . .] Both territorially and eco-
nomically, it is impossible to separate Jews from Arabs, and
any attempts to divide them up risk stifling the development
of both peoples.

> From the resolutions of the Tenth Congress of
> the Palestinian Communist Party, 1946

Almost all Zionist parties have at one time or another
advocated binational, federal, confederative, or
cantonal solutions. Indeed, when immigration and
colonisation first began and the Jews represented between

10 and 30 per cent of the population, it was difficult to openly call for the kind of Jewish state with sovereignty over the whole Land of Israel that Theodor Herzl's generation had dreamed of at the end of the nineteenth century. Almost all leaders, both on the left and on the right, made vague proposals and general remarks about a plan for Jewish–Arab coexistence within one framework or another, in full knowledge that a significant proportion of these somewhat malleable proposals were just for show.[1]

Zionist Marxism

Within the Hashomer Hatzair Party, which grew out of a Galician youth movement, more specific and sincere binational positions were formulated, confirming the party's difference from other Zionist currents. When Kibbutz Artzi (Hashomer Hatzair's federation of kibbutzim) was founded in 1927, the project of creating a 'binational socialist society in and around Eretz Israel' was a core part of its credo. The argument was that, given that Palestine is in essence a country with two distinct cultural communities, it is destined to be the homeland of the people that has returned to it, but equally the homeland of the people that lives there; the latter is not just a mass of anonymous persons, hence it must be part and parcel of any future plan. The proletarian revolution, and the idea of brotherhood among peoples that it embodies, it was argued, would ultimately bring together the two nations about to take shape in the country and would thus establish peaceful coexistence between them.

In fact the binational socialism of Meir Yaari and Ya'akov Hazan, the two Marxist leaders of Hashomer Hatzair, looked less like a concrete political objective than like a vision of the future in which the historical role of the capitalist nation state would come to an end. For them, this 'internationalist' stance was more of an emotional and mobilising myth than a political programme designed to be implemented immediately. But this did not prevent the party from calling for membership of the Histadrut trade union (the General Federation of Workers in the Land of Israel), whose principal aim was to work towards the Zionist project. Of course, there was no place for Arab peasants or workers in the kibbutzim's 'conquest of the soil'. A multinational workers' unit would emerge later, after the foundation of the Jewish National Homeland, but for the time being the principle of Hebrew labour reigned supreme.

And yet unease about the Arab question continued to pose problems of conscience for Hashomer Hatzair for several years. Its leaders made contact with local Arab representatives and endeavoured to instil in its members a spirit of brotherhood among peoples. The Hashomer Hatzair–Kibbutz Artzi movement joined the League for Jewish–Arab Rapprochement and Cooperation from the moment of its founding in 1939, initially as an observer, then as a full member in 1942. Two leading figures from Hashomer Hatzair, Mordechai Bentov and Aharon Cohen, became active members of the League, albeit in a personal capacity rather than as representatives delegated by their party.

But in November 1940, when a commission was set up in the League to explore possible relations between Jews and Arabs and to propose political solutions to the conflict, Bentov was appointed its chairman. The committee prepared a detailed report that was intended to serve as a basis for Hashomer Hatzair's adherence to the League's new platform. The text, written in English, was not supposed to be made public, but it was leaked, and the Zionist establishment subsequently slandered it, dubbing it 'the Bentov Book'.

Bentov, who had come to Palestine in 1920, was one of the founders of Kibbutz Artzi and was himself a kibbutznik. He had sent the newly drafted report directly to Meir Yaari, the leader of the party, with the following apology: 'This report was written in the name of the committee, which is not completely socialist, and in several places I had to use compromise formulas, and also to resort to non-Marxist discourse and terminology.'[2] This comment was intended to placate Yaari, who was always suspicious of figures such as Leon Magnes, Robert Weltsch, Ernst Simon, and others who, in his view, were prepared to collaborate with *effendis* and rich Arab businessmen in the name of peace. Hashomer Hatzair accordingly called for a working-class, antibourgeois binationalism, whereas the members of Brit Shalom, of bourgeois descent, opted for a minimalist Zionism, ready to give up on a Jewish majority in Palestine.

In fact Bentov and the other members of the League sincerely supported binationalism, because they feared that Jews, who were in favour of partitioning the country, planned to lord over whatever Arab minority remained in the future state. In the League's project for a common state, the issue of a majority, although important, remained secondary and was not seen as a prerequisite for the coexistence of the two peoples: 'Sovereignty can be achieved through joint and equal participation, for the benefit of all concerned. We have established this common sovereignty as the basic principle of our efforts to find a solution. This is the root and the essence of binationalism.'[3] The state was to be based on power sharing and would take the form of a territorial federalism or a community federation. The model of territorial federalism was inspired by the Canadian and Swiss models, in other words two interconnected territorial entities, one with an Arab majority and the other with a Jewish majority, with Jerusalem as their common capital. The community model was based instead on two groups, each managing its own affairs, while the federal state would be run by the two of them together.

Hashomer Hatzair's preference was for community federalism rather than territorial federalism, as the party was keen to avoid any future partition of the country. Two members of parliament would represent the two communities; two Jews and two Arabs, elected every four years, would be appointed to head the federal government, one of them being elected as president. A special joint board would set the immigration quota each year. Federal Palestine would later be integrated into a regional confederation and become part of a Middle East on the road to socialism.

Obviously, one very important question remained: would this whole programme be conditional upon obtaining a Jewish majority? The response from Hashomer Hatzair left no room for doubt: 'It's quite clear. When we talk about a Jewish–Arab agreement, we are talking about an agreement that will allow us to become the majority in Eretz Israel. Any other agreement is out of the question.'[4] But it was too late; the damage had been done. Ben-Gurion, in typical demagogic style, slated the Bentov Book as an anti-Zionist pamphlet, and made sarcastic public attacks on it. In the 1940s he viewed any serious move towards binationalism as a real danger to the progress of 'national settlement and immigration'.[5]

In April 1942, at the sixth congress of Kibbutz Artzi, the idea of a federation, put forward by Bentov, was rejected out of hand, before eventually becoming the subject of a compromise according to which '[t]he Zionist Organisation should include in its programme a provision to create a binational political regime allowing the Zionist enterprise to progress unhindered while establishing equal power, without stipulating any numerical ratio between the two peoples'.[6]

Germany's aggression against the Soviet Union in 1941 and the Soviet Union's subsequent entry into the Second World War encouraged Hashomer Hatzair and afforded its Marxist–Zionist doctrine renewed prestige: the movement obtained more than 20 per cent of votes in the Histadrut congress elections. It continued to advocate binationalism up until 1948: this was a constant note in its electoral platforms, regardless of the attacks it invited.

In the 1946 memorandum, which Bentov and Hazan had contributed to drafting and which Hashomer Hatzair presented to the Anglo-American Commission, binationalism was put forward as the most equitable solution for resolving the increasingly acute confrontation between the two 'national communities'. With the help of a detailed diagram, the authors described the role to be played by each community in establishing a common power structure. The limits of community power in relation to central government, the constitution and the framework of its application, parliament and government, education and health, economy and monetary arrangements are all covered with care and attention, and one can discern the authors' sincere wish to find a stable and lasting modus vivendi for the two interdependent communities. The text was unambiguous about the future:

> In fact, [binationalism] is the inevitable postulate of the non-domination principle. The latter is intrinsically incapable of implementation in an either wholly Arab or wholly Jewish state. A state in which two component national elements carry equal weight politically irrespective of their numbers cannot simultaneously by [sic] a mono-national state whose character is defined by one single entity [. . .]. We suggest that the logical and realistic way out of the situation is an Arab-Jewish state or a Palestinian State which would merit the appellation 'Jewish' or 'Arab' as little as Belgium deserves to be called Walloon or Flemish, or South Africa – Boer or English.[7]

Aharon Cohen states in his book *Israel and the Arab World* that 'the written evidence of the Hashomer Hatzair Workers' Party was of considerable assistance to the commission, and had an effect on its conclusions'.[8] And indeed some of the Commission's conclusions, in particular its opposition to partition, came close to the views of Hashomer Hatzair. Shortly afterward, the Soviet Union began to move towards the recognition of a Jewish entity as a national political body in Palestine.

Communists in Palestine

Communism was founded in Palestine in 1919, by Jewish immigrants who had left the Zionist movement to create the Hebrew Socialist Workers' Party, which in 1922 took the Yiddish name Palestinishe Kommunistishe Partei (Palestinian Communist Party, PCP). The PCP joined the Third International (Comintern) led by the Soviet Communist Party. Conscious that the Jewish population was a very small minority at the time, the party tried to recruit more Arabs to its cause. Arabs did indeed swell the ranks of the party and one of them, Radwan Al-Hilo, a manual worker from Jaffa, was elected general secretary in 1935, even though the majority of the militants was made up of Yiddish-speaking Jews. The communists saw the Arab Revolt of 1936 as a genuine anti-imperialist uprising and lent it their support, although they denounced acts of vandalism, terrorism, and violence against Jews.[9]

Throughout its existence, the PCP rejected Zionism as an illegitimate colonialist movement. Communists did not believe that the Jews of the world constituted a specific nation. They gave no credence to the idea that, after two thousand years, Jews could claim historical rights in Palestine. They rejected the Balfour Declaration as an act of pure imperialism and called for the expulsion of the British and the creation of a democratic state with an Arab majority in which Jews, including those who arrived after 1918, would be citizens with equal rights.

The PCP focused its efforts largely upon opposing the expulsion of peasants, while remaining unconditionally loyal to Soviet communism. But these positions earned it the hatred of the Jewish community throughout the Mandate period and it remained isolated, since it was just as difficult to win the support of Arab sympathisers. However, the Great Revolt of the 1930s enabled the PCP to recruit more non-Jewish members, and its influence increased somewhat among urban workers. Throughout this period, in the name of 'proletarian internationalism', the party constantly called for solidarity between the local population and the immigrant community.

The party's isolation from the Jewish community was significantly reduced when the Soviet Union entered the war in 1941. The victory over Germany in 1945, the conquest of Eastern Europe by the Red Army, and the communist seizure of power in China in 1949 increased public sympathy. A change of position on Jewish settlement also helped the party to widen its audience among the Jewish community. At the end of the war, when the reality of the Nazi extermination enterprise came to light, there was a turning point, albeit slow to begin with. The continued existence in Germany of camps for survivors and refugees whom no western state was prepared to welcome created an untenable situation, which led the Jewish communists in Palestine to revise their position.

In 1943 the PCP split; the Arab members founded the National Liberation League under the leadership of Emile Touma, a brilliant young intellectual from Haifa who had become a Marxist while studying at Cambridge. These communists did not appreciate the shift among their Jewish comrades towards the recognition of a developing Jewish national identity. The Arab members, however, sought to integrate fully into the nascent nationality and, as a result, toned down their criticism of the Mufti and his supporters.[10]

The Arab members broke away and therefore did not participate in the PCP Congress held in 1944, where the Jewish communists decided to maintain their support for an independent democratic state in Palestine, but without specifying this time whether it should be Arab or Hebrew. Meir Vilner, who had come to Palestine from Vilnius in 1938 and was one of the party's dynamic young leaders, declared once more that '[t]he creation of an independent democratic republic will guarantee full equal rights for the Jewish minority'.[11]

The party's spokesperson, Shmuel Mikunis, and the other leaders were cautious; they hesitated and questioned the shift, which was driven by Vilner and his partner Esther Vilenska and supported by many young people. Vilner and Vilenska unhesitatingly accelerated the breakthrough, formulating an original political line. In March 1945, addressing local party committees, Vilner declared: 'The exclusively Arab character of the country has indeed changed, both in the composition of the population and in its economy. Palestine is now a binational country. This is the historical change that is underway [. . .] and, as far as our policy is concerned, this will lead to far-reaching conclusions.'[12]

This was apparently the first time that a local communist leader had paid lip service to the concept of binationalism. At the Ninth Congress held in the same year, the PCP decided to come out explicitly in favour of an indivisible Arab–Jewish state that should be founded on the principle of equal rights, without distinction of race, nationality, religion, or gender, and hence on a principle of national rights that should be equal between Jews and Arabs – rights to free national, cultural, and economic development without artificial obstacles, in cooperation and brotherhood among peoples, and in mutual understanding and recognition of each other's rights. A year later, at the Tenth Congress held in 1946, it was finally decided that Palestine is a binational country.

Jewish communists began indeed to replace their usual anti-Zionism with positions that could be cautiously described as 'a-Zionist'. They did not advocate a mass migration of Jews to Palestine but were not opposed to it either, on humanitarian grounds – in view of the harsh reality of survivor camps in Europe; and they denounced even the measures put in place by the British to stem 'illegal' immigration. However, they stood against the creation of an exclusively Jewish state and refused to countenance the idea that such an entity would put an end to the diaspora and that all the world's Jews should gather in Eretz Israel.[13]

However, proposing a binational state without being able to reassemble a communist party made up of activists from both peoples was viewed as an absurdity by many grassroots members. Thus the 'Jewish' party sought to renew the agreement with the National Liberation League, with a view to uniting with it in a common Jewish–Arab movement. But the League firmly rejected a union that rested on a binational project. It feared that, if it set itself the declared objective of achieving an Arab–Jewish state, Arab currents would suspect it of being a secret agent of Zionism. Hence it persisted in vindicating a democratic state: a 'free Arab homeland', genuinely protective of all its minorities.

Various actions were carried out jointly – strikes and demonstrations with Jews, for example – but the Arab side continued to firmly refuse to endorse the reception of refugees from Europe, since other countries in the world were not ready to do it either. It should also be pointed out that a small organisation called 'the Hebrew Communists' emerged in correlation with the National Liberation League; it seemed to be a kind of inverted version of the League. They were opposed to binationalism and, despite their muddled and apologetic rhetoric, advocated the partition of the country and the creation of a sovereign Hebrew state alongside the Arab state, according to the principle of self-determination.

In February 1947, an assembly of communist parties active throughout the British empire met in London: Emile Touma represented the Liberation League, while the Communist Party was represented by Shmuel Mikunis. In his speech, Touma put forward the traditional position that an appropriate solution to this complex situation would be a unified democratic state, respectful of the civil rights of the Jewish minority but not of its national rights. Almost all the representatives of Arab communist parties shared this point of view. Mikunis, on the other hand, set out Vilner and Vilenska's binational position, emphasising that '[t]wo national groups live in the country. Any plan to resolve the problem must take this reality into account and guarantee both peoples equal rights and opportunities for development'.[14] Mikunis also expressed his opposition to a democratic Arab state on the one hand and, on the other, to a partition of the country accompanied by the creation of a separate Jewish state.

A number of communist parties were sympathetic to Mikunis's speech on account of the extermination of a large proportion of the European Jewry, but there was also one party from the Middle East that endorsed these arguments: the Egyptian National Liberation Movement, the most important Egyptian communist movement at the time, which in 1945 had come out in favour of a binational solution in Palestine. Its leader was Henri Curiel, a Marxist with a Jewish background; he had authored an account of the situation of the Jewish community in Palestine in which he highlighted the growing opposition between Zionism and Great Britain, while criticising not only the positions of the Zionist left but also the platform of the League led by Emile Touma. Curiel was also sympathetic to the Palestinian Communist Party's new stance in favour of binationalism. Other currents on the Egyptian left (in particular those led by Jews, Karaites, and Copts) radically rejected these 'binational' positions, in which they saw camouflaged sympathy for the Zionist enterprise.[15]

It is important to remark here that the shifting of the PCP and of Curiel's group towards binationalism took place autonomously and was not dictated by Moscow. The Comintern had been dissolved in 1943, but the Jewish and Egyptian communists had probably sensed, during their contact with the Soviet communists, that there would be no strong opposition to a point of view that recognised the national character of the Jewish Yishuv under construction in Palestine. Just like the western countries, which had little appetite for taking Jewish survivors in, the Soviet Union apparently did not care to see East European refugees, who were still held in camps in Germany, return to their countries of origin. The Soviets had also identified the possibility of an alliance with the Jewish Yishuv, whose opposition to the British presence in Palestine was mounting.

And indeed, in May 1947, Andrei Gromyko, the Soviet foreign minister, made the following declaration before the UN General Assembly, to the surprise of all the communists in the region and worldwide:

> All this leads the Soviet delegation to the conclusion that the legitimate interests of both the Jewish and <the> Arab populations of Palestine can be duly safeguarded only through the establishment of an independent, dual, democratic, homogeneous Arab–Jewish State. [. . .] Thus the solution of the Palestine problem by the establishment of a single Arab–Jewish State with equal rights for the Jews and the Arabs may be considered one of the possibilities and one of the more noteworthy methods for the solution of this complicated problem. Such a solution of the problem of Palestine's future might be a sound foundation for the peaceful coexistence and co-operation of the Arab and Jewish populations of Palestine. [. . .] If this plan proved impossible to implement, in view of the deterioration in the relations between Jews and Arabs – and it will be very important to know the special committee's opinion on this question – then it would be necessary to consider the second plan, which, like the first, has its supporters in Palestine and which provides for the partition of Palestine into two independent autonomous states, one Jewish and one Arab. I repeat that such a solution of the Palestine problem would be justifiable only if relations between the Jewish and <the> Arab populations of Palestine

indeed proved to be so bad that it would be impossible to reconcile them and to ensure their peaceful coexistence.[16]

A few months later, the Soviet Union and its Eastern European satellite states supported the UN General Assembly resolution to partition Palestine and to create two separate states, Jewish and Arab. The PCP and the National Liberation League (with the exception of Touma and a few other prominent members) accepted the Soviet directive and united under a new name: the Israeli Communist Party (Maki). Vilner signed the Declaration of Independence of the State of Israel on behalf of the party, while other party leaders travelled to Eastern Europe to gather arms for the defence of the new Jewish state. There is no doubt about it: for a brief period, Moscow was more pro-Zionist than Washington.[17]

End of an Idea

Hashomer Hatzair equally changed its name; uniting with the Socialist League and Poale Zion Smol, it became Mapam (the United Workers' Party) from 1948 on. The party completely abandoned binationalism and, despite the reservations of many members, enthusiastically took part in the coalition government led by Ben-Gurion. The fact that the UN General Assembly had divided Palestine, creating a Jewish state that was 45 per cent Arab, and yet did not respect the Arabs' right to self-determination did not seem to be a problem for the two parties of the Marxist left. All the earlier arguments of these two parties about the impossibility of separating two such intertwined communities all but disappeared from their 'materialist' historical accounts. For Mapam, the national dream had become a reality: a state with a Jewish majority had finally been proclaimed. For Maki, loyalty to the overall strategy of the

Soviet Union, in other words, to a bright and promising future for all humanity, had always taken precedence over any partial or 'marginal' historical right.

Fortunately for the newborn Jewish entity, the Arab High Committee, the Arab Higher Committee, and the Arab League immediately declared war on it. This was fortunate because, with a 45 per cent Arab population that had a particularly high birth rate at the time, it was likely that, regardless of the number of immigrants who arrived from Europe, a Jewish state with a Jewish majority would not have remained democratic for long.

The fact that, during the 1948 war, more than 750,000 refugees had to leave the territory of the future Jewish state and the territories allocated to the Arab state that were eventually conquered and annexed by Israel in order to escape the fighting, or were forced to do so, greatly facilitated the consolidation of the new Jewish state. Added to this was the fact that, for the next eighteen years, a regime of military administration was imposed on the weakened and stunned Arab minority that remained in Israel (around 150,000 people). This military regime effectively annihilated the principle of civil equality, limiting the freedom of movement of the majority of non-Jewish inhabitants and drastically reducing their living space. It also did a great deal to prevent the spontaneous return of refugees and facilitated the accelerated confiscation of lands until then cultivated by absentees, as well as the expropriation of the 'present absentees' (persons who had clandestinely remained in Israel or returned there, and were not included in the census of citizens).

Had it not been for the Nakba, which significantly reduced the presence of local Arabs, we may assume that a 'binational apartheid' state would have been established by the end of 1948. In other words, the situation that was gradually created in the decades after 1967 would have begun to be put in place immediately after the birth of the State of Israel. While taking care not to overgeneralise, one could suggest that the regime of military administration imposed upon the Arabs of Israel between 1948 and 1966 prefigured the continued military domination suffered today by the majority of Palestinians in the West Bank, who have been deprived of basic civil rights for fifty-five years.

7

Semitic Action and an Arab–Hebrew Federation

The founders of 'the Jordan Union' [*sc.* the Hashemite Arab Federation] seek to create the tools that will enable a gradual and organic transition from a federal framework to that of a unified state, through the gradual transfer of sovereign powers from the states to the union. This transition will take place, in each of its phases, as a result of the free will of the two peoples, through the mutual development of relations of trust and partnership, and through the equalisation of the standard of living in Palestine with the one that will be in force in Israel.

Uri Avnery, 'The Jordan Union',
HaOlam HaZeh [*This World*], 2 June 1957[1]

It should be pointed out that only some of the members of HaPeulah Hashemit (Semitic Action) were Canaanite in their outlook. But all of them accepted that Zionism had fulfilled its role by obtaining a state and by welcoming refugees from Europe and from Muslim countries and any Jew who wished to live there. From now on, the state would have to be neutral from an ethnic and religious point of view, and Zionist activity would have to be separated from the state, which belongs to all its citizens; this is the condition for peace and integration into the environment.

Boaz Evron, *Athens and Oz*, 2008[2]

The binational paradigm suffered a certain setback in the Israeli arena between 1948 and 1967. For nineteen years, the Arabs of Palestine virtually disappeared from public discourse, and the conflict took the form of what we might describe as an inter-state problem. As we saw earlier, the small Ihud group continued to exist after the death of Leon Magnes, but ceased to advocate the establishment of a common Jewish–Arab framework and confined itself to fighting for the political equality of Arab citizens, the abolition of martial law, and the return of some of the refugees. The organisation's journal *The Candle*, edited by Rabbi Binyamin, reached only a very small audience. Martin Buber and Ernst Simon continued to lend their support, but the circle of sympathisers and readers was constantly dwindling.

At the end of 1956 two events shook the small Israeli peace camp. On 29 October Israel joined France and Britain in an unprecedented attack on Egypt, which had 'dared' to nation-alise the Suez Canal; and the same day saw the perpetration of the Kafr Qassim massacre, in which forty-nine men, women, and children were killed by the Israel Border Police.[3]

In his autobiography, Uri Avnery, editor of the weekly news magazine *HaOlam HaZeh* (*This World*), recounts that he con-tacted Nathan Yalin-Mor three days after the start of the war and that their conversation led to the creation of a new move-ment.[4] An interview with the founders of HaPeulah Hashemit in 1962 about the circumstances surrounding the creation of the group gives a slightly different version, however. One of its oldest members, Benyamin Omri, recounts:

A few days after the political collapse of the Sinai campaign, I went to a restaurant, and there I came across a copy of *Yediot*

Aharonot (*Latest News*) that contained an interview with Nathan Yalin-Mor. In the interview, Nathan said that the State of Israel could not continue to ignore the refugee problem if it really wanted to unite Eretz Israel. These words surprised me, because they suggested a political and not just a moral approach to the refugee problem [. . .]. I got in touch with Uri Avnery, whom I had known a few years earlier as someone well versed in these ideas and with whom I had had several discussions. He recommended that I contact Nathan. I did, and we agreed to meet at the Herlinger café. After two meetings, we thought it made sense to involve Avnery in these meetings and discussions.[5]

In December 1956 the ties between them became closer, which led to the creation of Semitic Action.

The 'Canaanite' Background

First of all, the term 'Semitic' needs to be clarified. After the Second World War and the crushing of Nazism, the presence and weight of concepts related to the existence of 'races' went into significant decline, particularly among liberals and in left-wing circles. Members of Brit Shalom and Kedmah-Mizraha, and many others at the time, had explicitly believed in the existence of a Semitic race that included both Jews and Arabs, which they felt justified the rapprochement and integration of the two groups. During the 1950s, however, race was removed from progressive discourse, and ideas of a biological origin became the preserve of the arrogant and segregationist far right.

Uri Avnery reports that he was the one who proposed using the term 'Semitic':

I adopted this term because it is the only one that has a common meaning in both Hebrew and Arabic, since it emphasises what is common to both peoples – the Semitic language and the ancient Semitic culture. I excluded definitions such as 'Jewish–Arab' or 'Hebrew–Palestinian', which mark precisely what separates the two. The term 'Semitic' emphasises what unites us, what we have in common. This is how the name Semitic Action came about.[6]

What Semitic Action had in common with other pacifist organisations during the Mandate period was a desire to integrate into the environment and to participate in it. The future of the Hebrew state, whose formation was a direct result of the national enterprise, depended upon its ability to bring the local population closer to itself, while it brought itself closer to the culture of that population. The alternative to such a policy of reconciliation would be an interminable bloody conflict, sure to end in catastrophe sooner or later.

Unlike Brit Shalom and Ihud, the new group saw itself as nationalist but not Zionist, Hebrew but not Jewish, secular, even atheist, and certainly not a modern heir to the ancient Prophets. There was another important distinction: its socio-professional profile was totally different from those of its predecessors. For the most part, the core members of Brit Shalom and Ihud were academics: many members of these groups were teachers, or even faculty heads at the new Hebrew University. By contrast, the new generation of academics in the 1950s, for instance the sociologist Shmuel Noah Eisenstadt, had ceased to see themselves as moral and political pathfinders and tended instead to confine themselves to their scholarly fields. The rise of researchers in the humanities and social sciences who wrote in Hebrew as supposedly apolitical specialists reached its peak around the mid-1960s.[7] Most of the critical intellectuals in the public arena were in fact journalists, essayists, writers, and poets.

Semitic Action was founded by Avnery and Yalin-Mor, who at the beginning of their political careers had been on the 'revisionist' right. In his youth Avnery had been a member of the right-wing militia Etzel (an acronym for Irgun Tzvai-Leum, the National Military Organization in the Land of Israel). Once he became director of a popular weekly paper, he made a significant mark upon Israeli cultural life and, with great flair and originality, facilitated the expression of new sensibilities among the younger generation. As for Yalin-Mor, who had already garnered a reputation as a former ideologue and leader of the group Lehi (i.e. Lohamei Herut Israel Lehi, Fighters for the Freedom of Israel), this move represented for him a major political shift, which was to make him one of the most consistent activists in the Israeli peace camp.

Avnery brought with him Amos Kenan, Benyamin Omri, and Shalom Cohen to the new organisation. Yalin-Mor introduced to the group Boaz Evron, his brother Yair, and Yaacov Yeredor, all former members of Lehi who were now leaning to the left. Kenan and Evron were 'sabra' (i.e. Israel-born Jewish) intellectuals from the extremist secret anti-British resistance, and had also been part of the trend that called itself Canaanite. This trend, along with the group's basic terminology, indicates the existence of an important underground network that fuelled the ideological formation of Semitic Action.

The term 'Canaanite' was applied by the poet Abraham Shlonsky to the young Hebrews or, more precisely, to the members of the Hebrew Youth Constitution Committee. This novel intellectual movement, which emerged in the late 1930s and early 1940s, based its ideology on the writings of Adya Gour Horon (Adolphe Gourevitch) and drew mythical inspiration from the articles and poems of his friend Yonatan Ratosh. The historian and the poet had met in Paris, where a fruitful symbiosis had flourished between them. Horon, who was living in France, had specialised in the study of antiquity, archaeology, and linguistics, fields in which he was recognised as a leading figure, although he had not managed to obtain an academic post because he did not have French nationality.

He got close to Vladimir Jabotinsky and his revisionist movement, becoming the first leader of its French branch, Betar
– a Hebrew acronym for Joseph Trumpeldor Alliance. He
also befriended Boris Souvarine, one of the founders of the
Communist International, also known as Stalin's biographer
and radical critic. Before the Second World War, Horon had
participated in the creation of Shem, a theoretical discussion
circle in Paris, and had published, in French, a journal entitled
Shem: Journal of Hebraic Action.[8]

Horon seems to have been the first twentieth-century
thinker to reconnect to the historical logic of Isaak Markus
Jost, the pre-Zionist pioneer of Jewish historiography, and to
shake up and reinvigorate the traditional Zionist narrative by
relying on up-to-date historical and linguistic research. In his
view, that falsified narrative, initiated by the historian Heinrich
Graetz, had deliberately persisted in portraying the Jews as
a people or nation driven from its land and that had lived in
exile for nearly two thousand years. Horon, on the other hand,
insisted that, 'whether willingly or not, the vast majority of the
millions of Jews who appeared in the ancient world were not
descended from Judeans, but were the descendants of con-
verts'. And the linguist and historian added:

> There is therefore no truth in the assertion that the 'exile'
> took place mainly after the destruction, when Titus and then
> Hadrian drove 'the Jews' out of Palestine. This view, based on
> historical ignorance, was in fact adopted from the invented and
> hostile account of the Catholic Church fathers, whose concern
> was to show that God had punished the Jews for having cruci-
> fied Jesus.[9]

Thus, according to Horon and Ratosh, contrary to the
received wisdom, the age-old Jewish presence has always been
based on a specific, internal culture, which came from Babylon,
not from Jerusalem. Jews have never been an ethnic people,

and they must not be presented as such by an erroneous and misleading Zionist mythology, which is in reality but a mirror image of traditional anti-Semitism.

Christian Judeophobia in Europe, which uprooted the descendants of faithful Jews and drove them from one place to another, forced some of them to leave, not for Eretz Israel, but for Canaan, a country that was never truly Jewish; it was Canaanite. This ancient country, whose space extended from the Euphrates to the ocean, constituted a geographical entity in which populations who spoke similar dialects lived under a similar cultural cloth. This, then, was the ancient homeland of the Hebrew nation, which was to be revived in the modern era.

The migrants to Palestine, whose numbers were growing, acquired a Hebrew language and culture with Canaanite–Semitic roots. In the old–new country into which they integrated and where they gave birth to new generations, their task was to develop an original indigenous culture, linked for many centuries, by thousands of threads, to the emblematic geopolitical sources of the Fertile Crescent. The discovery, at the end of the 1920s, of the remains of the important Ugaritic culture, north of the Syrian coast, which exhibits quite a few similarities to Hebrew culture in the form the latter is described in the Bible, supported the development of the Canaanite myth, which constituted the starting point and the objective of the revival of modern Hebrew in Canaan.

Two decisive phenomena have contributed to the formation of a Hebrew ethics and ideology. The first is the compromises made by Vladimir Jabotinsky's *revisionist* movement with the Jewish religion and institutions. This kind of conformism led directly to an ideological split within the radical right and to the birth, within it, of the Canaanite trend. Second but no less important is the specific cultural context in which the new right emerged – a right that was not truly Zionist. French-style secular nationality, founded on *ius soli*, the right of soil (or birthright), culture, and language rather than on *ius sanguinis*, the right blood, was a priority for this new Hebraic sensibility, which, not coincidentally, was born in Paris rather than in Berlin or Eastern Europe. From the outset, 'Canaanism' claimed to be a civic and political nationalism, totally different from traditional Zionism, which from times immemorial right up to the present day has remained fundamentally ethnocentric and ethno-religious.

The lack of separation between religion and state in the young Israel of the post-1948 period reinforced the rejection of religious imposition among the generation that returned from wars – especially, albeit not exclusively, because it was impossible to define who was Jewish on the basis of secular criteria. The influence of the Canaanites in artistic and literary circles increased in direct proportion to what they denounced as the submission of institutional culture to the religious values of 'exile'. On both the right and the left, secular circles mobilised against Ben-Gurion's policy of compromise with religion, which they accused of reinforcing the future risk of a theocratic Jewish state, something that would be a great misfortune for 'Hebraicity'.

But the division between right and left among Canaanites and their supporters concerned relations with the local Arabs and the states that neighboured the young Israel. Of course, they all spoke Semitic languages, but would it not be better if they all became Hebrews, so as to continue to live in the great land of the Euphrates? Isn't Arab nationalism in fact an artificial imperialist invention devoid of any real substance or power, one that should be reduced, or even rejected?

Canaanites such as Ratosh and Aaron Amir, his direct heir, had reservations about Arab culture, which, although Semitic, was in their view overly impregnated with Islam. They therefore sought alliances with cultural or religious minorities: Copts and 'Pharaonians' in Egypt, Maronites, and other Lebanese who identified with the ancient Phoenicians. But above all they set their sights on broadening and strengthening the 'Hebraicity' that resulted from the territorial expansion of the Zionist enterprise, explicitly aspiring to assimilate Arabs and others into the Hebrew national culture. Given that biological 'ethnic' origin was not the main factor, what mattered was acquired culture, which would enable civic equality within the Hebrew state.[10] After all, what is there to stop it? Hasn't France 'Frenchified' the Bretons and the Alsatians? Hasn't England made its neighbouring lands more and more English? Haven't the Sicilians become Italianised? In the United States, haven't the various 'ethnic' immigrants – Germans, Italians, Poles, Russians – eventually become proud Americans?

A Semitic Left?

As an intellectual trend, Canaanism enjoyed great popularity among former members of the Lehi such as Amos Kenan and Boaz Evron, but also within the ranks of the Etzel, and even in the Palmach (Strike Force). Uri Avnery, General Matti Peled, the writer Benyamin Tammuz, the sculptor Yitzhak Danziger: many were seduced by this unusual vision of Hebraicity, which sought to open up new cultural channels.[11] But the most 'realistic' ones among them eventually came to two conclusions: first, ancestral Jewish religious culture must not be artificially cut off from a reborn Hebrew culture; and, second, integration into the Semitic cultural space requires above all that an alliance be forged between the newly formed Hebrew people and its close neighbours – in other words the Arabs of Palestine, some of whom have become 'Israeli Arabs', whereas the majority continue to live in refugee camps all around Israel's borders.

While Canaanite journals leaned to the right on the national question, the weekly *HaOlam HaZeh* looked leftward. Avnery was the driving force behind a non-Marxist bloc of doves. He was one of those who pioneered the use of the concept of 'the Palestinian people' within the Hebrew-reading community in the 1950s, a period when the term 'Palestinian' was virtually non-existent. Essayists, journalists, and politicians in Israel, including Arab editors, sometimes used the phrase 'Arabs of Palestine', but never spoke of a Palestinian 'people' or 'nation'. Avnery and the other members of Semitic Action were among the first Israelis to introduce this new identity to the Israeli public.[12] The demand for the recognition of a Hebrew people distinct from the Jews of the world made it easier for members of the group to begin to identify the Arab population living in Eretz Israel as a specific Palestinian people.

On this matter it should be pointed out that, until the disintegration of the United Arab Republic of Egypt and Syria in 1961, an event that marked the beginning of the rollback of the idea of a unitary pan-Arab nation, there was still a fair amount of hesitation about the existence of a 'Palestinian nation' with the right to a state of its own. Explicit debates on the creation of a Palestinian entity did not begin until 1959. The Iraqi leader Abd al-Karim Qasim, distancing himself from pan-Arabism, was apparently the first to mention a 'Palestinian entity', thus indirectly contributing to the recognition of a specific 'Palestinian nation'. It is true that in Egypt students had cautiously begun to define themselves as 'Palestinians' in the 1950s, but the 'Palestinian Charter', the major founding text of the Palestine Liberation Organization (PLO), was not drafted until 1964. Around the same time, the Israeli left of all persuasions was calling for peace between Israel and neighbouring countries, making no reference to the notion of a Palestinian national state.

In 1957 Avnery published the essential positions that were soon to form the core of the political programme of Semitic Action:

Two peoples claim ownership of the whole of Eretz Israel: the Hebrew people and the Palestinian people. For two generations, these two mixed peoples have lived alongside each other. The war of partition established a closed political border between them and concentrated them into two separate states. However, both deny these borders. A Hebrew leader who claims that Israel's borders are definitive is lying, or lying to him- or herself. An Arab leader who says the same thing about the borders of the Arab state would also be lying. Neither of them believes what the other says. For the Hebrew, Israel's borders, the result of a transient necessity, are only temporary. For Palestinians, Israel is a fait accompli that must be abolished. No amount of talking will change that. Hebrews see their homeland in Tel Aviv and on Mount Hebron, in Haifa and Nablus, on Mount Zion and in front of the Wailing Wall. The teachings of the Bible, in elementary school, remind them of this in a thousand different ways. Palestinians see their homeland in Jericho and Jaffa, in Bethlehem and Nazareth, in Gaza and Ramleh. Refugees in Yavneh teach it to their children and their children's children, the schoolmasters remind their pupils of it. In the hearts and minds of all the inhabitants who belong to these two peoples, citizens of the two states, Eretz Israel is whole for eternity, and any partition is a temporary and passing fact; it is an illness that must be cured as soon as possible.[13]

In 1957 Avnery called for a Hebrew nation that, contrary to Jewish Zionist ideology, would adopt a flexible and open identity for its imagined community. The criteria for membership of this community would allow openness to others, without distinction of origin; in other words they would not reflect ethnocentric, racist, or religious principles. According to Avnery, the political union between Israelis and Palestinians had to be voluntary and federal, its aim being to break down the idea of the Jewish ghetto living in fear that has been a feature of Zionism since its inception. It was not a demand for assimilation between Hebraicity and Arabness but a call for binational reconciliation, with recognition and respect for different identities. This union could not be achieved by force or coercion. The only legitimate force that might intervene would be Israeli aid – requested by Palestinians – to overthrow the puppet Hashemite government or to annex Gaza and integrate it into the new federation.

In Avnery's vision, the two sovereign states would create between them a federation called Ihud HaYarden in Hebrew, Itihad al-Ourdane in Arabic. A central authority above the two national governments would manage defence, foreign relations, and customs. The separate governments would be responsible for culture, education, and the economy, as well as for immigration – *aliyah* for persecuted Jews and victims of anti-Semitism, return for Arab refugees uprooted from their homeland. The Hebrews would have a legitimate relationship with the Jews of the whole world, as would the Palestinians with the entire Arab world. Both entities would have a president elected jointly by all citizens. If the president is Palestinian, the vice-president would have to be Israeli, and vice versa.

Furthermore, 'the project of the founders of the "Jordan union" will be to create the instruments for the gradual and organic transition from a federal structure to a unified state framework'.[14] Consequently the logic of the 'Jordan union' points to a single state; the fact that Avnery's newspaper supported the federal principle was an exception and went against the grain in the 1950s.

The Hebrew Manifesto

The Hebrew Charter was Semitic Action's manifesto; published in 1958, it had taken over a year to draft and complete.[15] The first part, on relations between Israelis and Palestinians, was largely penned by Avnery himself, and is closely related to his long article published the previous year in *HaOlam HaZeh*. Once again, it expresses an aspiration for the federal unification of the complex consisting of Eretz Israel and Palestine, with Gaza and Transjordan. The emphasis is on the creation, alongside the Hebrew nation, of a Palestinian nation with the right to independence. Initially there is no question of a binational state; the full sovereignty of the two nations has to be preserved. But in the final phase, when mutual trust breeds loyalty to the common homeland, the federal union is expected to generate a fully shared collective citizenship, so that all the citizens of the union will have the right to settle freely anywhere they wish.

Nathan Yalin-Mor wrote the second part of the *Manifesto*, on Semitic culture and Israel's international relations. This was in the 1950s, at the time of the great Nasserite fervour, the Ba'ath Party, and the anti-imperialist revolution in Iraq. It is therefore unsurprising that in the *Manifesto* the former head of Lehi enthusiastically calls for the unification of a Semitic space and the progressive foundation of the United States of Asia Minor and North Africa. According to Yalin-Mor, the struggle against foreign powers, their military bases in the region, and the vestiges of colonialism would eventually bring various nationalist movements together and lead to the creation of a great Semitic confederation. In this context Israel would cease to be the satellite of a foreign power; it could thus contribute to a neutral stance between the two blocs – the United States and the Soviet Union. Regional and 'non-aligned' agreements of this kind in the postcolonial world would be beneficial for world peace.

The lawyer Yaacov Yeredor drafted the third part of the *Manifesto*, which details the constitutional system envisioned by the members of Semitic Action. The emphasis is on democratic and liberal principles and on the desire for a secular state that belongs to all its citizens, regardless of origin or gender. Citizens, men and women alike, should be able to join the religious community of their choice without interference from the state. One of Israel's major problems during this period was the clerical nature of the state; there was no written constitution, and this was no accident! A constitution and the complete separation and autonomy of powers are the foundation of a future liberal democratic state in which human rights and citizens' freedoms must be enshrined in a constitution. All individual rights must be the responsibility of the secular state, while freedom of religious belief must be respected. All this means abolishing Zionist government institutions – the Jewish Agency and the Zionist Organization – while preserving the link with Jews throughout the world and continuing to welcome into the Hebrew state all those who wished to belong to it.

The section on culture, history, and education was written by Boaz Evron and is entitled 'The Cultural Renaissance'. It forms the most densely theoretical part of the *Manifesto* and reflects the humanist principles that motivated most of the group's members. Education in the emerging Hebrew state must not wallow in the past but must rest on a moral vision of the future. Regarding the past, it is crucial to combat traditional Jewish isolationism, to seek out the Semitic Hebrew foundations of every place and build connections with them, while constantly maintaining a universalist approach. The measure of all things is not the beauty of the state and admiration for it, or God's almighty greatness; only what is good for humans, their freedom and happiness should serve as a compass for the choice of values. Human freedoms refute all totalitarian ideologies, and this is why the spiritual and ideological constraints of Zionism, which invades and strangles all areas of intellectual and cultural life within the state, must be opposed. The authors of the *Manifesto* then add:

> Our intention is not only to abolish coercion, but also to put an end to the official myths that distort the Hebrew mind. The main false myth is that there is a Jewish nation – of which the 'Jews of Israel' are only a part – which is in essence different from all humanity. According to the myth, this nation has

existed since Antiquity, since the time of the Prophets; this is an exceptional people which has always been set in opposition to the Gentiles, who harbour a hatred for it. This myth [. . .] fuels a racist, nationalist mystique, which arouses in its victims feelings of hatred, fear, and secession, isolation from the best of world culture and from free contact with other peoples. It erects a mental barrier to sincere cooperation, on a basis of equality and mutual respect, between the Hebrew nation and other nations.[16]

The time he spent as a Lehi representative in the United States at the end of the 1940s and beginning of the 1950s did much to consolidate Boaz Evron's view of the world, which evolved from a non-Zionist liberalism to a national civic republican vision he would never abandon.[17] In the *Hebrew Manifesto* he asserted the need for a free and common school system for all pupils in the young state of Israel – but one that allowed everyone to choose whether to attend a school where teaching was in Hebrew or one where teaching was in Arabic. In any case, all Arab pupils would have to learn Hebrew and all Hebrew pupils would have to learn Arabic. The teaching materials would be identical, with variations in the field of literature. Education would also be designed so as to give the children of both nations a sense of belonging to the same homeland. The separation of state and religion, too, would have to be reflected in the education system. Those who wished to receive religious instruction would do so on an individual basis, outside the public school timetable. The state would, however, be able to provide them with some financial assistance.

For the rest of his life, Evron continued to set out his theoretical positions in dozens of articles and essays. The synthesis of his reflections on the history and essence of Judaism, Hebraicity, and Israelism, as well as his intense aspiration for reconciliation with the Palestinians and the Arab world, found expression in *The National Balance Sheet*, his great work published in 1988. In 2010 he made a final attempt to explain the unifying theoretical ideas that had led to the creation of Semitic Action in the 1950s:

> There was unanimity that, after the creation of the State of Israel and the reception of refugees from Europe and the Middle East and of any Jew who wished to join it, the state must cut itself off from the nationalist–ethnic base upon which it was founded, in order to create a legally egalitarian structure, like all modern democratic structures, in accordance with what had been promised in the Declaration of Independence. Jews, Christians, Scots, Irish, Welsh, and Pakistanis in Britain may differ culturally, linguistically, and in their world views, but despite the fact that Britain conquered most of these peoples and groups by force, they are now all subjects of Queen Elizabeth II, and are effectively equal in civil rights and obligations.[18]

Just like Brit Shalom and Ihud, Semitic Action did not become a mass movement or even a political party, although the will was there. However, unlike its two predecessors, it did manage, for seven years (1960–7), to publish its own journal, which was largely aimed at the cultural sphere. *Etgar* (*Challenge*) was published fortnightly to begin with, then monthly. Yalin-Mor was its editor-in-chief, alongside Avnery, Evron, Benyamin Omri, Yaacov Yeredor, Maxim Ghilan, Haim Hanegbi, and others.

Unlike *HaOlam HaZeh*, *Etgar* eschewed political populism and cultivated an intellectual aura: it published interviews with Martin Buber, Yeshayahu Leibowitz, and Aharon Cohen, and also poems by David Avidan and Dahlia Rabikovitch along with translations of articles from the Arab press. It also continued courageously and stubbornly to defend the need for a solution to the refugee problem, in the belief that Israel ought to participate by taking in some of the refugees and compensating others. *Etgar* also lent its full support to the Algerian struggle for independence. Until its demise on the eve of the Six-Day

War in 1967, the journal remained faithful to the federalist principles of Semitic Action.

At the beginning of 1964, however, a peculiar article written by one of the group's collaborators was published in the pages of *Etgar*. Yaacov Yeredor, a lawyer, a former Lehi member, and a consistent pacifist, who had vigorously defended the Arab nationalist group El Ard, unexpectedly published an article entitled 'What Path to a Greater Israel?'[19] The editorial board prefaced the article with a 'warning', stating that the journal did not endorse the author's positions, and Avnery wrote a reply that was published in the same issue. Yeredor, who had recently lodged a complaint against the exclusion of the El Ard group from elections, confessed in the article in question that he had always been a supporter of 'Greater Israel', in other words of the territory between the sea and the river Jordan.

> Perhaps it will be easy for the reader to understand that the homeland of the author of these lines is Eretz Israel, as defined in all the international documents from 1922 [. . .] up to the UN Assembly resolution of 27 November 1947. [. . .] I have no choice in the matter. Eretz Israel is one and unified. It was divided by those who divided it on the basis of the principle of the self-determination of peoples. It is my all-encompassing homeland, and I cannot be more loyal to Tel Aviv than to Hebron, to Nataniya than to Tulkarem, to Ashkelon than to Gaza [. . .] even though I do not forget for a moment that the people residing in Eretz Israel are not one, but that there are two peoples – the Hebrew and the Palestinian Arab [. . .]. No one could imagine that such a sharing of a homeland by two peoples would be a simple matter, and that its problems can be solved easily. But once again, there is no choice in the matter. There is no other homeland – neither for us nor for them.

These comments contradicted neither the spirit nor the theses of the *Hebrew Manifesto*, but according to the members of the editorial team they lent it an 'annexationist' hue that most of them rejected. The *Hebrew Manifesto* did indeed advocate the unity of Eretz Israel, but Avnery made a point of reminding the reader that it recommended above all a federal framework of two sovereign states, whose union could be achieved only by moving towards a Semitic confederation across the whole region.[20]

Three years later, history would concretely bring about the realisation of Yeredor's 'territorial' hopes. Semitic Action disbanded before the 1967 war, and the remarkable *Etgar* remained a parenthesis, as significant as it was brief, in the history of Israeli intellectual life.

8

1967

A Land to Be Shared or a Land to Be Unified?

Binationalism means paying less attention to border issues, diplomatic decisions, and 'road maps' and far more attention to principles such as political equality, human respect, mutual recognition, and justice. [. . .] In the end, the coexistence of the two national communities will be an irrevocable decision.

Meron Benvenisti,
The Dream of the White Sabra, 2012[1]

The fact is that recently, ideas have been raised in both the national camp and the peace camp about various sorts of federations and confederations, along with plans for 'two states in one homeland' and other notions. I consider all these to be highly positive efforts amid the conceptual stagnation that has seized large segments of the Israeli public, and certainly many political circles. It's true that wherever a new idea leads, a land mine, real or possible, will immediately go off beneath you, but the apartheid process that is striking deep roots in our life is far more dangerous, and uprooting it will soon be impossible.

A.B. Yehoshua, 'Time to Say Goodbye to the
Two-State Solution: Here's the Alternative',
Haaretz, 19 April 2018[2]

In June 1967, after the Israeli blitzkrieg, Nathan Yalin-Mor and Uri Avnery, overcome by the giddiness that seized the nation, let themselves be caught up in the intoxication of victory. Both were ecstatic about the 'liberation' of East Jerusalem; Avnery even voted in the Knesset for the unification of the city. They soon sobered up, though, and realised that a new occupation of densely populated territories would not necessarily bring the peace with the Arabs any closer but would constitute a further phase in the oppression, and perhaps expulsion, of the indigenous population. Later on they deeply regretted having succumbed to the nationalist–territorial enthusiasm that had gripped them during that moment.

Unlike in 1948, this time there was no serious attempt to displace the population in the West Bank and Gaza, although in the Golan Heights inhabitants were expelled from their homes. But in the West Bank almost 250,000 Palestinians, most of them living in refugee camps, had fled the fighting and were not allowed to return home. In the Latrun region three villages had been completely destroyed.[3]

Three Petitions

On 12 July 1967, a month after the fighting ended, the veterans of Semitic Action came together again to publish a petition entitled 'A Fundamental, Just, and Lasting Solution':

> Let us hope that the war of June 1967 will go down in history as the last of the wars between Israel and its neighbours [. . .] that a federation of Eretz Israel (Palestine) will be created on the territories of the State of Israel, the Gaza Strip, and the West Bank, with 'Greater Jerusalem' as its capital.[4]

Alongside Avnery, Yalin-Mor, Boaz Evron, and Amos Kenan, a number of creatives and artists from the antigovernment peace camp signed the petition: Dan Ben-Amotz, Dani Karavan, Yigal Tumarkin, and Uri Zohar, who were joined by an honorary academic, Ernst Simon (Martin Buber and Rabbi Binyamin had passed away by then).

On 22 September 1967, the daily newspaper *Haaretz* published a small insert written by the painter Shimon Tzabar and the journalist Haim Hanegbi and signed by a dozen sympathisers of the socialist organisation Matzpen (Compass), which read as follows:

> The occupation brings with it a foreign power, this power brings with it resistance, resistance brings with it repression, repression brings with it terrorism and counter-terrorism. The victims of terrorism are generally innocent people. The occupation of the territories will turn us into a people of murderers and murdered victims. Let us withdraw from the occupied territories immediately!

It was symbolic that on the same day, 22 September 1967, the daily *Maariv* published the manifesto of the Movement for the Liberation of Eretz Israel. In this case, the ninety signatories included some of the biggest names in the Israeli intelligentsia: Nathan Alterman, Shai Agnon, Moshe Shamir, Haim Gouri, Uri Zvi Greenberg, Aaron Amir. . . . Two renowned geographers from the Hebrew University also signed the manifesto, alongside Yitzhak Zuckerman and Zivia Lubetkin, two former fighters from the Polish ghetto. In a burst of enthusiasm, the signatories proclaimed:

> Greater Israel is now in the hands of the Jewish people, and just as we cannot give up the State of Israel, we have a duty to keep alive what it has given us: Eretz Israel [. . .]. We owe it to ourselves to be faithful to our entire country – both for the past and for the future of the people. And no government in Israel has the right to renounce such plenitude.

Looking at these three petitions today, it is clear that, far more than the other two, it is the third that most profoundly reflects the hegemonic ideology of Zionism, by virtue of the number and notoriety of its signatories; and that this is the ideology that triumphed. In June 1967 Israel annexed Arab Jerusalem and the surrounding villages. The Palestinian inhabitants of this annexed territory were granted autonomous resident status, but not citizenship. A month later, emergency regulations were imposed throughout the occupied territories. These measures made possible an absolute differentiation at the judicial level: on the one hand, the Israeli civil law for Israeli citizens who had moved beyond the Green Line; on the other, a draconian administration and military power for the indigenous population. This is how colonisation could begin in the new territories under Israeli control – without any officially declared annexation, in order to avoid attracting global public opinion on the question of the basic civil rights of the population under occupation.

Since 1967, the main objective of the Israeli peace camp, all its persuasions combined, has been to evacuate most of the occupied territories in order to reach a peace agreement. When the option of handing over some of the occupied regions to Jordan proved hopeless, some peace activists supported the creation of a Palestinian state in the occupied territories. It was in this context that the Movement for Peace and Security was founded; it was led by the historian Yehoshua Arieli and remained active until the October War of 1973. This organisation was succeeded in 1977 by the movement Peace Now. At that point, the smaller parties of the parliamentary left, including the Israeli Communist Party, were advocating a two-state solution. All of them were opposed to the continuation and expansion of the settlements, and in 1993 approved immediately the Oslo Accords, which they saw as a step towards resolving the conflict. The reality would prove them wrong and disappoint their hopes.

The first settlement, Kfar Ezion, was established in September 1967, and the first nucleus of settlers in Hebron was established a year later. In 1993–4, at the beginning of the Oslo Accords process, the number of Israelis in colonies and illegal settlements in the West Bank exceeded 134,000, not counting the thousands already settled beyond the Green Line, on the outskirts of Jerusalem. By the end of 2021, 880,000 Israelis were living throughout the West Bank – 375,000 of them in Jewish neighbourhoods around Al-Quds (i.e. Arab Jerusalem). This represents 12 per cent of Jewish Israeli citizens and around 25 per cent of all residents on the left bank of the Jordan. Within Israel's pre-1967 border lines there are almost 2 million Palestinian Arabs, a figure that amounts to 21 per cent of Israeli citizens.

The geopolitics and demography of Palestine or Eretz Israel have undergone significant changes in the half-century since 1967. But political awareness of this historical process has been slow to emerge.

Menachem Begin against Apartheid

The Israeli right of all persuasions immediately supported the annexation of the territories conquered in 1967. At the head of this camp was Menachem Begin, a former leader of Etzel, who had dreamt of Greater Israel all his life. But this leader of the revisionist right was a firm liberal: in the 1950s and 1960s he had stood against the military government imposed by Ben-Gurion and by the Mapai party – the Workers' Party of the Land of Israel. In Begin's view, the annexation of Judea and Samaria, and also that of the Gaza Strip, which was so close to his heart, had to remain nonetheless subordinate to fundamental democratic principles.[5] Begin won the elections in 1977 and was appointed head of government. On 28 December of that year he presented to the Knesset his plan for the autonomy of the 'liberated territories'.[6]

Begin denied the Palestinians the right to national self-determination and rejected out of hand the idea of creating a new sovereign state between the river Jordan and the sea. In his view, the Palestine Liberation Organization (PLO) was corrupt and abhorrent, and he called upon the Israeli army to crush it once and for all. However, this courteous Polish Jew could not imagine human beings, even Arabs, being deprived of their civil and political rights under a foreign regime, so the status of administrative autonomy that he sought to put in place included a number of integration mechanisms for all those called upon to live under Israeli rule.

In paragraphs 14 to 16 of his plan, Begin envisaged something that no Israeli leader had ever dreamt of presenting to the public:

> Residents of Judea, Samaria and the Gaza district, without distinction of citizenship, including stateless residents, will be granted free choice of either Israeli or Jordanian citizenship. A resident of the areas of Judea, Samaria and the Gaza district who requests Israeli citizenship will be granted such citizenship in accordance with the citizenship law of the state. Residents of Judea, Samaria and the Gaza district who, in accordance with the right of free option, choose Israeli citizenship, will be entitled to vote for, and be elected to, the Knesset in accordance with the election law.

Paragraphs 20–21 complete this radical vision:

> Residents of Israel will be entitled to acquire land and settle in the areas of Judea, Samaria and the Gaza district. The Arabs who live in Judea, Samaria and the Gaza district and who, in accordance with the free option granted them, become Israeli citizens will be entitled to acquire land and settle in Israel.
>
> A committee of representatives of Israel, Jordan, and the Administrative Council will be established to determine norms

of immigration to the areas of Judea, Samaria and the Gaza district.

During the parliamentary debate on this proposal, Begin explained why he advocated this liberal democratic political line, which at the time was characteristic of neither the left nor the right:

> I will now explain why we have proposed free choice of citizenship, including Israeli citizenship. In any case, I have been putting forward this idea for years – in government when I was a member, in the Knesset, and in the press – and once again, the answer is quite logical. I shall put it simply, without attacking anyone: we never wanted to be like Rhodesia. This is the way to show honesty to all those of good will. You accuse us of Rhodesianism and so on. But here we are, proposing full equal rights. Antiracism, the same rights for all. If, of course, they opt for citizenship.[7]

At the end of the 1970s, Rhodesia was, even more than South Africa, a hideous exemplar of a regime of apartheid and racial exploitation; it had been so ever since the unilateral proclamation of independence by the white settlers in 1965. As head of government, Begin sought to warn Israel of the risk of deteriorating into a situation of anti-egalitarian and antidemocratic relations that would be impossible to reverse.

At the same time it was clear that, from a strictly legal point of view, the aim of Begin's programme was not to create a federal state. Logic would dictate, however, that autonomy within the framework of a democratic state was likely to lead to an original cultural mix between two increasingly intertwined peoples that could no longer be separated.

Begin did not have time to realise his annexationist dream, and his self-rule plan never even got off the ground. Struck with fear, his successors entirely marginalised this idea, which could have transformed Israel into a binational state – the only exceptions being the minister of defence, Moshe Arens, and perhaps Reuven Rivlin, the former president.[8] Begin's successors preferred to continue colonisation and to consolidate the formation of an apartheid-like regime of separation and expulsion, maintaining the existing structure of the Jewish state while expanding its territorial base.

Begin's proposal hardly found more enthusiasm among the institutional Zionist left, which preferred a cautious annexation, in small steps, of the least populated territories, without granting the indigenous people any citizenship – all this being accompanied, of course, by fervent declarations of peace . . . In the 1970s, only the small groups of the radical anti-Zionist left were talking about a one-state solution. In fact they tended to adopt the platform of the PLO, which had been calling for the creation of a secular democratic state since 1969, or the proposals of the Palestinian left for a single socialist state. In both cases, the collective rights of Jewish Israelis were discounted and the idea of binationality was hardly ever mentioned.[9]

The Distress of the White Sabra

'In the summer of 1977, after Likud's victory in the Knesset elections, I, like many of my friends, felt as if my world was collapsing in on me.' This is the opening of Meron Benvenisti's 1988 book *Slingshots and Batons: Territory, Jews, and Arabs*. Benvenisti, a member of the Labour Party and former deputy mayor of Jerusalem, played an active role in the annexation of Arab Al-Quds, while unhesitatingly offering support, as a man of the left, for a 'territorial compromise' and a withdrawal from most of the occupied territories, with the exception of Jordan Valley, which represents 20 per cent of the West Bank.

Faced with the urban reality created in Jerusalem and its environs and with the expansion of colonisation across the rest of the West Bank, Benvenisti had come to the conclusion that the geo-demographic reality was simply irreversible. The Zionist colonisation process, based as it was on a mixture of territorial myth and economic interest, could not be stopped. But Benvenisti did not join the annexationist right; on the contrary, he embarked upon a critical revision of the foundations of the Zionist enterprise, in which he had been a firm believer right up to that point. He began to see Zionism as a colonial enterprise, fundamentally no different from earlier European colonisations.

The facts on the ground were not the only factor that convinced Benvenisti of this 'irreversibility'. He was lucid enough to recognise the impact of politics upon history. 'There is no doubt about it', he wrote, 'any political situation is reversible, provided that a political force is built up to bring about change. In theory, we can dismantle settlements and "plough up" roads, but will the facts and, above all, the passage of time strengthen the political forces that support the continuation of the occupation or, on the contrary, the political forces opposing it?'[10] The fact that the cautious left was now following the ever determined right can be explained by the deeply rooted philosophy of 'one more dunam (900 square metres), one more goat', which had led to the sanctification of the bulldozer and the creation of the State of Israel. The peace camp found itself unable to provide a significant counterweight to the intransigence of the annexationist forces, especially as the Zionist lobby in Washington had ruled out putting any pressure on the State of Israel.

According to Benvenisti, the second Israeli republic, born in 1967, differed in several respects from the first republic, founded in 1948. The second republic was more ethnic and less territorial, in that it reigned over the whole of 'Mandate Eretz Israel' but granted fundamental civil rights only to Jews. The old border, the Green Line, applied only to Palestinians, who had no such rights and were subject to a draconian military administration.

Benvenisti's moral conscience led him to continue to oppose the despoiling of land and water resources, the brutal use of the 'carrot and stick' approach by the occupation authorities, cynical exploitation by building contractors, and the funding of colonisation out of the state budget. However, he remained cautious and hesitant in his search for a political alternative to 'territorial compromise' – the great mantra of the Zionist left, always in favour of 'peace' yet hungry for 'homeland soil'. In return, the left did not forgive the former deputy mayor for betraying the programme of his past comrades, and showered him with insults. He was also strongly criticised by Palestinians, who saw him as a Zionist who had rejected self-determination for the Palestinian nation. Throughout the 1980s Benvenisti was a voice in the wilderness. Having studied intercommunity conflicts at Harvard – particularly the troubles in Northern Ireland and the struggles against apartheid in South Africa – Benvenisti nonetheless energetically sought new solutions. His mind gradually opened up to the binational option, but not as an idealistic vision to turn into reality; as a Zionist, he always preferred the exclusive Jewish state. Moral honesty, however, led him to recognise a reality that could not be ignored: the *de facto* presence, within the territories, of a binational entity, which therefore ought to be legally ratified.

Initially the Palestinian insurrection of the 1980s – the Intifada – did not alter Benvenisti's original vision. He did not imagine that Israel would allow the Palestinians to create their own sovereign state. The Oslo process led him to question his position, but he continued to state that the peace agreement that was currently drawn up would not definitively resolve the problem and that the truth showed, beyond public proclamations, that in the best case scenario some kind of Israeli–Palestinian confederation was on the horizon.

Neither the assassination of Yitzhak Rabin nor the coming to power of Likud, Benyamin Netanyahu's party, surprised Benvenisti; Ehud Barak's manoeuvres to marginalise the

Palestinians, followed by those of Ariel Sharon – from the withdrawal from Gaza to the 'cantonisation' of Palestinian society in the West Bank – confirmed his prediction that Israel would never agree to give up Judea and Samaria.

In his book *The Dream of the White Sabra*, published in 2012, Benvenisti takes a hard look at the various phases of his life and summarises his views. Comparing various multinational countries, he concludes that 'binationalism is the code word for any agreement, comprehensive or partial, that seeks to deal in an egalitarian and unforced way with the conflicts arising from the inherent tension between ethnic divisions and liberal democracy'.[11] 'Equality' is the key concept here: the bloody conflict that tore Northern Ireland apart resulted in an agreement based on 'equal respect' – respect for the identity and cultural specificity of both communities. According to Benvenisti, only the pursuit of such equality could reduce injustice and eliminate the apartheid-like regime that was establishing itself in the territories conquered in 1967.

Cracks on the Left

In 2003, the newspaper *Haaretz* published an interview with two figures on the opposite ends of the political spectrum, who had nonetheless come to the same conclusion about binational coexistence.[12] And there was an important biographical commonality between Benvenisti, a former dignitary of the Zionist establishment, and Haim Hanegbi, a former left-wing journalist: both were sabras, born each to a mixed couple (a Jew and a native) in Jerusalem in the 1930s. Through their families and social environments, they had been immersed in a Judeo-Arab atmosphere from childhood. Having people of non-Jewish origin around was not unusual for them, as it was for Ashkenazi immigrants and their children who had settled in Tel Aviv, far away from Jaffa.

'Their way of life was not foreign to me; it was part of me', Benvenisti stated in the interview, adding: 'So today I live their tragedy even though I perhaps caused it. I feel myself attached to them. Emotionally, I am very attached to them. But for years I didn't know how to translate that attachment into political language. Now the binational mode of thought may give it political expression.' Likewise, Hanegbi reflected: '[T]he Arabs were never strangers to me. They were always part of my landscape. Part of the country. And I never doubted the possibility of living with them: house next to house, street next to street.'

Benvenisti acknowledged that his thinking on the issue had undergone a change:

> [W]hat is taking place here is a struggle between two national movements for the same land. It followed from this that the rational solution was two states for two nations. [. . .] However, in the past two years I reached the conclusion that we are dealing with a conflict between a society of immigrants and a society of natives.

Benvenisti thus came closer to Hanegbi, who since he became an adult had not been a Zionist but had long believed in the solution of two states for two peoples, both created by the Zionist enterprise.

The two ageing sabras acknowledged that, although they were sceptical, they had supported the Oslo process – Hanegbi had even joined the Labour Party – but their great disappointment made them realise the impossibility of partitioning the country. Without concealing his sadness, Hanegbi summed it up as follows:

> Then I understood that Israel could not free itself of its expansionist pattern. It is bound hand and foot to its constituent ideology and to its constituent act, which was an act of dispossession.

I realized that the reason it is so tremendously difficult for Israel to dismantle settlements is that any recognition that the settlements in the West Bank exist on plundered Palestinian land will also cast a threatening shadow over the Jezreel Valley, and over the moral status of Beit Alfa and Ein Harod. I understood that a very deep pattern was at work here. That there is one historical continuum that runs from Kibbutz Beit Hashita to the illegal settler outposts; from Moshav Nahalal to the Gush Katif settlements in the Gaza Strip. And that continuity apparently cannot be broken. It's a continuity that takes us back to the very beginning, to the incipient moment.

It is therefore important, Hanegbi insisted, to continue to fight against the colonialist model and to understand that the walls built by Israel around the Palestinian presence *de facto* enclose the Israeli nation too – and that the destiny of those walls, like that of all walls that separate populations, is to crumble, sooner or later.

Benvenisti and Hanegbi are not the only ones who ended up abandoning the left's dream of a two-state solution after the collapse of Oslo and the subsequent expansion of colonisation. Three months after this interview, the Anglo-American historian Tony Judt published an article that shook up Zionist circles in the United States and earned him the ire of many Jews.[13] The ensuing controversy saw Judt – who as a young man had been a Zionist, had worked on a kibbutz, and learned Hebrew, then throughout his life had cared about both Israelis and Palestinians – accused of anti-Semitism, self-hatred, and treachery.

Judt, until then a supporter of the Israeli Labour Party, decided to stop beating about the bush in his criticism of Israeli policy: he blamed mainly the national character of Zionism for causing the interminable conflict and for leaving no way out. Like other currents in Eastern Europe at the end of the nineteenth century and up until the First World

War, from Warsaw to Odessa to Bucharest, Jewish nationalism is ethnocentric or, more precisely, ethno-religious, which
means that it excludes the other: 'The very idea of a Jewish
state – a state in which Jews and the Jewish religion have
exclusive privileges from which non-Jewish citizens are forever excluded – is rooted in another time and place. Israel,
in short, is an anachronism.' According to Judt, this type of
isolationist Jewishness is totally at odds with identities that
are open to one another, the kinds of plural identities that
communication networks are helping to proliferate. Pluralist
western democracies are characterised by a diversity of reli-
gions and languages; cultural plurality is developing within
them as part of an ineluctable historical process that over-
comes difficulties and separatism.

Judt argues that an ethno-religious state that rules over
a large non-Jewish population is bound to become less
democratic and less liberal. Moreover, the evacuation of the
territories conquered in 1967 has become impossible, and it
seems that no Israeli leader would dare, now or in the future,
to displace several hundred thousand settlers. Israel is moving
towards a regime of quasi-apartheid, and the desire to preserve
its Jewish character may ultimately push it to carry out a mass
transfer. It seems that the only remaining moral and humane
solution is to work toward an equal binational state for Jews
and Arabs, Israelis and Palestinians, but the realisation of such
a democratic vision seems highly unlikely.[14]

Judt's article was widely discussed in the American Jewish
community, giving rise to a mixture of hostile reactions and
growing interest among young readers. A great many letters,
some highly emotional, were received by the newspaper, and
Judt was accused of wanting to destroy the Israeli state. A campaign of denunciation against his views was waged in Israel,
and even some liberal publicists in the peace camp distanced
themselves from his trenchant arguments. On the other hand,
Gary Sussman, an immigrant from South Africa and a lecturer

at Tel Aviv University at the time, agreed with much of Judt's article and expressed the view that binationalism would eventually come about, because '[s]eparation is discredited and impossible'.[15] Between the type of solution applied in Algeria and that of South Africa, Israel is moving towards the latter, even though this is not what anybody wants.

The Disillusionment Continues

Since that time, cracks have continued to appear in the dam. More and more people in the peace camp have had to face the idea that demanding separation and the creation of an independent Palestinian state alongside Israel amounts to an alibi that preserves the status quo, allowing for uncontrolled colonisation and for the unwitting emergence of an apartheid regime. As we approach forty years of military rule over a population deprived of fundamental civil rights and self-determination, a realisation, still small, has dawned upon people in a few circles that the occupation is not temporary and will not be ended either by external pressure or by a change of government.

Three main theoretical approaches have been formulated as a way out of the political stalemate. One proposes a democratic and secular state based on the principle 'one person, one vote' – independently of any specific criteria and of the national rights of each community. At the other end of the spectrum is the paradigm of a confederation of two sovereign states, each voluntarily relinquishing some of its sovereignty in order to integrate with the other under a single political umbrella. Between these two options there is a third, which proposes a binational state based on a democratic principle that embodies civic equality but scrupulously preserves the collective rights of each nation.

Supporters of the first solution are mainly Jewish Israelis who live abroad and, together with Palestinian and Arab intellectuals and activists who likewise live in the United States and the United Kingdom mobilise public support for the creation of a single state – or, more precisely, for the transformation of what is in their view an apartheid state into a democratic, egalitarian, secular republic. Ilan Pappé, a professor at the University of Exeter in the United Kingdom, and Haim Bresheeth, from the University of London (SOAS), may be considered prominent figures in this camp.[16]

These two Israelis were among the first to reach the conclusion that, in spite of all its embarrassments, Israel is incapable of withdrawing from the occupied territories. They were soon joined by others: Gabriel Piterberg, a professor at UCLA in Los Angeles, Neve Gordon, a professor at Queen Mary University in London, Ran Greenstein, a professor at the University of Johannesburg, Jeff Halper, an anthropologist who lives intermittently in Israel and the United States, and Miko Peled, the son of General Matti Peled. These are some of the most prominent supporters of a 'secular democracy' or a 'state of all its citizens' that would stretch from the sea to the river Jordan.[17] The aims of achieving total equality for all those who live under Israeli control and of asserting all their individual rights, regardless of origin, religion, language, or nationality, are at the forefront of these people's concerns.

Alongside this first trend, other positions have been formulated, in response to a desire to ask another important question in the context of this universal project for the one-and-indivisible republic: can national identity be totally disregarded? Shouldn't the collective rights of the two nations be preserved, together with individual civil rights, in the future representation of a binational Israel–Palestine?

In 2011 the Israeli sociologist Yehouda Shenhav published a book titled *Beyond the Two-State Solution*. In his conclusion, the author sets out the binational paradigm as the best solution to the conflict.[18] His model is based on cantonisation and 'concordance democracies'. Above all, Shenhav focuses on the rights of religious traditionalists, who are a strong presence in both communities. He is convinced that we live in a postsecular world, although he underestimates the rise of the radical symbiosis of nationalism and religion, in both Judaism and Islam. He therefore proposes a theological–political approach headed by religious leaders; this approach would ultimately contribute to the elusive rapprochement between the two communities. Shenhav's initial premise is that the painful confrontation between Jews and Palestinians does not stem from the 1967 war, but was produced by the 1948 war. Hence a return to that date is likely to pave the way for binational reconciliation. However, this original thesis makes no mention of the clashes between Zionist settlers and the indigenous population that took place between the end of the nineteenth century and 1948.

Shortly after the publication of Shenhav's book, Avraham Burg, former Chairman of the Jewish Agency and the World Zionist Organization, began to abandon his convictions about the two-state solution. In 2011 he came to the following conclusion:

> The new political formula to replace 'two states for two peoples' will be a citizens' formula. Everyone between the river Jordan and the sea has an equal right to equality, justice, and freedom. In other words, there is a strong probability that between the river and the sea there will be only one state, neither ours nor theirs, but a common state.[19]

On the twentieth anniversary of the Oslo Accords, Burg honed and clarified his binational vision: 'Everyone who lives (or will come to live) between the river Jordan and the Mediterranean Sea will be guaranteed equal individual, political, economic, and social rights [...] the collective rights of Israeli Jews and Palestinians – linguistic, cultural, religious, and political, will be guaranteed in all political structures.'[20]

The pages of the daily newspaper *Haaretz*, which gave Burg a platform to set out his views, are also home to a journalist who has embraced the new paradigm. Gideon Levy, a long-time correspondent for the paper in the occupied territories, now a talented and prolific polemicist, has begun to express Israeli fears about federalism. In 2014 he resolutely joined Benvenisti, stating:

> the one-state solution has been in place for a long time. It is a solution for Jewish citizens, but a misfortune for Palestinian residents. Those who are afraid of it – that is to say, almost all Israelis – ignore the fact that the single state already exists; they are only afraid of its changing in nature: from a state of apartheid and occupation to an egalitarian state; from a *de facto* binational state disguised as a nation state (that of the dominant nation), to a legally ratified binational state.[21]

This was not a facetious comment on the part of the valiant journalist, who disapproves of hypocrisy almost more that he does of wrongdoing. Levy had clearly understood that the majority of Palestinians and Israelis can no longer be separated territorially:

> The Palestinian in Hebron and the Israeli in Tel Aviv are ultimately subject to the same power, even if it is democratic in Tel Aviv and dictatorial in Hebron, even if one is civilian and the other military. The original authority is identical in both cases: it is the Jewish government in Jerusalem, which decides the fate of both. The Palestinian Authority has less freedom of action than a regional council.

Once started, Levy wouldn't let go: in another article he refined his position yet further:

Theodor Herzl founded the Jewish State in Basel, and this state ended in 1967 and became binational. For most of its existence, therefore, it has been binational. [. . .] So would it be worse if binationalism were to become democratic? And why wouldn't the Jewish character, whatever that means, be preserved in a binational democracy, alongside the character of other peoples?[22]

Although increasingly numerous, the supporters of the binational view in Israel have not organised themselves into a political or ideological movement. The 'confederalists', on the other hand, came together fairly early, to form an organisation that called itself A Land for All or Two States, One Homeland. This initiative materialised in 2012, as a result of contacts between Meron Rapoport, previously a journalist at *Yedioth Ahronoth*, and the Fatah activist Awni Al-Mashni from the Dheisheh refugee camp. They were soon joined by the geographer Oren Yiftachel from Ben-Gurion University, the composer Eliaz Cohen from Kfar Ezion, and, later, Said Zeedani from Al-Quds University. According to its spokespersons, the movement has several thousand sympathisers, so it is hardly surprising that it has been warmly received by Uri Avnery, a veteran supporter of 'confederation'.

The organisation's manifesto proclaims that the country is a unique historical and geographical entity in which two peoples are destined to realise their right to national self-determination. The green line will be the border between the two states, both of which will be democratic. Each state will be able to offer the right to immigration and citizenship: 'refugees of 1948' for Palestine, 'Jewish immigrants' for Israel. However, 'citizens of both countries are free to move and live in all parts of the land'. Citizens will vote in their home state, but may reside permanently in the neighbouring state. Jerusalem will be the capital of both states, and they will have common institutions: courts for human rights, economic establishments, offices for the management of natural resources, and so on. Palestinians who are Israeli citizens will enjoy the rights of a national minority, as will Israelis who prefer to reside in the Palestinian state.[23]

In a public lecture delivered at Tel Aviv University in 2011, Oren Yiftachel outlined this future confederation, which was designed to put the 1947 UN Resolution 181 on the partition of the country back on the agenda.[24] The difference between a confederation and a federation is that the former is founded by 'sovereign states or political entities with the right to self-determination'. According to Yiftachel, Israel is a legitimate legal entity that cannot be called into question. The proposal for a single, common democratic state for the two communities undermines 'the supreme value of the Zionist people', which is why it is unworkable, irrelevant, and even harmful. Yiftachel is convinced that 'Israel would rather shrink than lose its Jewish sovereignty'. Confederation, unlike the other options – a single democratic state or a binational federation – is a gradualist project, which preserves two national spaces without undermining them. Yiftachel thinks that it is no coincidence that Canada, the United Kingdom, and Switzerland all opted for a confederal framework and that this choice explains their success. Unfortunately, he fails to point out that in these three successful cases, unlike in his Israeli–Palestinian project, the entire binational or multinational population benefits not only from 'the freedom to come and go' across the various regions of the confederation but also from a single, common, and egalitarian citizenship.[25]

Despite the harsh criticism levelled at their optimistic proposals, the members of A Land for All have continued to spread their ideas and highlight their political realism, continually emphasising that their project calls for 'two sovereign states, Israel and Palestine, within recognised and precise but open borders, with freedom of movement and residency for all, with institutions common to both states'.[26] The settlements, however, are supposed to remain within the Palestinian state, and there is virtually no mention of the presence or departure of the Israeli army from Palestinian territory.

Avnery was one of the first to campaign for the idea of confederation. A Land for All reminded him of Semitic Action, and he did his best to elide the differences between confederation and federation: 'Germany is a federation, and Switzerland a confederation. What's the difference?' he asked, with affected candour, concealing from his readers the fact that in both countries the inhabitants enjoy full common citizenship, and that was not a feature of the confederal scheme he was advocating.[27]

A few years later, two renowned jurists also spoke out in favour of the confederal solution: in 2021 Menachem Mautner of Tel Aviv University and Joel Singer, former director of the International Law Department of the Israel Defense Forces, published a long article in which they started from the premise that the project of two separate states had become impossible. The creation of a separate Palestinian sovereignty, 'with Israeli and Palestinian islands extraterritorially linked to their metropolitan state by a network of tunnels, ex-territorial roads and bridges', is no longer feasible.[28] This is why, in their view, it is necessary to create a confederation of two independent states with common institutions. Palestinian refugees would be allowed to return and, in exchange, a significant number of settlers, Israeli citizens, would continue to live on Palestinian territory. 'This solution will enable the Israeli army to extend its presence in the demilitarised Palestinian state, not as an army of occupation, but as a military presence in peacetime. [. . .] The Palestinians will be allowed to retain an urban police force in their state.'

It seems that at least some of the 'confederalists' have preferred to sidestep the fact that the precondition for the creation of a future confederation, according to their own logic, is the creation of a sovereign Palestinian state. In other words, an impetus must be given to the principle of 'two states for two peoples'. Once again, according to this very logic, the effort must focus first and foremost on creating a reconciled and friendly neighbouring state, which would have to voluntarily keep most of the settlers, while accepting a common political structure with a foreign army, which would continue to patrol its lands.[29]

Heightened Sensitivities

The publication, in July 2020, of a *New York Times* article by Peter Beinart entitled 'I No Longer Believe in a Jewish State' came as a shock to many readers. A journalist, writer, and guest lecturer at a number of universities, Beinart has always been regarded as a liberal Jew and a religious and observant person, moderately critical of the State of Israel and Zionism. But this American Zionist had come to the conclusion that the two-state project was a dead end. He frankly admitted: 'For decades I argued for separation between Israelis and Palestinians. Now, I can imagine a Jewish home in an equal state.'[30]

In fact Beinart was returning to Ahad Ha'am's central idea: a Jewish spiritual centre within an egalitarian binational state. The Jewish state of Israel has denied the fundamental rights of Palestinians for over half a century; such an undemocratic situation can no longer be tolerated by American Jews, as it damages their liberal image in the United States. Therefore, to ensure the present and the future of Jews in the Middle East, Israel must grant civic equality to the Palestinians under occupation – in other words it must implement the same law for all the citizens under its jurisdiction. Although it would preserve Jewish cultural autonomy, such a state would, of course, cease to be Jewish.

Beinart's new stance provoked particularly aggressive reactions from American Zionist organisations, which feared that the influence of this renowned intellectual over young

Americans of Jewish origin would lead them to withdraw their support for Zionism. Dan Shapiro, former US ambassador to Israel, in fact an Israeli–American citizen who is close to the Zionist lobby in Washington, rebuked Beinart, describing his article as 'utopian nonsense'.[31] Many others accused him of denying Jews the right to self-sovereignty and of seeking the disappearance of Israel, especially as he made no secret of his support for exerting international pressure on Israel in order to alter its exclusive nature: Beinart deems legitimate any non-violent pressure aimed at changing Israel's aggressive, invariably US-backed policy.

Shortly after the publication of Beinart's article, a stimulating essay by Ian Lustick was published.[32] A professor of political science at the University of Pennsylvania, Lustick is also the founder and former president of the Association for Israel Studies (AIS). He has published dozens of articles and several books on Israel, and is recognised as one of the leading experts on the subject in the American academic world. In an article published in 2013, he wrote: 'Obsessive focus on preserving the theoretical possibility of a two-state solution is as irrational as rearranging deck chairs on the Titanic rather than steering clear of icebergs.'[33] Over the years, his doubts about a political agreement have grown to the point of becoming all-encompassing.

Lustick argues as follows: the paradigm of partition is long dead, and a binational state exists in reality between the river and the sea. So why has Israel locked itself into a historical situation that is likely to erode it year upon year? The author attempts to answer this question in three main chapters. First, since its creation, Israel has applied an uncompromising 'iron wall' policy lest any sign of weakness jeopardise its existence. Second, 'Holocaustia' – the psychosis of the Shoah – takes centre stage in the collective memory and automatically equates any potential enemy with Nazi anti-Semitism. Finally, the third factor in Israel's political blindness is the United

States' unquestioning support for Israel, which is linked to the weight of the pro-Zionist lobby in Washington.

For Lustick, the number of settlers in the West Bank, in addition to those Israelis who reside in the belt surrounding Jerusalem or Al-Quds, has created an irreversible situation, which must serve as the entry point for any empirical analysis today. No paradigm is available other than to take account of the binational reality as it stands and to act within this framework so as to transform it into an egalitarian democracy. Long-term civic struggles such as those of black Americans for equality should orient and drive progressive policies in Israel on a day-to-day basis.

While Lustick tries to remain cautiously realistic and to avoid, as far as possible, being seen as a utopian, Omri Boehm, an Israeli by birth and now a professor of philosophy at the New School for Social Research in New York, has broken free of this limitation. His book *Haifa Republic* develops a startling and thought-provoking vision of the future.[34] If you want to imagine what a binational Israeli–Palestinian state would look like, Boehm suggests, all you have to do is think of the whole country as being like Haifa. The shared daily life of Jews and Arabs in this northern city – in the hospital, at the university, at the theatre, and in other sectors and institutions – can serve as a model for the future creation of a lively and ebullient federative democracy in other parts of the country. Unfortunately, this optimistic breath of fresh air has not yet been translated into either Hebrew or Arabic.

The great writer Avraham B. Yehoshua, a long-time resident of Haifa, has also joined, unexpectedly, the ranks of those who question the call for a two-state solution. Like most intellectual celebrities on the Israeli left, he had repeatedly come out, in the past, in favour of partition and of separation from the Palestinians as the only possible solution to the interminable historical conflict. Yehoshua was both a unique writer and an original Zionist. It was perhaps his prolonged sojourn in

Paris during the 1960s that strengthened the territorial dimension of his conception of the nation. He felt far more Israeli than Jewish, far more of a secular republican than an ethno-religious one. Not truly a Canaanite, he adhered with all his strength to 'being Israeli' as the primary expression of his self-determination as a Jewish man.[35]

For all that, he did not turn away from the cultural pluralism deeply rooted in Israeli society, nor did he try to lend to it a uniform and fictitious sabra image like the one set in stone by the ministry of education, its thousands of teachers, and a good many canonical authors.[36] Like a great many Israelis and a number of great intellectuals, he never felt any alienation or instinctive reticence towards Arabs. Just like Meron Benvenisti and Haim Hanegbi, Yehoshua came from Jerusalem, belonged to the same generation, and, what's more, was married to a Sephardic woman from Morocco. Being very attached to his birthplace, something he was keenly aware of, he sought to rid himself of the usual resentment towards the hegemony of the European Ashkenazi, even if he never quite succeeded in doing so.

The process of opening up to the idea of binationality was slower for Yehoshua than for Hanegbi and Benvenisti. Writing in 2011, he was still deeply apprehensive about the inevitable emergence of binationality, which was expected to stretch all the way between the river and the sea; he returned to the subject three years later, accusing both the Palestinians and the Israelis of secretly banking on becoming the dominant majority in a future common state.[37] But the writer was morally troubled, and his unease left him no respite until, in 2015, he came for the first time to doubt his traditional world view: 'As a stimulating mental exercise, the project of a "Greater Israel", giving Israeli citizenship to all Palestinians who want it, as the president of the State Reuven Rivlin has outlined, has shattered certain clichés and given rise to new ideas.'[38]

For the moment, this was no more than a mental exercise. But a year later Yehoshua cautiously proposed the annexation

of Area C – the 60 per cent of the West Bank where most settlers were concentrated – and the granting of resident status, if
not citizenship, to the 100,000 Palestinians who lived there.[39]
These heretical initial reflections, which ran counter to the
classic 'two states for two peoples' mantra, immediately provoked an indignant reaction from intellectual representatives
of the Zionist peace camp; but their reaction did not dissuade
Yehoshua, who stubbornly persevered and even went further
in his unexpected views.

In 2018 he published another article, in which he writes, not
without sadness:

> I hope I am wrong, but, along with some of my good friends,
> I feel that the two-state project, for which we have fought for
> fifty years, will not come to fruition, and that it serves only as a
> cunning and illusory cover for the slow but steep slide into the
> reality of a criminal occupation, and a legal and social apart-
> heid, which, in the peace camp, both Israeli and Palestinian, we
> have come to accept out of fatigue and fatalism.[40]

Then, a week later, Yehoshua complemented this first article with another, in which he explained what motivated his
thinking:

> It is not Jewish or Zionist identity that concerns me, but
> something more important than that: our humanity and the
> humanity of the Palestinians who live among us. We are not
> the Americans in Vietnam, or the French in Algeria, or the
> Soviets in Afghanistan, who one day will get up and leave. We
> will live forever with the Palestinians, and every wound and
> every sore will be remembered and passed on from generation
> to generation.[41]

In his view, Israel is faced with a simple choice: continue
to be an apartheid state or move progressively towards a

binational state founded upon equality. Yehoshua draws up a detailed scheme to demonstrate why it is the second option that should be chosen. In the final line he proposes an equal and common citizenship for Palestinians and Israelis within the framework of a federation: a part of its institutions will embody shared sovereignty, another part specific cultural and national aspirations.

Yehoshua was drawing here upon the long tradition of humanist Zionists who, from the time of Ahad Ha'am, Martin Buber, and Leon Magnes, were ready to renounce the idea of an exclusive Jewish state in return for a peaceful coexistence with the indigenous people, in the belief that this alone would safeguard the presence of Jews in the Middle East.

9

'You Can't Clap with One Hand'

There is a path to understanding and agreement between the two peoples. Agreement is a necessity for the development of the country and for the liberation of both peoples. The condition for agreement: the principle that one people cannot dominate the other, and the creation of a binational state on the basis of political equality and full cooperation between the two peoples in economic, social, and cultural fields.

Fawzi Darwish Al-Husseini, speech at
the Haifa Institute of Technology,
22 July 1946

I call for renewed support for the idea of a one-state solution, and for the opening of a debate in Palestinian society to replace the struggle for independence with the struggle for equal rights and the right of return. Within all the territories, this option is emerging as the default choice. We can promote it with the help of a peace movement, as in South Africa, and wait patiently. It will take as long as it takes.

Sari Nusseibeh, interview in
Haaretz, 14 August 2008[1]

As an old Arab proverb says, 'you can't clap with one hand'. In the long history of binational ideas in Mandatory Palestine, alongside Brit Shalom, Ihud, Martin Buber, and Leon Magnes, extremely few Arab voices have been heard expressing the wish to be integrated into a federative coexistence. The reason is simple and was mentioned in my first chapter: the colonisers came to settle in a small, narrow strip of land inhabited by almost a million people, claiming, on the basis of a nationalist ideology, that that place had belonged to them since the dawn of time. In the newcomers' historical imagination, the ancestors of their ancestors had been exiled in ancient times, and after two thousand years or so of tormented 'wandering' their direct descendants had decided to return home. It should come as no surprise that no educated Arab has been prepared to endorse this story, which stakes a claim to 'historical rights' to the very land where Arabs, their ancestors, and their ancestors' ancestors were born.

For centuries, Arab Muslims and Christians lived peacefully side by side with non-Zionist orthodox Jews, both Sephardic and Ashkenazi, without any serious issues arising between them. They considered Judaism a religion inferior to Islam, of course, but, although it suffered sometimes a few infringements, Judaism was not an object of hatred for Muslim believers; this contrasted with the hostility it received from the Christian tradition.

Furthermore, as we saw earlier, under the Ottoman empire the mass of practising Jews was almost always free to migrate to the Holy Land, with a few exceptions, and yet chose not to do so. Such emigration profoundly contradicted the Jewish faith, which was always concerned not to undermine the sacred and divine nature of that land. On the other hand, as a result of the existing hostility towards Jews in Eastern Europe, Zionists began to come to Palestine and founded in its heart an exclusive Jewish nation state, thus causing growing concern among the Arab population, which perceived this as an escalating threat.[2]

Curiosity and Reconciliation

Not all Arab writers have remained indifferent to the deteriorating situation of Jews within European civilisation. Many condemned anti-Semitism. For example the great Arab historian George Antonius, who was born in Lebanon in 1891 and lived in Jerusalem, dreamt of a Greater Syria–Palestine. In 1939, when he was a member of the Arab Executive Committee, Antonius wrote the following, in his famous book *The Arab Awakening*:

> The treatment meted out to Jews in Germany and other European countries is a disgrace to its authors and to modern civilisation; but [. . .] [t]o place the brunt of the burden upon Arab Palestine is a miserable evasion of the duty [viz., reception of the Jewish immigrants of Europe] that lies upon the whole of the civilised world. [. . .] The cure for the eviction of Jews from Germany is not to be sought in the eviction of the Arabs from their homeland.[3]

Antonius was not opposed to Jewish immigration to Palestine; he even expressed interest in Ahad Ha'am's idea of the creation of a Jewish spiritual centre, a source of cultural richness and diversity. However, he was extremely wary of the Zionist claim to the whole of Palestine. This is well documented in the memoirs of Ben-Gurion, who met the Arab historian in Jerusalem on several occasions, on Magnes's initiative. The future head of the Israeli government quotes extracts from a long conversation with Antonius in 1936:

> 'What is the area?' Antonius asked.
> 'The area is Erez Israel,' I replied.

He asked what the boundaries of Erez Israel were, and I answered that they were known from history.

Antonius said that a border was an artificial thing, today it was here, tomorrow it was there.

Those who regarded Palestine and Syria as a single country considered the border something artificial, I said, but we regarded Palestine as a historical and geographical unit and, while there might be many possibilities as to the exact boundary lines, the area itself was fixed and permanent.

'What is the area?' he asked again.

'It is the land between the Mediterranean to the West and the desert to the East, and between Sinai to the South and the source of the Jordan to the North.'

'Do you also include Transjordan?' Antonius asked in surprise.

'Of course,' I answered. 'Is the Jordan the boundary of Erez Israel? It is a river of Erez Israel.'

'In other words, you want more than the Mandate territory that was given to you by England,' he retorted.

I asked what the boundaries under the Mandate had to do with determining the territory of Erez Israel. That had been an artificial partition and it did not constitute the basis of our discussion.

'Then you also include the Hauran,' he said with even greater astonishment.

I said that I did not mean to include the part that had been outside of Erez Israel, but that both Gilead and Bashan belonged to it.

'You are in fact proposing that what England didn't give you, you should obtain from us,' Antonius said.[4]

It should come as no surprise that conversations of this kind did not help to make Antonius or other Arab intellectuals any more sympathetic to Zionist colonisation.

In spite of all this, a few isolated intellectuals continued to exhibit curiosity about the binational idea, which floated about on the fringes of the Zionist camp. For example the newspaper *Falastin* translated and published an article by the pacifist philosopher Hugo Bergmann, and liberal Egyptian journalists openly declared themselves in favour of the integration of Jews into Palestine.[5] Very early on, the jurist Musa Alami, a senior official in the Mandate administration and, later, a member of the Arab Higher Committee, sought to build bridges and to find a compromise with the Jewish nationalist movement. He declared himself in favour of a limited cantonisation project within the framework of an Arab state, and met with various Jewish figures such as Ben-Gurion and Magnes, in hopes of achieving this objective. He broke off contact later, when it became clear that the Zionist leadership would not accept any compromise on the demand for a Jewish majority in the future state. Ahmad Samih Khalidi, director of the Arab College in Jerusalem, also advocated solutions that involved the cantonisation of Palestine, and to this end established contact with Magnes. He proposed the creation of a state that included Palestine and Transjordan, with a large Jewish canton in the coastal plain; here again, contact was broken off when he raised the issue of a limit on Jewish immigration.

Others took steps in this direction within the framework of a larger organisation. This is particularly true of Fawzi Darwish Al-Husseini, a distant relative of the Mufti of Jerusalem, Haj Amin Al-Husseini. As a young man, Al-Husseini participated actively in the great Arab Revolt of the 1930s, for which he was imprisoned by the British authorities. During the 1940s he became more interested in the Zionist movement, even coming to the conclusion that the Arabs of Palestine would benefit from establishing relations with the moderate wing of Zionism. In April 1946 he initiated a meeting with two representatives of the League for Jewish–Arab Rapprochement and Cooperation. Six young intellectual friends of Fawzi attended the meeting, after which the decision was taken to found

Falastin Al-Jadida (the New Palestine). On 11 November 1946 an agreement was signed between this Arab organisation and the League for Jewish–Arab Rapprochement and Cooperation in which it was stated that the two groups should work together on behalf of the whole country, in the hope of reaching an Arab–Jewish cooperation agreement that favoured political equality between the two peoples, thus paving the way for the country's independence.[6]

Al-Husseini and his friends founded a club and set about energetically propagandising for the binational principle. Jamal Al-Husseini, a close friend of the Mufti and also a member of the Arab Higher Committee, warned his cousin to cease his reprehensible activity, but the latter refused to comply and even went so far as to ask the British authorities for a permit to carry a weapon for self-defence – which they refused. He was murdered by unknown assailants on 23 November 1946. When asked about the assassination, Jamal Al-Husseini replied: 'My cousin stumbled, and received his proper punishment.'[7]

We saw in chapter 6 how the National Liberation League, the organisation under which the Arab communists came together, had rejected the Palestinian Communist Party's (PCP) proposal to act together towards creating a federal state. They advocated an 'Arab democratic Palestine' that would grant rights to the Jewish minority and would respect those rights. The Soviet Union's change of position prompted the vast majority to support the UN partition plan without reservations.

The Palestinian National Idea

The creation, in 1964, of the Palestine Liberation Organization (Munadhamat al-tahrir al-Filastiniyah) made it clear that from then on it would be exclusively a question of representing the Palestinian people, not an Arab people or a pan-Arab nation. The Palestinian National Charter, drawn up on this occasion, confirmed the link between the nation–homeland and Palestinianness; the latter ran along similar lines to the Zionist concept of Jewishness, defined as 'an eternal congenital quality'. The Charter declared the 1947 partition plan null and void, and insisted that the State of Israel was destined to disappear as an independent entity. Only Jews living in Palestine before the start of the 'Zionist invasion' would be considered Palestinians and would have the right to continue to reside in their homeland. This charter would remain in force until the end of the 1980s.

In 1965, the Tunisian president Habib Bourguiba, having called for the recognition of Israel within the borders of the UN partition plan, was subjected to various attacks and accused of betraying the Palestinian people. The Palestinian left-wing organisations – the Popular Front (PFLP) and the Democratic Front (DFLP) – advocated the creation of a single state across the entire territory of Palestine and opposed any recognition of the Israeli national entity. However, at the end of the 1960s the first cracks began to appear. Leftist 'democrats' began to talk, albeit cautiously, of a single Palestinian state in which Jews and Arabs should live without discrimination and develop their national culture. In a speech to the UN General Assembly in 1974, Yasser Arafat urged the creation of a democratic state that would include all the Jews who lived in the entire Palestine, without exception. Around the same time, the National Council of the Palestine Liberation Organization (PLO) declared that any liberated territory would come under Palestinian authority. During the second half of the 1970s, more and more voices began to be heard in support of a gradualist policy, showing readiness to be somewhat more flexible about the existence of Israel, and also about the option of creating a Palestinian state side by side with Israel. PLO moderates willingly agreed to meet with Israeli pacifists. But this approach led to the assassination in 1978 of Said Hammami, the PLO representative in London, and to an attack in 1983 on Issam Sartawi, one of the leaders of Fatah who had been open to dialogue. In both cases, the perpetrators were radical Palestinians opposed to any compromise with Israel.

It took the outbreak of the Intifada at the end of 1987 – and the new sense of popular nationalist strength it gave to many people – for the PLO to adopt the Palestinian Declaration of Independence, drafted in 1988 by the poet Mahmoud Darwish and translated into English by the academic Edward Said. This PLO declaration recognised for the first time the 1947 UN resolution on the partition plan and, as a by-product, gave *de facto* recognition to the State of Israel and therefore to the parallel creation of a Palestinian state. With the Oslo Accords of 1993–5, the arrival of the PLO leadership in the West Bank, and the recognition of the autonomy of the Palestinian Authority, everyone was entitled to think that a two-state solution based on the 1948 borders was about to become a reality, and that this would finally regularise the troubled relations between the two peoples.

To this day, researchers continue to evaluate how much responsibility each side should take for the failure of the negotiations. However, in the context of an extremely asymmetrical power relation between Israel and the Palestinians, the first Oslo agreement and the Camp David summit demonstrated clearly that Israel was in no way prepared to accept the creation of a sovereign Palestinian entity alongside it, in other words upon 22 per cent of the territory of Mandatory Palestine. Because of the hubris deeply ingrained in its fundamental relationship with the Palestinians, Israel formally refused to withdraw to the borders of the green line, to dismantle all the settlement blocs, or even to commit to a definitive cessation of building in the occupied territories.[8]

Personalities such as Darwish – or Haider Abdel-Shafi, the leader of the Palestinian–Jordanian delegation to the Madrid Conference in 1991 and one of the first to demand full recognition of Israel – opposed making too many concessions in the negotiations led by Yasser Arafat, whose failure they foresaw very early on. For example, while it demanded exclusive ownership of the Wailing Wall and the Jewish Quarter, Israel rejected the Palestinians' claim to full sovereignty over the Holy Esplanade of Al-Aqsa Mosque. Israel's intransigent positions, along with its refusal to take seriously the search for a compromise solution to the refugee problem, enjoyed the full support of the United States, which, astonishingly, was presented to the world as a neutral mediator between the two parties and was seen as such by the majority of Israelis.

The total failure of diplomatic relations and the continued intensification of colonisation, which in fact had never ceased, further undermined any hope of reaching one day a peace agreement between two sovereign entities. In 2002, after a rise in armed resistance and acts of terrorism, Israel decided to start building a high concrete wall to prevent Palestinians from crossing into Israel, while Israelis were allowed to cross freely. In addition, bypass roads reserved exclusively for settlers have been built across a large part of the West Bank, which is increasingly divided up by new settlements, sealing the Palestinian population into isolated enclaves. The status of the Palestinian Authority in Ramallah has steadily deteriorated, while the Hamas refusal movement has grown in influence.

At a time when the Oslo and Camp David agreements had reached an impasse, a historical event of the utmost importance took place that was to leave a profound mark on the sensibility of many Palestinian intellectuals. The official dismantling of the apartheid regime in South Africa and the electoral victory of Nelson Mandela in 1994 fostered growing hopes that different populations with different sensibilities and social structures could overcome their difficulties and divisions to live together in a unified democratic state. Likewise, in Northern Ireland, the establishment of civil peace through the 1998 Good Friday Agreement stimulated a new mode of thinking and lent a torch in the search for new ways to resolve the Israel–Palestine conflict.

A Single Democratic State?

Towards the end of the 1990s, Edward Said expressed doubts about the possibility of creating a Palestinian state alongside Israel, although he had spoken out in favour of this solution ever since 1980, together with Darwish and Abdel-Shafi. Said's scepticism about Israel's sincerity only increased with each phase of the Oslo Accords. Israel's refusal to sign an agreement on a total cessation of settlements (or colonisation), in return for Arafat's commitment to put an end to the use of violence, had set off alarm bells. He deduced from this that Israel's real intention was to create a kind of Bantustan – in other words a state under trusteeship, divided up, like the apartheid regime in South Africa, and certainly not an independent Palestinian state. It increasingly appeared to Said that Arafat was leaning toward this arrangement in order to preserve a shred of artificial sovereignty in the West Bank and Gaza. Hence his radical conclusion on the need to bury the idea of two states and seek an alternative paradigm, which he himself formulated in 1999:

> Jewish Israelis and Palestinians are inextricably intertwined. The space is so small that it is impossible to completely avoid one another [. . .] Mutual involvement in one another's lives shows that an agreement must be reached that will make it possible to live together in peace. Separation is not the way to make this possible.[9]

From this moment until his death, Said maintained this stance. And his point of view spread, particularly among the descendants of refugees and Palestinian émigrés active in the English-speaking world.

Two significant articles that followed in Said's footsteps

were published in 2002 – one by Lama Abu-Odeh, a legal scholar at Georgetown University in the United States, the other by Ghada Karmi, a medical doctor and a lecturer at the University of Exeter in the United Kingdom.[10] Both authors come from refugee families exiled in 1948. They grew up and were educated in the West, and reached the same conclusion in the early 2000s: it is no longer possible to separate the two populations and to divide the country fairly. A democratic and secular state is an adequate solution – and probably the only solution – to the interminable bloody conflict.

In her article, Abu-Odeh pointed out that the national struggle of Palestinians does not benefit from enough sympathy in the world, whereas if, after years of occupation, this struggle were to focus more on the demand for equal civil rights, it could, on the contrary, gain greater support in the West, particularly in the United States. Karmi, for her part, expressed her certainty that the proximity between eastern Jews and Arabs would facilitate a cultural rapprochement between the two communities. However, there are hardly any clear references, in either of these articles, to the future of Israeli identity in the context of a single secular state that would replace the current State of Israel.

A few months later, the British newspaper the *Guardian* published an article by Ahmad Samih Khalidi, associate professor at Oxford and member of the editorial board of the *Journal of Palestine Studies*.[11] He, too, expressed scepticism about the ill-considered plan for two separate entities. He suggested reconsidering the solution of a single democratic state as a way out of the apartheid situation, which is taking hold with increasing violence in the occupied territories; and he made no attempt to conceal that the model of the solution applied in South Africa served as his reference.

It is no exaggeration to say that nowadays the influence of Palestinian intellectuals who intervene in the public debate of the West to advocate a one-state solution to the conflict acquires more and more weight. Two other representatives of this trend of ideas have emerged: Omar Barghouti and Ali Abunimah. Barghouti, who was born in Qatar to a refugee family, grew up and went to school in Egypt, before studying at university in the United States; he then married and moved to Israel. He was one of the founders, in 2004, of the Boycott, Divestment, Sanctions (BDS) movement, which calls for an embargo on Israel and has garnered a growing following. Barghouti believes that there is no alternative political solution to the establishment of a democratic and secular state between the river Jordan and the Mediterranean. Only such a political structure will ensure that Palestinians are no longer considered 'relatively human' and their human rights are fully realised.[12]

Ali Abunimah, journalist and founder of the website Electronic Intifada, is also the son of refugees, raised and educated in the United States. He joined forces with Barghouti. In 2006 he published *One Country: A Bold Proposal*.[13] According to Abunimah, the two-state paradigm is in its final throes, now serving as little more than a band-aid on a wooden leg. The Palestinians must return to the original position of the PLO or, more precisely, of Fatah in 1969: the demand for a democratic and secular state in which Jews, Muslims, and Christians live together with full equality of individual and civil rights.

Beyond a strong support for the right of Palestinian refugees and their descendants to return to their homeland, the publications of the majority of critical Palestinian intellectuals are characterised by the lack of any serious treatment of the issue of the current and future presence of Jewish Israelis between the sea and the river Jordan. It is true that most supporters of the secular and democratic state admit formally that all the Jewish-born residents of Israel should be able to continue to live in the common state, but they do not see fit to address the legitimacy of their retaining specific collective rights as part of an overall solution.[14]

The Binational Paradigm

Among Palestinian intellectuals living under Israeli rule, the range of approaches to Israeli identity and the Israeli state has, from the outset, revealed that diverse underlying principles are at stake. In 1999, As'ad Ghanem, a lecturer in political science at the University of Haifa, published a forward-thinking article entitled 'A Binational Palestinian–Israeli State'.[15] Ghanem writes like someone who knows the reality of Israel and is well versed in the processes of the 'Palestinianisation' and 'Israelisation' of its Arab minority. His innovative point of view on the federative paradigm does not stem, like many others, from registering the failure to create a Palestinian state alongside Israel, as envisaged by the Oslo Accords, but from an analysis of the painfully unresolved situation experienced by Palestinians in an ethnocentric Jewish state where inequality is enshrined in law: 'A change to the unhappy identity of the Arabs of Israel can take place only if their numbers can grow seriously through union with the Palestinians of the West Bank and Gaza in a single body. [. . .] Support for this binational arrangement by the Arab citizens of Israel is a necessary condition for its success.'[16]

Ghanem incisively criticises those who advocate the creation of a 'secular and democratic' state on the grounds that they underestimate the strength of national feeling among the two peoples. This oversight can only exacerbate antagonisms, and will not contribute to advancing the compromises needed to achieve equality between the two communities. Such compromises will have to focus in particular upon the distribution of power, resources, and space, which are essential to living together. The future Palestinian–Israeli state must be an associative democracy that will stimulate and develop both languages and both cultures while preserving the internal autonomy of each community.

Ghanem has continued to publish essays and articles on the binational principle, of which he may truly be considered the most visible standard bearer among Palestinian Israelis, although obviously not the only one.[17] In 2002 Azmi Bishara, a member of the Knesset, publicly expressed his support for the federative solution; in a major interview in *Haaretz*, the founder and charismatic leader of the Balad party – the National Democratic League – declared:

> Ultimately, I think that the framework should be binational. [. . .] From that point on, several solutions are possible. It could be a Belgian-type solution: a single binational framework across the whole territory, with two separate national parliaments and a single upper house; or it could be two political entities, both democratic, but where the relationship between them is not that of two separate states but one of close proximity in terms of borders, passports, and trade. In all cases, this country must be the whole of Palestine for the Palestinians and the whole of Eretz Israel for the Israelis. The partition between the two entities must be limited.[18]

This was not exactly the official position of Bishara's party, nor is it likely to be adopted as such, but it did reflect a new state of mind among many of the movement's voters.[19] It should be noted that in the same interview Bishara strongly insisted that 'we must recognise the fact that Zionism has succeeded in bringing together a Jewish population here, which today has the right to self-determination [. . .] and that a Judeo-Israeli nationality based on the Hebrew language has been established here'.

In Israel and in the West Bank, a growing number of Palestinian and Palestinian–Israeli intellectuals have criticised current ideas for partitioning the country and have proposed that Jewish Israelis engage in debates designed to promote different paths to reconciliation between the communities. Constant talk of the impossible division into two states seems discouraging to many; most prominent among these are Diana

Butto, lawyer and former PLO adviser; Nadim Rouhana, director general of Mada al-Carmel, the Arab Centre for Applied Social Research; Mazin Qumsiyeh of the Palestine Museum of Natural History; Mohammad Dahleh, one of the founders of Adala, the Legal Centre for Arab Minority Rights in Israel;[20] and Jonathan Kuttab, one of the founders of the independent human rights organisation Al Haq.

Before the outbreak of the first Intifada, Sari Nusseibeh of Birzeit University gave an interview on the future of the occupied territories to a popular Israeli weekly.[21] This philosophy professor, the son of a former Jordanian minister, stated without hesitation that he was in favour of their annexation by Israel. Of course, he continued, the creation of a Palestinian state alongside Israel remains the ideal but, to achieve this end, any political approach should be deemed legitimate. So, if participation in Israeli democracy helps to promote Palestinian rights, the West Bank and Gaza must be annexed. To the question: 'How do you see life inside the State of Israel?' Nusseibeh replied: 'We will be the Arabs of 1967, not the Arabs of 1948 [. . .]. If we are in one state, there will be no difference between an Arab from Tulkarem who votes in the Knesset and an Arab from Umm al-Fahm. [. . .] If I am asked to choose formally between autonomy or annexation, I say annexation!'[22]

When the first Intifada began in 1987, Nusseibeh emerged as one of the most ardent supporters of the idea of two states for two peoples. Together with his friend Faisal Husseini, he contributed to establishing contacts between PLO activists and Israeli leaders, including some from the right.[23] He was one of the first to dare to speak of the possibility of a compromise on the return of Palestinians and to establish close contacts with the Peace Now movement. None of this prevented his being placed under administrative detention in 1991. Released after three months, he discreetly participated in the Oslo Accords and publicly criticised the suicide bombings. His increasingly moderate positions elicited concern from senior Palestinian officials but posed no obstacle to his nomination as PLO representative in Jerusalem, in Faisal Husseini's place, or to his appointment as president of Al-Quds University.

In 2002, together with the Israeli Ami Ayalon (former head of Shabak, Israel's Internal Security Service), Nusseibeh founded an organisation called the People's Voice whose stated aim was to move towards peace and the recognition of two states on the basis of the 1967 green line, with complete evacuation of the settlers.

But in 2008 he returned to his 1985 starting point:

> We have been trying for fifteen years (since 1993) to found an independent state, and we have failed. We convinced ourselves that Jerusalem would be our capital and that we would be pure: a model for the rest of the Arab world. Jerusalem remains out of the question, and we have lost Gaza. Ramallah is all we have left, along with corruption and inefficiency. That's not what I was aiming for when I talked to my students about the two states. Fatah, the mouthpiece of the central current and the only alternative to the fanatics on both the Right and the Left, helped fuel a certain ideology, which now seems to have been a misjudgement. This ideology is disintegrating, along with Fatah itself. The time has come to reconstitute the organisation around a new political doctrine. Otherwise, in a few years' time, it will surely be our undoing.[24]

Thus far, Nusseibeh has failed to formulate a theory that opens up a new perspective. Other Palestinian intellectuals, just like their Israeli Jewish counterparts, have repeatedly demonstrated their inability to develop a serious alternative strategy, which could extricate Israelis and Palestinians from the spiral that has produced this persistent situation, in which one people dominates the other.

10

Alternatives

Apartheid? Transfer?
Or a Binational Compromise?

And the land is divided
into districts of memory and regions of hope,
and the residents mingle with each other,
like people returning from a wedding
with those returning from a funeral.

Yehuda Amichai, 'Love of the Land'[1]

He and I
are both terrified
and don't speak to each other
about fear, or other than fear
since we are enemies . . .
What might happen if a serpent
were to appear in front of us
out of one of the scenes and hiss
before engulfing both the
terrified ones,
And the script says:
We will team up together in killing the snake.

Mahmoud Darwish, 'A Ready Script'

Shortly after the 1967 war, the Lebanese-born author Cecil Hourani, who had served for ten years as an adviser to the Tunisian president Habib Bourguiba, published an article in reaction to the fighting that had just ended. He wrote:

> It is clear that the Zionist movement as a whole, and the Israeli leaders in particular, must now face a dramatic dilemma as a result of their blitzkrieg of June 5. This dilemma is the following: If the Israeli Government accepts the Arabs within the territories she controls as full Israeli citizens, with equal civil and political rights, the concept of Israel which has hitherto been incorporated into her laws will have to be changed. Israel will no longer be a Jewish State in which, as it does now, full citizenship requires not only membership of the Jewish religion, but Jewish ancestry: it will become a Jewish–Arab State in which nationality will be a function of residence or citizenship. Israel, in other words, as she has been since 1948, will no longer exist, and Palestine, with Arabs and Jews living together, will have been restored. If, on the other hand, the Israeli authorities refuse to accept the Arabs as full Citizens with equal civil and political rights, Israel will have on her hands a large population which she will be unable to liquidate or to govern.[2]

Hourani was not considered to be hostile to Israel. He had always been an uncompromising critic of the Arab world, and in 1965 had played a significant role in Bourguiba's call for the recognition of the State of Israel. His analysis of 1967, brief and logical, is surprisingly simple and straightforward – indeed, the reader may be surprised that, for more than half a century, Israeli leaders have ignored this elementary historical logic. Such blindness may have stemmed from the fact that, contrary to Hourani's prediction about Israel's inability to withdraw from the newly occupied territories in the heart of Palestine, most Israeli leaders, intoxicated as they were then with national euphoria, could not imagine what the future might hold.

The Homeland Expands

At the end of the war in 1967, many Israelis indeed feared that the new territories that had been conquered, especially those with a large non-Jewish population, would end up undermining the Jewishness of the State of Israel. And yet, from 1968 onwards, every opportunity to reach some kind of compromise with the Kingdom of Jordan on the return of the West Bank was rejected. So why, after more than half a century, does Israel continue not only to rule over areas densely populated by non-Jews but also to implant into these areas ever more Israeli Jewish settlers, who could soon number one million?

There are several answers to this question, but no explanation is entirely certain. The new 'living space' conquered in 1967 quite naturally provoked a kind of intoxication among Israel's intellectual elite. Similarly, most political leaders were unsurprisingly enthusiastic. Over time, irredentism (a term drawn from the Italian political lexicon) – that is, the demand of a linguistic and cultural group to be restored, like Trieste, to the territory of its mother country – has morphed into a habitual demand for the expansion of the 'original' homeland. Indeed, any territory annexed to the nation state over the past century and a half has generated great enthusiasm among the people in the process of being constituted, in the same way as a sudden increase in an individual's private wealth. This was the case with Alsace-Lorraine for the French, California for the Americans, the Sudetenland for the Germans, and Arunachal-Pradesh for the Chinese (who call it South Tibet); and it is now the case for the Russians when it comes to the Russian-speaking provinces of Ukraine. In the process, countless border conflicts have given rise to armed clashes between peoples, causing the deaths of a great many victims.

The same was true of the Sinai Peninsula, the Gaza Strip, the West Bank, and the Golan Heights, which were labelled territories of the 'great homeland' as soon as they were conquered in 1967, and soon saw prosperous settlements established upon them. Many Israelis are convinced that they have returned within the borders of the historical homeland promised to their ancestors more than three thousand years ago – be that in Ofira near Sharm el-Sheikh in the southern Sinai Peninsula, a settlement already established in 1956 that had nonetheless to be evacuated when Israel withdrew from Sinai, or in Merom Golan in the north, where a kibbutz was founded on 14 July 1967 on the land of the Syrian village of Aleika, whose inhabitants had been expelled (to give just two examples). In 1936, during the discussion with George Antonius mentioned earlier, David Ben-Gurion described the borders of the territorial imaginary of the Zionist movement, knowing full well that they certainly could not be secured in their entirety. After the crushing victory of 1967, on the other hand, Moshe Dayan, Ben-Gurion's closest disciple, was convinced that anything was possible. He declared, in the arrogant tone characteristic of the sabra, that Sharm el-Sheikh without peace was preferable to peace without Sharm el-Sheikh.

But historical circumstances and a number of political constraints forced Israeli leaders to abandon a significant proportion of the territories of the Jewish colonisation. The peace agreement with Egypt at the end of the 1970s led to the dismantling of settlements in the Sinai Peninsula, to great public dismay. On various occasions during talks with Syria, Israel showed itself willing to evict settlers from the Golan Heights in return for a peace agreement but, as the peace process failed to materialise, the settlers remained in place. In 2005 Jewish settlers were uprooted from Gaza too, one of the most densely populated places in the world; This gave rise to public expressions of grief and unprecedented cries of distress from settlers and their supporters. But the indigenous population paid a heavy price for its violent and determined resistance, a price that was disproportionate to the achievements of colonisation.

The evacuation of Gaza did not signify any real break with the past; it was carried out under the leadership of Ariel Sharon, then head of government and one of the architects of the policy of deliberate occupation of land with the aim of preventing a withdrawal from the West Bank. Gaza was still Gaza: an immense camp of overpopulated and starved refugees, whom Sharon, in *de facto* coordination with Hamas, had decided to keep locked up, as in a ghetto, under draconian external Israeli control. The West Bank, which the Israeli authorities officially renamed 'Judea and Samaria' on 22 July 1968, has remained to this day a territory that Israel cannot bring itself to relinquish, despite the large population under its domination there. It is also significant that, since the late 1960s, the State of Israel has never produced an official geographical map on which its eastern border is not the river Jordan.

At the time of the Intifada, which had been a huge popular uprising in 1987, it might have seemed that a growing number of Israelis were beginning to recognise the impossibility of indefinitely maintaining military power over a population deprived of human and civil rights and of any self-sovereignty. Indeed, awareness of this situation paved the way for the Oslo Accords and for the faltering and ultimately abortive attempt to withdraw from most of the West Bank. This led to the creation of the Palestinian Authority, which was supposed to become autonomous but in reality was totally dependent on Israel; and not even the slightest effort was made to dismantle a single Jewish settlement in Judea and Samaria. This situation hampered all peace negotiations and undermined Palestinian confidence in the process.

There were other reasons for this impotence and for the lack of a sincere desire to withdraw completely from the West Bank. For example, wouldn't a sovereign Palestinian entity so close to Tel Aviv be a bridgehead for all the enemies in the region? Wouldn't terrorists take advantage of it to infiltrate Israel all along the border? Wouldn't missiles rain down on

Israel's international airport? Wouldn't a Palestinian state constitute a growing locus of identification for Palestinian Israelis,
who would certainly be recognised as citizens, but in a country
that is not their own?

The Zionist right – of all persuasions, nationalist–religious and secular alike – immediately and wholeheartedly
pronounced itself in favour of the full annexation of Judea
and Samaria, which it regards as having always been a part
of its heritage. The picture was different for the Zionist left:
from time to time it tabled plans for a partial withdrawal from
the West Bank, paying heed to the feelings of ownership so
strongly present in Israeli opinion. Yigal Allon, an eminent
figure on the Israeli left who had been for a long time deputy
head of government and then minister for foreign affairs,
labour, and education, was the first to propose, on 26 July 1967,
a plan to return territory to Jordan, mainly in order to be rid
of the areas most densely populated by Palestinians. But the
plan also envisaged including into Israel not only the entire
Jordan Valley, expanded for security reasons, and the entire
Gush Etzion region, but also the already annexed Arab Al-
Quds, with all its neighbourhoods, and the major Palestinian
city of Hebron (Al-Khalil). Allon was also the first to approve
the illegal establishment of settlers in the heart of Hebron and
went so far as to grant them ministerial funding and equip
them with weapons.

During the Oslo negotiations, Yitzhak Rabin, who, like
Allon, was deeply committed to separation from the great mass
of Palestinians, was unable to endorse a halt to settlement in
the heart of the country.[3] In 1994 Baruch Goldstein's assassination of twenty-nine worshippers in the Ibrahim Mosque, right
in the Cave of the Patriarchs, sent huge shockwaves through
the Israeli public, handing Rabin a golden opportunity to evict
illegal settlers from the centre of Hebron – and Goldstein was
one of them. But the head of the Israeli government dithered:
he knew perfectly well that this decision would have effectively

sounded a note of reconciliation, which was sorely lacking in the accords process, and could perhaps have prevented the terrible wave of Palestinian attacks that followed the massacre, but he did not have the courage to take such an 'un-Zionist' decision.[4]

Years later, in 2021, as one of his first actions, Isaac Herzog, a member of the Labour Party who had just been elected president of Israel, decided to light a candle in Hebron, in the bloodstained Cave of the Patriarchs. He justified his action by saying: 'We all share deep roots branching out of this tomb.'[5]

'National roots' were to be found not only in the city of Abraham. Bethlehem (Bayt Lahm in Arabic) was David's birthplace, where he was anointed king, too, but the tomb of Rachel 'our mother' is also located at the entrance to the city. Jericho (Arīḥā) was the first city liberated by Joshua, the son of Nun, with the help of a divine miracle, and for a time Shechem (Nablus) was the capital of the kingdom of Israel. It was between these cities, not in Sinai or Gaza, that the biblical 'people of Israel' once lived. In the background of the Zionist imagination, Judea and Samaria has always been coextensive with a terminology that has strong territorial connotations. The area was seen as the beating heart of mythological Eretz Israel, and many Israeli Jews soon learned to regard its possession as the raison d'être of the colonisation of the land of Zion – far more than the possession of Tel Aviv, Haifa, Galilee, or the Negev.

The spatial references of Israeli citizens are primarily based on the Bible. In accordance with a directive from the ministry of education, pupils must begin memorising the biblical epics already in kindergarten. The Bible is taught in all state schools as a credible historical text, long before pupils develop any critical faculties. This intensive 'brainwashing' uses a 'geographical–patriotic' imaginary that incorporates not only a 'reunited Jerusalem' (which 'will never again be divided'), but also Hebron, Jericho, Bethlehem, and so on. Immediately after the 1967 war, dozens of Israeli archaeologists set off in search of ancient rubble to confirm the biblical account. This did much to anchor the idea that the conquered territories were national property.

The New Pioneers

Ahead of the archaeologists, pioneers of a new kind had already rushed to the West Bank. On 27 September 1967, a religious kibbutz, Gush Etzion, was created on the ruins of a settlement conquered by the Jordanian army in 1948. Among the militants who took part in this action were members of the Bnei-Akiva movement, soon to be at the forefront of colonial expansion. At the very beginning, a few small outposts of colonisation were established. The claim was that they were built in the image of the pioneering kibbutzim, but in fact they represented a new symbiosis between religion and nationalism that in the last third of the twentieth century would come to characterise Judaism in Israel, and then vast segments of Middle Eastern Islam, as well as Christian evangelism in the United States and Brazil. God was no longer king, the master of the world capable of restraining the earthly ruler, as Martin Buber and Leon Magnes had taught. Total human possession of the earth was now the supreme expression of the will of God – both the nationalist Jewish God and the fundamentalist Muslim God. Before its creation and after its foundation, the State of Israel was based primarily on a myth that combined nationalism and socialism; from this point on socialism is consigned to the dustbin of history and all that remains is the national myth, increasingly cloaked in the garments of a pioneering and original religious faith.

The end of the 1973 war saw the emergence of Gush Emunim (the Bloc of the Faithful), a dynamic movement made up of disciples of the extremist Rabbi Zvi Yehuda Kook, which managed to attract the entire national–religious fringe of the Zionist movement. Its members – wearers of 'knitted skullcaps', which were made of coloured wool and given this name for differentiation from the presumably sad black Jewish skullcap – enjoyed the support of the entire 'secular' right and made repeated attempts to establish settlement outposts throughout Judea and Samaria. The first settlements to spring up were Elon Moreh near Nablus, Kedumim, Elkana, Beit El, Shilo, and Ma'aleh Adumim. When the right came to power in 1977, the number of such outposts increased in parallel with the expansion of the existing settlements, many of which were built on land that belonged to Palestinian peasants. The vanguard settlers did not feel isolated, since a large part of the public empathised with them; one could now see knitted skullcaps being increasingly worn by ordinary citizens.

The number of Jewish Israelis settling in the West Bank has risen year upon year, but not all are motivated by ideology. Indeed, living half an hour away from Jerusalem and forty-five minutes away from Tel Aviv, at prices well below the cost of housing inside Israel, is an attractive prospect for many. Despite the risk of attacks, the proximity of Arab villages does not seem to be a deterrent, especially since roads reserved exclusively for Israelis have been constructed since the 1990s. As a result, a non-negligible number of Mizrahim or Mozrahi Jews ('easterners') have come to live in Ma'aleh Adumim and other large settlements. Many of them have supported the colonisation drive without really being an organic part of its vanguard.[6]

The settlements have been populated also by new immigrants from the former Soviet Union whose standard of living has greatly improved thanks to this *aliyah* – this emigration to the soil of the homeland. At a certain point, poor Orthodox clerics, driven by material and economic interests, also joined the celebration of colonisation, and in doing so were able to taste for the first time the benefits of modern territorial nationalism, from which their ancestral Jewish faith had hitherto deterred them.

Strangely, according to official government statistics and media coverage, Jewish Israelis who live in the West Bank are considered, demographically and legally, to be residents of the State of Israel, even though this territory has not been formally annexed.

The construction of a university in Ariel is a flagrant example of the unbridled Israelisation that has been successfully achieved in the West Bank. A small settlement halfway between Nablus and Ramallah was founded in 1978 and named Ariel. Four years later, under the aegis of the Israeli Bar-Ilan University, a college was set up there. The college became autonomous in 2005, adopting the name of Ariel University Centre in Samaria, which enabled it to receive state subsidies and, in 2012, to be recognised as a university by the Council for Higher Education in Judea and Samaria. Initially the Committee of University Presidents opposed the recognition of the institution as a university, given its location outside the borders of the state, but after the American Zionist patron Sheldon Adelson donated 20 million dollars in 2018 the Israeli parliament finally amended the law by extending the powers of the Council for Higher Education beyond the official borders of the state. In 2022 the Committee of University Presidents finally decided to recognise Ariel officially, for fear that its prolonged sidelining may cause an international boycott. The decision was accepted by most academic staff and by all Israeli academic institutions, which naturally considered Ariel to be a 'sister university'.

To this one should add a not insignificant fact: Ariel University, located as it is in the heart of Samaria, is not and will not be open to the Palestinian population that lives and works nearby; young people who are not Israeli citizens are not allowed to study there, even if they live a kilometre away from the gates. The mission of the university is to provide education to settlers, to Israeli students who have crossed the green line, and to Jewish students from elsewhere. In other words, like other cultural activities reserved exclusively for Jews, this university in Samaria is one of the strong signs of the success of a stealth colonisation of the West Bank, carried out without any real planning.

Not the vigorous resistance of the harshly repressed population, not the theft of land, not the half-hearted talks, and not international pressure, either, have been able to put the brakes on this process of rampant colonisation. Whether it comes from the United Nations, from Europe, or from the Arab countries, all pressure just hits a wall (literally as well as figuratively). Although the entire world is aware that Israel's domination of these territories is more like a brutal repetition of the dominations practised in colonies throughout the nineteenth century and the first half of the twentieth, Israel continues to enjoy an astonishing level of indulgence.

Two main factors have enabled Israel to continue and extend its appropriation of territories without encountering any significant international opposition. First, in Europe, the weight of the guilt linked to the memory of the Holocaust has for the most part disarmed any critical attitude. This state of mind also happens to converge with Europeans' traditional mistrust of Islam and of Muslim immigrants. Second, in the United States, the intensive and sophisticated activity of the pro-Israel lobby – with the American–Israeli Public Affairs Committee (AIPAC) at its centre and with the added weight of the Christian evangelical Zionists – has effectively erected a barricade in defence of Israel, the country's 'democratic ally'. This, among other factors, explains the United States' provision of unparalleled financial and military aid to Israel since 1962.[7]

Israel's effective penetration into new territories at the heart of 'the land of the ancestors' has continually expanded. To what extent has it also colonised the hearts of the majority of Israeli Jews?

Hegemony on the Ground

It is no easy task to work out up to what point Israeli Jews have approved of colonisation over the years, and whether they still identify with it today. Numerous testimonies show that many wavered, either because they did not want to end up living with Arabs all around them, or for ethical reasons related to the refusal of theft and of the appropriation of land taken from Palestinians, who were born in their own homeland and lived in it. The Israeli Labour Party, at its peak, expressed the tergiversations of this dilemma. Levi Eshkol, then head of government, made a famous joke at the end of the Six-Day War: 'We only want the dowry, not the bride.'[8] In other words we want the core of our homeland, but without the people who live there. The contradiction was insoluble, so the solution was constantly postponed by means of terminological contortions, while time was left to do its work.

The leaders of the Zionist left, who ran the country in the decade immediately after the conquest of the West Bank, were ideologically and mentally torn between retroactively legitimating the 'pioneers' who colonised the Jezreel Valley and refusing to grant similar legitimation to the contemporary 'pioneers' in the Jordan Valley. There is also a disparity between their justification of the expulsion of the Arabs from Safed in 1948 and the establishment of a Jewish colony in the heart of Hebron, at the expense of local inhabitants. The Zionist 'one more dunam, one more goat' approach reared its ugly head behind every decision, constantly annihilating even the most moderate proposals.[9]

As we have seen earlier, at the beginning of the twentieth century the justification for colonisation was not based upon the idea of finding a refuge for Jews persecuted in Europe who aspired to live under their own sovereignty; it was based explicitly upon the claim to ownership of a land that had always been the exclusive heritage of an exiled people that had been driven away from it two thousand years ago. It is apparently more difficult to renounce one's property rights, the cornerstone of modern bourgeois civilisation, than to fight for the fundamental human rights of others kept in a state of subjection.

In Israel, the middle classes, concerned above all to consolidate their socioeconomic advantages, were not quite as overjoyed by the extension of colonisation as they had been in 1967, when the old city of Jerusalem was annexed; but they were never really opposed to it, and even got used to it gradually. The less privileged strata of Israeli society were not actively in favour of the settlers' conquest of the land, but supported it, buoyed up by that natural desire for national power, which in the modern world generally compensates for the miseries of daily life. In any case, in the eyes of most Israelis, even if the settlers do not always obey the law, even if they commit acts of aggression against their neighbours, fraudulently obtain subsidies, and end up living a life of state-sponsored privilege, they nonetheless remain a member of the body of a Jewish people that is constantly growing stronger and, thanks to them, extends its Zionist living space.

In the Israeli consciousness, settlers do not enjoy total hegemony in the sense given this term by the Italian Marxist Antonio Gramsci, whose example was bourgeois ideology in the contemporary world. The bourgeoisie dominates not only through its economic power but also through its ability to establish, especially with the help of its intellectuals, the set of values and representations at the base of social relations. Colonisation has a dominant, but far less secure status in Israeli consciousness. The values proclaimed by Jews settled in Judea and Samaria are not fully shared by the majority of Israelis. However, what plays in the settlers' favour is the fact that the wavering majority has not formulated any coherent system of alternative norms; all Israeli governments have taken note of this and have continually adapted to the spontaneous hegemony that emerges on the ground.

The democratic liberal values of most Israelis have always been subordinated to an ethnocentric conception of the definition of Judaism and of the State of Israel. Any democratic state, even a non-liberal authoritarian state, is considered in principle to be the property of all citizens who live under its authority, and this in principle includes cultural and linguistic minorities. The State of Israel, on the other hand, does not belong, either *de iure* or *de facto*, to all Israeli citizens. It does not define itself as an Israeli state, in conformity with any national democratic logic, but as a Jewish state that belongs to the Jewish people of the whole world, even though formal adherence to this identity is exclusively religious. This implies the discrimination enshrined in law against Palestinian Israeli citizens, along with the political will to acquire additional Israeli Eretz territory and to live alongside non-Jews deprived of rights, as has happened for more than half a century.

Moreover, so long as the political imagination continues to be fuelled by a dimension of 'timeless temporality' – and given that Israel is not actively annexing the West Bank – consistent liberal Zionists can turn a blind eye to the suffering of others, as they continue to prattle on about 'two states for two peoples' in the distant future while in reality endorsing the historical process that has taken shape between the river Jordan and the sea and is increasingly perceived as uncontrollable and inevitable.

Stychic and Catastrophic

Writing in the early twentieth century, the Zionist Marxist thinker Ber Borochov introduced a novel use of the term 'stychic' (elemental) in his analysis of the situation of Jews in Eastern Europe and the prospect of their emigration from Russia. A stychic series of events or processes is one that is not deliberately planned but occurs haphazardly, in a manner somewhat reminiscent of a series of natural phenomena. For example, the emigration of Jews to Palestine cannot be explained either by the publication of Theodor Herzl's pamphlet or by the very minor Zionist movement that was emerging at the time; it was the result of a succession of unforeseeable and uncontrolled historical circumstances that prompted Jews to leave their homes in order to return to their ancient homeland, where some of their people already lived – although in fact they had long since been converted to Islam. At the time, Borochov wrongly thought that this stychic process would make Jewish emigration turn toward Palestine when in fact it spontaneously headed west, in particular towards the United States, until the latter closed its doors to immigration in 1924. But Borochov's analysis was going to be indirectly validated by a catastrophic event: I mean of course the Nazi extermination of Jews, which, more than any other factor, led to forced emigration to the Middle East and the creation of the State of Israel.

One could say, in summary, that many historical events result from a combination of the stychic and the catastrophic. For example, the abolition of slavery in the United States was not simply the result of a gradual socioeconomic stychic process involving a change in the previous capitalist relations of production; it took a cruel civil war to accelerate and complete that change. The same was true of the revolution in Russia: tsarist power had begun to crumble long before the First World War, but the global and deadly nature of the hostilities propelled the Bolsheviks to power, at the end of a radical insurrection. Catastrophes, which are generally associated with global military confrontations, participate in the movement of history along with stychic processes in the *longue durée*.

Since 1967, unchecked colonisation has given rise to a stychic process of this kind, a process not pre-planned at government level that brings the two peoples between the sea and the river Jordan to intersect. The majority in each of the two communities would not have voluntarily and consciously opted for this form of integration, but they have accepted it because they had no choice in the matter. No political, diplomatic, or military force has proven capable of halting it. After all, it is hardly plausible that any government could simply remove 850,000 Israeli Jews from the heart of the historical homeland.

Although Israel has never taken an official decision to annex the West Bank, the day-to-day situation has long been a binational one, and it takes a good deal of blindness and pretence to ignore it and to continue to talk about a future two-state solution. Many realise that this *de facto* binationalism in which we live is twisted and deadly, with one people dominating another, imposing its national and social agendas, and then having to absorb the desperate, violent reactions of the dominated. Palestinians live under the same sovereignty as Israelis do, but unlike Israelis they are deprived of freedom of movement and expression and of the right to protest; they suffer persecution, detention without trial, the imprisonment of their children, night-time searches of their homes, body searches at roadblocks, live ammunition fired at demonstrators, deadly repressions of unarmed rioters ... This unequal treatment has bloody consequences, and there is no end in sight.

Walls, barbed wire, bypass roads, and suspension bridges do little to reduce tragic clashes between people who enjoy national freedom and a population utterly dependent upon these people's goodwill. The difference in legal status between the two, brought about by emergency decrees and military administration acts, has created a relationship similar in many respects to apartheid, which is designed to divide the two populations completely. Of course, the situation is not exactly identical to the one that was in force in South Africa from 1948 to 1992, but it is similar in principle, this similarity being based on the complete separation between two human groups that live side by side, or even one within another.[10] The day-to-day reality in the West Bank recalls, broadly, other colonial situations of the recent past. The Europeans who lived in their colonies almost always enjoyed the civil rights offered by the metropolis, from which they and their ancestors had descended, even though the colonies were not legally annexed to it; and it was simply assumed that they would live like this for decades, alongside natives deprived of citizenship and fundamental human rights.

The Secret Option

Unlike the British in India or the French in Algeria, but like Australians or the whites in South Africa, Israelis cannot just decide to separate themselves completely from the natives. More than 21 per cent of Arabs live within the green line, and Palestinians make up more than a third of the population of the Jewish capital. But there is, apparently, another option: what happened in 1948 could be repeated, by creating the conditions for another massive 'transfer' of the indigenous population.[11]

In the history of settlement colonialism, the idea of transferring a population had not been put aside. The idea of evacuating the natives has been present since 1830, when Andrew Jackson, the seventh president of the United States, had Congress pass a law aimed at deporting indigenous Indian populations westwards in order to allocate their land to white settlers. Reflecting on the possibility of Jewish colonialism outside Europe – but in Argentina, it would seem, not in Palestine – Herzl wrote in his diary on 12 June 1895: 'We shall have to take careful possession of land that is privately owned. We shall try to move the poor population across the border without attracting attention, by providing them with work in neighbouring countries, but we shall refuse to provide them with employment in our country. People with means will come to us. The confiscation and removal of the poor will have to be carried out with tact and caution.'[12]

In the 1930s, and especially after the 1936 Palestine Royal Commission – the Peel Commission – had recommended a population transfer, Ben-Gurion was referring quite openly to this idea, which Chaim Weizmann and Berl Katznelson introduced from time to time with caution. At a joint meeting of the management of the Jewish Agency and the Zionist Executive Committee, Ben-Gurion said: 'I support compulsory transfer. I don't see anything immoral in it.'[13] Following the logic of this position voiced by Ben-Gurion, the young State of Israel would seize the opportunity of its victory in the 1948 Arab–Israeli War to 'rectify' the 1947 partition resolution, which had stipulated that 45 per cent of the citizens of the Jewish State would be Arabs, by expelling more than 700,000 people across the ceasefire lines. The refugees left behind four million *dunams*, which were confiscated; many tried to cross the borders in order to return to their land, but these attempts were forcibly prevented and the land was swiftly allocated to Jewish settlers. The transfer continued until 1950, when the Arab inhabitants of the town of Al-Majdal were expelled to the neighbouring Gaza Strip so that the Jewish town of Ashkelon could be built in its place.

Some 150,000 non-Jewish inhabitants remained within the green line. A tentative Ben-Gurion did not dare to see the transfer through to the end, and for this he came under fire from the historian Benny Morris: 'If he had already expelled them, perhaps the job would have been finished [. . .] I feel that this place would be calmer and less painful if the matter had been decided, if Ben-Gurion had carried out a major expulsion and completely cleaned up the country, all of Eretz Israel, right up to the Jordan. One day it will become clear that this was his fatal mistake.'[14]

However, a secret plan from the 1950s that survives under the name 'the mole' was designed to transfer the population of the so-called Triangle (Umm al-Fahm, Tayibe, Qalansawe, and the surrounding area) to Jordan, should the opportunity arise. The massacre at Kfar Kassim, which took place in 1956 on the first day of the Sinai War and claimed between forty-nine and fifty-one Palestinian victims, was carried out in a context designed to induce fear and to transfer as many Arab villages as possible to the east in order to reduce the population of the Triangle.[15] This transfer project was apparently abandoned after the massacre and the strong reactions it provoked. Nonetheless, some members of parliament publicly supported the idea. These were Rabbi Meir Kahane of the New York Jewish Defense League and Rehavam Zeevi, a former general who had become a minister. There is no doubt that a number of Israeli right-wing activists still dream of displacing the Arabs and believe that a West in sympathy with Israel will eventually accept this state of things, especially if it is followed by desperate acts of madness committed by Palestinians in Israel or in Europe.

Any mention of the expulsion of Palestinians beyond the river Jordan is totally excluded from Israeli discourse and is not to be debated publicly under any circumstances. Such a transfer, which would result in the displacement of hundreds of thousands of Palestinians towards the east, would risk toppling the regimes in Jordan, Saudi Arabia, and the United Arab Emirates, and would thereby clash head-on with western interests in the region, particularly American; so 'don't mention it'! Similarly, the eviction of 1.2 million Gazans could destabilise the Egyptian regime. In the meantime, the State of Israel is content to stand by and watch the slow but steady emigration from the West Bank of young intellectual elites who leave behind them a mass of Palestinians deprived of any clearly identified political leadership, ready to throw in their lot with explosions of desperate anger, and resigned to a totally fatalistic world view.

Can we envisage anything but the continuation of this 'stychic' process, which has nothing to do with democratic principles and constantly manages to ignore them by resorting to brute force? An inescapable and virtually uncontrollable process of unequal and repressive binational coexistence, accompanied by murderous outbursts of violence followed by merciless reprisals: is this the fate to which this small territory is condemned?

Imaginary Options

One may well harbour serious doubts about many of the ideas and positions formulated by Menachem Begin throughout his long and eventful life, but it would not be an exaggeration to say that he understood, better than some leading figures on the Zionist left, that the future of this small country would perpetually bring Jews and Arabs together. This is why he explicitly talked about the need to begin promoting equal rights between them, courageously; otherwise Israel would remain a racial state of lords and vassals, just as Rhodesia was at the time. Remember the dreams of Ahad Ha'am, Martin Buber, Hans Kohn, Leon Magnes, and Hannah Arendt before 1948, of Uri Avnery and Boaz Evron in the 1950s, of Meron Benvenisti and A. B. Yehoshua in the 2000s, of Tony Judt and Peter Beinart in recent years in the United States, of Asad Ghanem and Sari Nusseibeh in Haifa and Al-Quds: will all these dreams eventually come true, or will all these people's efforts have been in vain?

There are two cities that may be seen as alternatives in the vision of a future for Israelis and Palestinians: Haifa and Jerusalem. In Haifa, Jewish and Arab citizens live together as neighbours; overcoming friction and discrimination, they accept each other and prosper thanks to a fruitful cooperation in work, education, and culture. In the capital city, on the contrary, Israel uses all possible means to hinder the citizenship of Palestinians who live under annexation, alienating them and constantly inciting them to leave the city or to resort to desperate acts of insurrection. For the time being Israel prefers the unequal situation in Jerusalem to the relatively more egalitarian one in Haifa, and this for the sake of preserving the 'Jewish character' of the state.

In this narrow space between the river and the sea, two peoples live in an unbearable atmosphere of conflict that can no longer continue. Can the trend be deliberately reversed, and if so, in what direction? Four proposals have been put forward to block the way to the looming catastrophe: two states for two peoples, a confederation of two sovereign states, a democratic secular state, and a binational federal state. There is an inherent relationship between the first two on the one hand and the last two on the other.

Since the 1970s, the Israeli left, both Zionist and non-Zionist, has spoken out in favour of the creation of a Palestinian state alongside Israel. In the 1980s the Palestinian national movement adopted the same position and, although not without hesitation, went on to construct its entire strategy on this base. As the principle of the self-determination of peoples is now dominant throughout the world, many thought that the creation of a Palestinian state alongside Israel would be a symbolic and complementary act in the vast process of decolonisation that began at the end of the Second World War. As we have seen, however, Zionist colonisation was unable or unwilling to set itself borders: driven from the outset by the idea of Jewish sovereignty, it was equally carried away by the justifying myth of ownership of the Land of Israel.

This myth began by undermining the pragmatism of reasonable Zionism, which effectively came to an end with the penetration of almost 1 million settlers beyond the green line. From that point on, appeal to the slogan 'two states for two peoples' reflects, at best, a form of naivety on the part of the last 'beautiful souls' on the Israeli left and, at worst, the cynicism of liberals, who are unable to admit that they were wrong and continue to delude themselves in order to salve their conscience. The same applies to the western states, particularly the United States: they are happy to talk diplomatically about a two-state solution even though most of them are perfectly aware that such an option is now obsolete.

The idea of a confederation of two sovereign states is similar to the first proposal, but adds an extra level of illusion, since, in order to achieve this supposed confederation, one must first make the 'two states for two peoples' paradigm a reality. The idea of confederation explicitly rejects the principle of a common citizenship and resigns itself to a separation, albeit incomplete, between occupier and occupied. The European Union is currently the best known confederation and could serve as a model here.

The concept of a secular democratic state constitutes a return to the position of the Palestine Liberation Organization (PLO) before its recognition of the existence of Israel as an entity, at a time when it still viewed the Jews of the region solely as a religious community. This concept does include the higher principle of a common and equal citizenship, rather than that of a single chosen sovereignty, but offers no institutional or legal expression to the cultural and national specificity of each of the two entities. Post-apartheid South Africa may be considered the most illustrative example of this option.

The paradigm of the binational state was first put forward by Ahad Ha'am and was subsequently advocated by Martin Buber, Leon Magnes, and others; more recently it has reached A. B. Yehoshua and is taking shape among Palestinian intellectuals. It envisions a federation of two or more national entities, as in Belgium, Canada, Switzerland, Great Britain, Spain, India, Bosnia–Herzegovina, and other countries, which have a common sovereignty and citizenship but have maintained cultural and linguistic particularities, autonomous governance bodies, elected assemblies attached to a supreme parliament, and so on. This is the scheme at the heart of the vision of eminent intellectuals on the fringes of the Zionist movement. Similar ideas are increasingly found today on the critical fringes of Israeli political commentary, as well as in current Palestinian thought.

Utopias and Calamities

Hopes for the gradual realisation of a moderate, egalitarian vision seem unlikely to be fulfilled in the current hostile atmosphere. The construction of a federation that respects cultural specificities and bestows a common and equal citizenship, just like other states, is possible only when two communities, in spite of cultural differences and economic disparities, can see beyond a conflictual past and the persistence of antagonistic interests and aspire to strengthen the relations of trust and solidarity between them, having realised that there is no other choice. This is what brought about the relative decline in tensions between Flemings and Walloons in Belgium, between Basques and Castilians in the Spanish state, between Catholics and Protestants in Northern Ireland, and between whites and Blacks in South Africa.

Ethnocentric, religious, and pseudo-religious postures, the concept of superiority linked to the feeling of being the eternal victim of history whether among Israelis or Palestinians, political fragmentation and rivalry, the discrediting of the Ramallah Authority, and the rise of a radical Islam that seeks to gain hegemony in the region – all these are factors that, for the time being, raise an obstacle to any possibility of cultural and political rapprochement between the two sides.[16] An egalitarian binational federation is seen by many Israelis as a nightmare, a demographic and cultural threat that would call the 'Jewish identity' into question. The fact that this identity, whatever it may be, has existed for two thousand years outside any sovereignty does not seem to constitute an argument that Zionist discourse wants to address.

Palestinian civic resistance organisations, which work to create a peaceful mass movement for equality and human rights and intervene legally too, at the local and international level, suffer the wrath of Israel, which bans them. Those Israelis who express indignation at the perpetuation of a discriminatory racist Jewish policy are pilloried and constantly accused of treachery by the burgeoning extreme right and by the current government. For the moment, there are hardly any political forces capable of bringing the two communities together so as to promote a federal structure on a new, humanist basis.

Meanwhile the stychic process continues, in spite of everything, to move towards an ever-growing demographic and economic integration. More and more Israelis settle in the West Bank, being driven not by idealism but by a desire to find ease and comfort, while more than thirty thousand Palestinians cross the separation barriers every day to work long hours in Israel. Thousands of construction workers come equally from the walled Gaza Strip, while Israeli industrial and agricultural products are permanently routed to Gaza, where the most widely traded currency, as in the West Bank, is the Israeli shekel, and postal mail destined for Gaza and the West Bank passes through Israel.

While Israel continues to define itself as a Jewish state rather than as an Israeli state that belongs to all its citizens, its Palestinian inhabitants are undergoing a process of accelerated cultural Israelisation: their importance to the economy and to society is gradually increasing, but this makes them oppose the dominant ethnocentric ideology more and more. Their Arab identity gets indirectly consolidated, making them feel that they are sub-tenants in the nation state of the Jewish people. The fact that, since 2003, the law on citizenship and entry into Israel prohibits Palestinian Israeli men and women married to a Palestinian man or woman from the West Bank from living together in Israel has no doubt broken the last link in the illusion of egalitarianism.[17]

In my view – and I very much hope that I am wrong – this uncontrolled process, of which few are aware in all its aspects, is likely to end in disaster. The coexistence of two increasingly intertwined populations with no civil, legal, or political equality may well continue for a while yet, but the truce will eventually come to an end. On the Israeli side, if extremist nationalists continue increasingly to occupy decision-making positions and openly promote an apartheid policy accompanied by mass expulsions, this process could trigger a generalised conflagration, which would risk leading to the senseless bombardment of the Al-Aqsa Mosque.

Will such radicalisation result in massive destruction, with tens of thousands of victims, or *only* in a brief, targeted bombardment of Hebron, Nablus, and, who knows, even Jerusalem? Can Israel's nuclear weapons prevent a conflict that threatens to spread outside the region? Or, on the contrary, amplify it to excess? Would Israelis' continued existence in the region be assured in the wake of a huge cataclysm, or would it be called into question altogether?

None of us can answer these questions. It is up to each and every one of us who wants to guarantee the future of our children and grandchildren in the Middle East to begin struggling in the dark, perhaps apparently against all hope, for equality and fundamental rights for others, for those who live next to us and opposite us. And, perhaps, like our ancestors, on both sides of the confrontation, to prepare for another great catastrophe, the prelude to yet more waves of emigration.

Old hopes, now faded, have had to give way to new, more audacious hopes; they have been transformed into historical utopias and inspirational myths, which grasped the stychic process, integrated themselves into it, and steered it towards much needed rational solutions. If we cannot share land, with

all the difficulties that entails, then we must learn to share
sovereignty. Palestinian–Israeli binationalism must, when the
time comes, tear from its heart the dividing wall of hatred built
like a fortress upon a mount of fears, so as to enable us all,
Israelis and Palestinians, to live together.

Afterword

> Should we be unable to find a way to honest cooperation and
> honest pacts with the Arabs, then we have learned absolutely
> nothing during our 2,000 years of suffering and deserve all that
> will come to us.
>
> Letter from Albert Einstein to Chaim Weizmann
> after the Hebron massacre, 25 November 1929[1]

Both Hamas's violent uprising in Gaza and Israel's crushing military response, which has been equally devastating, have raised concerns shared by many in Israel and around the world. These concerns echo those expressed by Ahad Ha'am, Hans Kohn, Martin Buber, Leon Magnes, Hannah Arendt, and many others: that creating an exclusively Jewish state in the Middle East without considering the fate of the local *indigenous* Palestinians and without attempting to integrate them into the settlement project would result in a situation where every decade is marked by recurring wars.

Before 7 October 2023, many believed that, if Israel were to sign peace treaties with the more conservative Arab countries, then the conflict between Israel and the Arab world could be resolved and Arab animosity towards Israel would diminish.

It seemed as though the Palestinian problem could be swept under the thick rug of regional politics. The Palestinians' desperate and cruel uprising shattered those delusions and brought the suffering of those who have been and continue to be harmed by the Zionist national project back into local and international consciousness.

At the time of writing this Afterword, it is difficult to assess the long-term developments that will result from this latest twofold catastrophe. While political thought in Israel appears to be stagnant or lost in the intoxicating sound of war drums, many around the world have begun to seek solutions to this dangerous conflict. The instability it continues to cause poses a risk not only to the Middle East but to the entire world. Both liberal western countries and conservative Arab states have begun to look again at the two-state solution, which was apparently consigned to the dustbin of history after the failure of the Oslo Accords.

The idea of a two-state solution has been raised by the president of the United States, and others have expressed their support for it; but there is currently no significant political appetite for this project within Israel itself. The left-wing Zionist movement has dissolved entirely and, apart from a small communist party, not many believe that dividing up the narrow territory between the river and the sea is a viable or a positive solution.

Just a glance at a demographic map shows the difficulty inherent in any major attempt to separate the two national groups. Israeli Arabs, numbering 2 million, constitute the majority in the Galilee area. The Jordan Rift Valley is largely populated by Jewish settlements. In the West Bank there are 3 million Palestinians and 850,000 Israelis, 300,000 of whom live in the eastern Jerusalem area. There is currently no political force in Israel that is willing or able to remove them from their homes. Neither is there any significant Zionist movement that would agree to divide Jerusalem and make Al-Quds the capital of an independent Palestine with the Al-Aqsa Mosque at its centre (a territory which would also include the destroyed Gaza Strip, geographically completely separate from the West Bank). It is unlikely that many Israelis would accept the existence of a Palestinian security force, even if it were limited and unarmed, positioned along the 1967 borders.

Apart from that, the Palestinian Authority in Ramallah, which usually cooperates with Israel, does not have the support of the majority of the Palestinian population and has consequently refused to hold elections for years. It cannot therefore be considered a democratic government. The political temperament of the Authority in Ramallah is far from liberal; the Authority has eradicated any organisation that disagrees with it. It is unclear whether basic human rights, which have been refused by the Israeli government for many years now, will be honoured under this Authority. Neither the United States nor Saudi Arabia are interested in the nature of the imagined Palestinian state. As far as they are concerned, it might as well be a type of Vichy state like that (which existed in France during the Nazi occupation), or even something like the South African Bantustan states.

In summary, from many points of view, a binational federation appears to be a more realistic and humane solution than a two-state entity. Quite obviously, any solution – even a flawed or incomplete one – that might reduce the constant violence in Gaza or the West Bank, end the apartheid regime, and promote even a small degree of equality between the two peoples is to be supported. At present, however, there are no political options in sight, to prevent another impending disaster.

Notes

Notes to Preface

1 Visit https://apnews.com/article/israel-apartheid-palestinians-oc cupation-c8137c9e7f33c2cba7b0b5ac7fa8d115.

2 Anita Shapira, *Israel: A History* (Waltham, MA: Brandeis University Press, 2012), 271.

Notes to Chapter 1

1 Mahmoud Darwish, *A River Dies of Thirst*, trans. Catherine Colburn (Brooklyn, NY: Archipelago Books, 2009), p. 145.

2 *The Poetry of Yehuda Amichai*, ed. Robert Alter (New York: Farrar, Straus and Giroux, 2015), p. 381.

3 Vladimir Jabotinsky, 'The Iron Wall', *Razsviet* (*Dawn*), 4 November 1923. https://www.jewishvirtuallibrary.org/quot -the-iron-wall-quot.

4 'The Ethics of the Iron Wall', *Razsviet*, 11 November 1923. https://david-collier.com/ethics-iron-wall-zeev-jabotinsky.

5 Israel Belkind, *The Arabs in Eretz Israel* [Hebrew] (Tel-Aviv: Ha-Meïr, 1928), p. 8.

6 David Ben-Gurion and Yitzhak Ben-Zvi, *Eretz Israel Past and Present* [Hebrew] (Jerusalem: Editions Yad Ben-Zvi, 1980), p. 196. This did not prevent Ben-Gurion, one of the drafters of

the 1948 Declaration of Independence of the State of Israel, from allowing the inclusion of the claim that, '[a]fter being forcibly exiled from their land, the people kept faith with it throughout their Dispersion'. It is a shame that this blatant historical falsification has apparently posed no problem for Israeli historians, who knew very well that, to this day, there is no trace or testimony of a forced exile of Jews imposed by the Romans, and hence no research whatsoever was conducted on this subject.

7　The five Jewish kingdoms were Adiabene (now northern Iraq) in the first century AD, Himyar (modern-day Yemen) in the fifth century, the Berber kingdom of Al-Kahina (North Africa) in the seventh century, Khazaria (southern Russia) in the eighth century, and Beta Israel (southern Ethiopia), probably in the fourteenth century.

8　See Yakov Rabkin, *Au nom de la Torah: Une histoire de l'opposition juive au sionisme* (Quebec: Presses de l'Université Laval, 2004).

9　During the four centuries of Ottoman rule over the region, the Jews of the Muslim world were able to abandon their 'exile' without difficulty and return to their 'desired homeland'. Only a few small groups made the journey; most Jews from the Arab East emigrated to Israel under duress, as a result of deterioration in the Arab regimes' relationship with them after the intensification of the conflict in the 1950s and 1960s. A significant proportion of Jews from the Maghreb opted to emigrate to Europe, and 90 per cent of Algerian Jews preferred to go to France, since they were already French citizens.

10　On this subject see Issam Nassar, 'Palestinian Identity: The Question of Historiography', in I. Hjelm, H. Taha, I. Pappé, and T.L. Thompson (eds), *A New Critical Approach to the History of Palestine* (London: Routledge, 2019), pp. 43–59.

11　Quoted in André Draznin, *What Do the Palestinians Want?* [Hebrew] (Jerusalem: Carmel, 2022), p. 82.

12　Also India, with its federal system of twenty-eight states, and Spain, with its seventeen autonomous regions and a diversity of linguistic heritage, may largely be considered multinational states. And we could add Bosnia–Herzegovina and Northern Ireland.

13 Hans Kohn, *The Idea of Nationalism: A Study in Its Origins and Background* (New York: Macmillan, 1946).

14 The Dutch researcher Arend Lijphart coined the phrase 'consociational democracy' to describe countries in which different communities live together and have a coordinated representation of their collective interests, within a framework of full civil and political equality. See his article 'Consociational Democracy', *World Politics* 21.2 (1969), pp. 207–25.

15 Moshe-Leib Lilienblum (*Jugendsünde*, Vienna: Brag, 1876, 196), one of the first members of the Lovers of Zion, emphasised this in his 1876 autobiography: 'We are Semites among the Aryans, sons of Shem among the sons of Japheth, an Asiatic Palestinian tribe in the land of Europe.' On 'pan-Semitism' within Zionism, see Hanan Harif, *We Are Brothers: The Eastward Turn in Zionist Thought* [Hebrew] (Jerusalem: Zalman Shazar Center, 2019).

16 The ancient biblical myth also asserted a common origin for the sons of Israel and Ishmael, the 'biological' descendants of 'Abraham our father' or 'Abraham their father'.

17 On this subject, see the detailed work by Yossef Gorny, *Politics and Imagination: Federal Ideas in Zionist Political Thought 1917–1948* [Hebrew] (Jerusalem: Yad Yitzhak Ben-Zvi, 1993).

18 David Ben-Gurion, *Zionist Policy and the Workers of Eretz Israel (Jewish State or Binational State?)* [Hebrew] (Central Publishing House of the Workers' Party of Eretz Israel, July 1944), p. 11. Ben-Gurion recalled a second meeting, in 1930, with members of Brit Shalom, and quoted himself as saying: 'The formula of a binational state, favoured by the people of Brit Shalom, means nothing, and has no political consistency [. . .]. Eretz Israel for the Hebrew people, and Eretz Israel for the Arab people, are not the same thing' (ibid., pp. 11–12).

19 See in particular his last book, *The Jewish War Front* (London: T.F. Unwin, 1940).

20 As quoted in Gorny, *Politics and Imagination*, p. 24.

Notes to Chapter 2

1 Ahad Ha'am, 'Truth from Eretz Israel' [1891], in Alan Dowty, 'Much Ado about Little: Ahad Ha'am's "Truth from Eretz Yisrael," Zionism, and the Arabs', *Israel Studies* 5.2 (2000), pp. 154–81, here 175.

2 Yitzhak Epstein, 'A Hidden Question' [1907], in Alan Dowty, '"A Question That Outweighs All Others": Yitzhak Epstein and Zionist Recognition of the Arab Issue', *Israel Studies* 6.1 (2001), pp. 34–54.

3 See Steven J. Zipperstein, *Elusive Prophet: Ahad Ha'am and the Origins of Zionism* (Berkeley, CA: University of California Press, 1993).

4 Ha'am, 'Truth from Eretz Israel', p. 162.

5 Ibid., p. 175.

6 Theodor Herzl, *The Jewish State* (New York: Dover, 1988), p. 96.

7 Theodor Herzl, *The Old New Land*, trans. Lotta Levensohn (New York: Markus Wiener / Herzl Press, 1987), p. 124.

8 Critical article on *Altneuland* [Hebrew], published in *Ha-Shiloah* 10 (1903), p. 6, https://benyehuda.org/read/5527.

9 Ahad Ha'am, 'The Law of the Heart' [1894], in his *Al parashat derakim* [*At the Crossroads*], vol. 1, p. 93, publication details unavailable; translated here from French. (Cf. another translation under the title 'A Judaism of the Heart', at http://www.ma tanel.org/wp-content/uploads/2017/01/SCHER-AHAD-HAAM -ENG.pdf.)

10 Quotation from Joseph Heller, *From Brit Shalom to Ichud: Judah Leib Magnes and the Struggle for a Binational State in Palestine* [Hebrew] (Jerusalem: Magnes Press, 2003), p. 167.

11 Preface to the new edition of the collection: Ahad Ha'am, *Am Scheidewege* (Berlin: Yiddishe Verlag, 1921), n.p. This and the

quotations in the previous para come from this piece and are translated here from French.

12 *The Complete Works of Ahad Ha'am* [Hebrew] (Tel Aviv: Dvir, 1956), p. 479.

13 See *Ha-Shiloah* 17, July–December 1907, pp. 193–206. The poet Hayim Nahman Bialik appended a comment as follows: 'This lecture was presented by the author at the "Ivriya" meeting during the Seventh Congress in Basel, but we think that the subject of the lecture is not outdated even now, and perhaps precisely now, as practical work in Eretz Israel has increased, it deserves attention. We do not agree with the honored author's opinion in several respects' (Epstein, 'A Hidden Question', p. 39).

14 Epstein, 'A Hidden Question', p. 40.

15 Ibid., p. 195 (only in Hebrew).

16 Ber Borochov, *Writings*, vol. 1 [Hebrew] (Tel Aviv: Sifriat Ha-Poalim, 1955), p. 148.

17 Epstein, 'A Hidden Question', p. 40.

18 On this subject, see Avi Glezerman: 'The Hidden Question' [Hebrew], *Matzpen* 89 (1981).

19 Epstein, 'A Hidden Question', pp. 42–3.

20 Ibid., p. 43.

21 Ibid., p. 48.

22 Ibid., pp. 50, 51.

23 We know by chance of the case of Aaron Aaronson, an agronomist from the Zikhron Yaakov colony who shared Epstein's point of view and had great admiration for him. See Harif, *We Are Brothers* (ch. 1, n. 15), p. 100.

24 On this original figure in the Zionist movement, see 'Rabi Binyamin et le pansémitisme', in Harif, *We Are Brothers*, pp. 95–210.

25 *Ha-Meorrer* newspaper, January 1907. Rabbi Binyamin had probably attended Epstein's lecture in 1905.

26 Shai Agnon wrote of him: 'Writers have a habit of honouring themselves with their non-Jewish degrees: a professor flaunts his

professoriality, and if he is a doctor, he *doctoralizes* his articles, but we have not found an author who designates himself by a title that would bring a kosher Jew to call him his brother. Until Rabbi Binyamin came along and referred to himself as *Rabbi Binyamin.' Me-Azmi el Azmi* [Hebrew] (Tel Aviv: Schocken, 1976), p. 174.

Notes to Chapter 3

1 Hans Kohn, *Living in a World Revolution: My Encounters with History* (New York: Trident, 1964 [1936]), p. 53.

2 Some members of the association lived in Europe, mainly in Germany: Robert Weltsch, editor of the *Jüdische Rundschau*, a widely circulated Jewish newspaper; and the philosopher Ernst Simon, who emigrated to Palestine in 1928.

3 On Albert Einstein, see Ofer Ashkenazi, 'Zionist, but Not Jewish Nationalist: Albert Einstein and Brit Shalom and the Events of 1929', in A. Gordon (ed.), *Brit Shalom and Binational Zionism: The Arab Question as a Jewish Question* [Hebrew] (Jerusalem: Carmel, 2008), pp. 123–48.

4 Preface to the first issue of the magazine *Sheifoteinu*, 1927.

5 Arthur Ruppin, *The Jews of To-Day*, trans. Margery Bentwich (London: G. Bell and Sons, 1913), p. 3.

6 On the racial conceptions of the father of Jewish colonisation see Etan Blum, *Arthur Ruppin and the Production of Pre-Israeli Culture* (Leiden: Brill, 2011).

7 Jacob Thon, a close friend of Ruppin's and a fellow member of Brit Shalom, also wondered: 'Who knows what scientific research will reveal? Perhaps, and this is very plausible, there will be descendants of the ancient Hebrews living in the Arab farming community, and a feeling of close racial belonging between the peoples will then be awakened; this will create a new basis for their life together in the country.' Cited in Harif, *We Are Brothers* (ch. 1, n. 15), p. 197.

8 In 1914, Ruppin was still imagining the possible transfer of some of Palestine's Arabs to Syria. Jacob Thon, for his part,

proposed transferring them to the other side of the Jordan. See Blum, *Arthur Ruppin and the Production of Pre-Israeli Culture.*

9 Cited in Nadine Gerling, 'The Practical Zionism of Arthur Ruppin', in A. Gordon (ed.), *Brit Shalom and Binational Zionism: The Arab Question as a Jewish Question* [Hebrew] (Jerusalem: Carmel, 2008), pp. 174–5. In August 1925, in his speech to the Zionist Congress in Vienna, Ruppin declared: 'Palestine will be a binational state [. . .]. This is a fact, a fact that many of you have not understood correctly'. This position was not yet seen as heretical, and many of Chaim Weizmann's supporters would have subscribed to it.

10 See Otto Bauer, *The Question of Nationalities and Social Democracy*, trans. Joseph O'Donnell (Minneapolis: Minnesota University Press, 2000). Other important researchers on Czech nationalism in Prague include Karl Deutsch, Miroslav Hroch, and Ernest Gellner.

11 Moshe Smilansky, 'Our Deeds', *Ha-Olam*, official weekly of the World Zionist Organization, 1913.

12 Cited in Tom Segev, *One Palestine, Complete: Jews and Arabs under the British Mandate*, trans. Haim Watzman (New York: Metropolitan Books, 2000), p. 114.

13 Translated (with minor changes) from the German version published in Yfaat Weiss, 'Central European Ethno-Nationalism and Zionist Binationalism', in A. Gordon (ed.), *Brit Shalom and Binational Zionism: The Arab Question as a Jewish Question* [Hebrew] (Jerusalem: Carmel, 2008), pp. 104–5.

14 Rabbi Binyamin (Yehoshua Radler-Feldmann), 'Around the Point' [Hebrew], *Sheifoteinu* 1.2 (1928), p. 21.

15 Quoted in Harif, *We Are Brothers*, p. 187.

16 Hugo Bergmann, 'On the Question of Majority' [Hebrew], *Sheifoteinu* (1929), pp. 24–9.

17 On the anti-imperialism of the group's members, see Zohar Maor, 'From Anti-Colonialism to Post-Colonialism: Criticism of

Nationalism. and the Secularisation of Brit Shalom' [Hebrew], *Teoria Oubikoret* 30 (2007), pp. 13–38.

18. Gershom Scholem, 'On What Principle', *Sheifoteinu* B.1 (September 1931), pp. 193–203.

19 On Scholem's religion and politics, see Amnon Raz-Krakotzkin, *Exil et souveraineté: Judaïsme, sionisme et pensée binationale* (Paris: La Fabrique, 2007), pp. 131–57.

20 In an interview in 1970, Scholem said: 'In retrospect as a member of Brit Shalom, at that time, I am today doubtful as to whether it would have made much difference had one thing been done then rather than another.' He added that the Arabs do have rights, 'but I think that the rights of the Jewish people are more important'. Ehud Ben Ezer (ed.), *Unease in Zion* (New York: Quadrangle / New York Times Book Co., 1974), pp. 271–2.

21 Quotation translated from the German published in the article by Hagit Lavsky, 'Nationalism, from Theory to Practice: Hans Kohn and Zionism' [Hebrew], *Sion*, B (2001), p. 196.

22 *Nationalismus: Über die Bedeutung des Nationalismus im Judentum und in der Gegenwart* (Vienna: R. Löwit, 1922).

23 *A History of Nationalism in the East* (New York: Harcourt, 1929). Despite his criticism of imperialism, Kohn remained markedly imbued with the orientalism characteristic of all his contemporaries.

24 *Sheifoteinu* A.1 (= initial pamphlet) (1927), pp. 28–39.

25 Jewish National and University Library 376/224, Kohn to Berthold Feiwel [1875–1937], Jerusalem, 21 November 1929.

26 Cited in Adi Gordon, '"Nothing but a Disillusioned Love?" Hans Kohn's Break with the Zionist Movement', in Ezra Mendelsohn, Stefani Hoffman, and Richard I. Cohen (eds), *Against the Grain: Jewish Intellectuals in Hard Times* (New York: Bergahn, 2014), pp. 117–42, here 123.

27 Ibid., p. 135.

28 Quoted in Lavsky, 'Nationalism, from Theory to Practice', 20. See also André Liebich, 'Searching for the Perfect Nation: The

Itinerary of Hans Kohn (1891–1971)', *Nations and Nationalism* 12.4 (2006), pp. 579–96.

29 See Yitzhak Conforti, 'East and West in Jewish Nationalism: Conflicting Types in the Zionist Vision?', *Nation and Nationalism* 16.2 (2010), 202–19, and Brian M. Smollett, 'The Rise and the Fall of the Jewish Vision in the Life and Thought of Hans Kohn', in B. M. Smollett and C. Wise, *Reappraisals and New Studies of the Modern Jewish Experience* (Leiden: Brill, 2014), pp. 268–85.

30 David Ben-Gurion despised 'the national and social character of this intelligentsia': 'so long as they are not a living organ of ourselves, we have no assurance that when a new wind blows, their true nature will not be revealed'. See Elek D. Epstein, 'From Brit Shalom to Circle 77', in A. Gordon (ed.), *Brit Shalom and Binational Zionism: The Arab Question as a Jewish Question* [Hebrew] (Jerusalem: Carmel, 2008), p. 199.

31 Natan Hofshi, *In Heart and Soul: The Struggle for the People and for Man* [Hebrew] (Tel-Aviv: private edition, 1965), p. 57. To add insult to injury, in the village of Nahalal Hofshi was regarded as the spiritual mentor of Moshe Dayan, the symbol of Israel's future belligerence.

Notes to Chapter 4

1 In Paul Mendes-Flohr (ed.), *A Land of Two Peoples: Martin Buber on Jews and Arabs* (Chicago, IL: University of Chicago Press, 2005), pp. 194–202, here 199.

2 In Hannah Arendt, *The Correspondence of Hannah Arendt and Gershom Scholem*, ed. M. L. Knott, trans. Anthony David (Chicago, IL: Chicago University Press, 2017), p. 207.

3 Gershom Scholem, 'Portrait of Martin Buber' [1953], in the collection of short writings *Explications and Implications: Writings on Jewish Heritage and Renaissance*, ed. Avraham Shapira [Hebrew] (Tel Aviv: Am Oved, 2 vols, 1975–6), vol. 1, p. 455.

4 Researchers have shown that the book is also a self-portrait of Hans Kohn. See Zohar Maor, 'Kohn's Buber, Buber's Kohn: Hans

Kohn's Biography of Martin Buber Revisited', *Leo Beck Institute Year Book* 63.1 (2018), pp. 255–72.

5 A summary of Buber's relationship with Ahad Ha'am appears in Martin Buber, *Between a People and Their Land* [Hebrew] (Tel Aviv: Schocken, 1948), pp. 157–62, where he states: 'Ahad Ha'am's Zionism is not "smaller" than the state, but much larger.'

6 Martin Buber, 'Judaism and the Jews' [1909], in his *On Judaism*, ed. Nahum N. Glatzer (New York: Schocken, 1967), 11–21: 17. Later on Buber tried to remove the clear biological dimension from his concept of blood.

7 See the moving letter from G. Landauer to M. Buber dated 12 May 1916, in Abraham Yassour, *Chapters on the Thought of Martin Buber* [Hebrew] (Tel Aviv: Alef, 1981), pp. 146–50. Landauer challenges his friend: 'In the future you will no longer be a participant in a German war against the nations of Europe and others, nor in a war of Europe against itself, as you are doing now, in the midst of confusion' (150). A few years later, in *The Ways of Utopia* (Tel Aviv: Am Oved, 1983), Buber devoted a fine chapter to the courageous anarchist (pp. 62–73, 236–352). See also M. Buber, *Paths in Utopia*, trans. R.F. Hull (Syracuse: Syracuse University Press, 1996).

8 Martin Buber, *I and Thou*, trans. Ronald Gregor Smith (New York: Charles Scribner's Sons, 1937), p. 28.

9 Ibid., p. 75.

10 On this anarchism, see Charles Bloch, 'Gustav Landauer', in E. Schaltiel (ed.), *Jews in Revolutionary Movements* [Hebrew] (Jerusalem: Shazar, 1982), pp. 125–32. On Buber's relationship with anarchism, see Shlomo Sand, 'Martin Buber, Proudhon et la vérité de demain', *Mille neuf cent: Revue d'histoire intellectuelle* 10 (1992), pp. 63–70.

11 On Buber's *Havruta*, see Buber, *The Ways of Utopia*, pp. 159–235.

12 From Buber's October 1929 article 'The National Home and National Policy in Palestine', in Mendes-Flohr, *A Land of Two Peoples*, pp. 81–91, here 84.

13 See the chapter entitled 'Truth in Myth" in Martin Buber, *With a Human Face* [Hebrew] (Jerusalem: Mossad Bialik, 1962), pp. 356–9.

14 Letter dated 4 February 1918, in Mendes-Flohr, *A Land of Two Peoples*, pp. 37–8.

15 'At This Late Hour', article from April 1920, in Mendes-Flohr, *A Land of Two Peoples*, pp. 42–6, here 46.

16 'Nationalism', article from April 1920, in Mendes-Flohr, *A Land of Two Peoples*, pp. 47–57, here 49–50.

17 See the article by Shalom Ratzabi, 'God Alone Is King: That's Why We Need a Binational State' [Hebrew], *Haaretz*, 8 May 2015.

18 The Muslim Brotherhood movement was formed in 1928. In its early days it emphasised opposition to violence, and its influence was limited. Rabbi Abraham Isaac Kook's first doctrinal statements appeared around the same time; they were later radicalised by his son.

19 'The National Home and National Policy in Palestine', lecture given in October 1929, in Berlin, to Brit Shalom supporters, in Mendes-Flohr, *A Land of Two Peoples*, pp. 81–91, here 84 and 87 – but translated here from French.

20 On 'Buberian sociology', see Uri Ram, *The Return of Martin Buber* [Hebrew] (Tel Aviv: Resling, 2015).

21 'A Letter to Gandhi', in Mendes-Flohr, *A Land of Two Peoples*, pp. 111–26, here 122.

22 Ibid., pp. 119–20.

23 See Joseph Heller, *From Brit Shalom to Ihud* [Hebrew] (Jerusalem: Magnes Press, 2003), p. 157.

24 'The Time to Try', in Mendes-Flohr, *A Land of Two Peoples*, pp. 304–5, here 305. See the fine obituary by Boaz Evron, 'The Figure of Martin Buber', *Etgar*, 24 June 1965.

25 On this subject, see Shlomo Sand, 'Bernard Lazare, le premier sioniste français', *Revue française d'histoire des idées politiques* 4 (1996), pp. 281–96.

26 On this subject, see Hannah Arendt, 'Bernard Lazare, the

Conscious Pariah', in her *The Jew as Pariah: Jewish Identity and Politics in the Modern Age*, ed. Ron H. Feldman (New York: Grove Press, 1978), pp. 76–9.

27 Hannah Arendt, *Rahel Varnhagen: The Life of a Jewish Woman*, trans. Richard and Clara Winston (New York: Harcourt Brace Jovanovich, 1974), p. 224.

28 Letter of 24 August 1936, in *Within Four Walls: The Correspondence between Hannah Arendt and Heinrich Blücher, 1930–1908*, ed. Lotte Kohler, trans. Peter Constantine (New York: Harcourt, 1996), pp. 20–1. Arendt admired the great German philosopher Herder's understanding of Judaism.

29 See now Hannah Arendt, *The Origins of Totalitarianism* (New York: Schocken, 2004). This wide-ranging essay was the subject of an avalanche of praise and criticism. Arendt's principal theories on the close links between the decline of the nation state and the rise of imperialism and the comparisons she makes between Nazi, fascist, and Soviet totalitarianism have been rejected by liberals (Raymond Aron) and Marxists (Eric Hobsbawm) alike.

30 Ibid., pp. 11 and 12. Despite her extensive knowledge of the Dreyfus Affair, Arendt fails to point out that the standard-bearers of extreme nationalism in France, figures such as Maurice Barrès, Charles Maurras, and many others, whether secular modernists or conservative traditionalists, were inveterate Judeophobes. Nor does her essay provide a sufficiently in-depth analysis of the differences between anti-Semitism in Poland, Romania, Russia, and France on the one hand and the specific conception of the Jew in Nazi nationalism on the other.

31 The variety of Arendt's positions is also apparent when it comes to the history and culture of the United States. In the 1960s, for example, she expressed her admiration for the American Revolution of the eighteenth century and praised its federalism and decentralisation. She also expressed reservations about abolishing racial segregation in schools in the South, arguing that white sensitivities had to be taken into account.

32 Hannah Arendt, 'Zionism Reconsidered', in her *The Jewish*

Writings, ed. Jerome Kohn and Ron H. Feldman (New York: Schocken, 2007), pp. 343–74, here 343.
33 Ibid.
34 Ibid., p. 344.
35 Ibid., p. 364.
36 Hannah Arendt, 'To Save the Jewish Homeland', in her *The Jewish Writings*, ed. Jerome Kohn and Ron H. Feldman, pp. 388–401, here 395. Throughout her life Arendt admired the communal life of the kibbutz and returned to it repeatedly. Despite her criticism of Zionism and Israel, she praised two particular achievements: the kibbutz and the Hebrew University.
37 Ibid., p. 400. On this point see Eric Jacobson, 'Why Did Hannah Arendt Reject the Partition of Palestine?', *Journal for Cultural Research* 17.4 (2013), pp. 358–81.
38 Arendt, 'To Save the Jewish Homeland', p. 401.
39 Hannah Arendt, 'Peace or Armistice in the Middle East', in her *The Jewish Writings*, ed. Jerome Kohn and Ron H. Feldman, pp. 423–51, here 450.
40 Ibid.

Notes to Chapter 5
1 Ernst Simon, 'Against the Sadducees', [Hebrew] *Sheifoteinu*, 3.5–6 (1932), pp. 152–67.
2 See Moshe Gabay, *Kedmah-Mizraha* [Hebrew] (Guivat Haviva: Institute of Arab Studies, 1983), p. 15, and also pp. 138–44 in Susan Hattis's pioneering doctoral thesis: Susan Lee Hattis, *The Binational Idea in Palestine during Mandatory Times* (Haifa: Shikmona, 1970).
3 In the following chapter we shall review the positions of left-wing political organisations on binationalism.
4 Walter Laqueur, 'The Arendt Cult: Hannah Arendt as Political Commentator', in Stephen E. Aschheim (ed.), *Hannah Arendt in Jerusalem* (Berkeley: University of California Press, 2001), pp. 47–64, here 57.
5 For an historical overview of the life of Leon Magnes, see Arthur

A. Goren (ed.), *Dissenter in Zion: From the Writings of Judah L. Magnes* (Cambridge, MA: Harvard University Press, 1982), pp. 3–57. See also David Barak-Gorodetsky, *Judah Magnes: The Prophetic Politics of a Religious Binationalist*, trans. Merav Datan (Lincoln: University of Nebraska Press, 2021), pp. 3–57.

6 On this subject, see the article by Hedva Ben-Israel, 'Binationalism versus Nationalism: The Case of Judah Magnes', *Israel Studies* 23.1 (2018), pp. 86–105.

7 Gershom Scholem, *From Berlin to Jerusalem* [Hebrew] (Tel Aviv: Am Oved, 1982), p. 230.

8 Leon Magnes was not universally liked, and Vladimir Jabotinsky in particular always found him insufferable. In the newspaper *Doar Hayom* of 22 May 1929, he described the situation at the university as 'a lot of loud bluffing', adding: 'This situation is nothing but a tragicomedy, and if we didn't feel sympathy for those involved, we could add [. . .] that the personality, qualities, and "scientific" status of the gentleman at the head of the institution tip the tragi-comedy over into pure comedy.'

9 After the Nazis came to power, Magnes expressed remorse, confusion, and serious doubts: 'It can be said, however, that the Jewish people are an emblematic example of the idea of blood, race, and community, an example of *You have chosen us*. Those who hate both Israel and the Germans claim that the Germans have inherited the arrogance of the Jews.' This comes from his speech at the opening of the academic year in 1933, in the volume *Chancellor's Address to the Hebrew University* [Hebrew] (Jerusalem: Hebrew University Publishing House, 1936), p. 165.

10 Ibid., p. 75.

11 See 'Students against the Rector: Political Student Trials at the Hebrew University in 1930', *The Librarians*, National Library blog, 23 October 2017.

12 Quoted in Norman Bentwich, *For Zion: A Biography of Judah L. Magnes* [Hebrew] (Jerusalem: Magnes Publishers, 1955), p. 129. On his strong link with Jeremiah, see Magnes's 1931 lecture, in the volume *Chancellor's Address to the Hebrew University*

[Hebrew] (Jerusalem: Hebrew University Publishing House, 1936), p. 95.

13 Schmuel Yoseph Agnon, *Shira*, trans. Zeva Shapiro (New York: Schocken, 1989), p. 103.

14 Leon Magnes, *Like All Nations?* [Hebrew] (Jerusalem: Portail de fleurs, 1929), p. 5; partial English translation in Arthur Herzberg (ed.), *The Zionist Idea: A Historical Analysis and Reader* (Philadelphia, PA: Jewish Publication Society, 1997).

15 Ibid., p. 10.

16 See Daniel P. Kotzin, 'An Attempt to Americanize the *Yishuv*: Judah L. Magnes in Mandatory Palestine', *Israel Studies* 5.1 (2000), pp. 1–23.

17 Magnes, *Like All Nations?* p. 93.

18 See *The Magnes–Philby Negotiations, 1929: The Historical Record* [Hebrew] (Jerusalem: Magnes Press, 1998), which contains Magnes's own testimony.

19 On the important role played by Magnes in organising meetings between Ben-Gurion and leading Arab figures, see David Ben-Gurion, *My Talks with Arab Leaders*, trans. Aryeh Rubinstein and Misha Louvish (New York: Third Press, 1973).

20 See Heller, *From Brit Shalom to Ihud* (ch. 4, n. 23), p. 157.

21 Cited in Goren, *Dissenter in Zion*, p. 385.

22 Speech to the executive meeting of the Jewish Agency, 26 February 1946. See Heller, *From Brit Shalom to Ihud*, p. 139.

23 Leon Magnes and Martin Buber, *Arab–Jewish Unity: Testimony before the Anglo-American Inquiry Commission for the Ihud (Union) Association by Magnes and Martin Buber* (London: Gollancz, 1947).

24 Ernst Simon, 'A Union of Two Nations', in *Palestine: Divided or United?* [Hebrew] (Jerusalem: Ihud Association, 1947), pp. 85–8.

25 See Simon's brief biography in Ernst Simon, *Fragments of Life: Construction in Destruction* [Hebrew] (Tel Aviv: Sifriat Ha-Poalim, 1986), pp. 29–56.

Notes to Chapter 6

1 On Ben-Gurion's relationship to binationalism, see for instance Yaacov Goldstein, 'David Ben-Gurion and the Binational Idea in Palestine', *Middle Eastern Studies* 24.4 (1988), pp. 460–72.

2 Quoted in David Zait, *Between Realism and Utopia: Constructivism, Common Organisation, and Binationalism in the Development of Hashomer Hatzair (1926–1942)* [Hebrew], MA thesis, Tel Aviv University, 1979, p. 314.

3 Ibid., p. 321.

4 Ibid., p. 327.

5 See Elkana Margalit, 'The Debate on the Idea of a Binational State within the Workers' Movement in Eretz Israel' [Hebrew], *Hatzionut*, D (1975), pp. 216–23.

6 Gorny, *Politics and Imagination* (ch. 1, n. 17), p. 93.

7 Hashomer Hatzair Workers' Party of Palestine, *The Case for a Binational Palestine: Binational Solution for Eretz Israel* (Tel Aviv: Executive Committee of the Hashomer Hatzair Workers' Party, 1946), p. 59.

8 Aharon Cohen, *Israel and the Arab World* (New York: Funk and Wagnalls, 1970), p. 343.

9 See Musa Budeiri, *The Palestine Communist Party 1919–1948: Arab and Jew in the Struggle for Internationalism* (London: Ithaca Press, 1979), pp. 58–81.

10 On this subject see Elie Rekhess, 'Jews and Arabs in the PCP: A Problem of Contemporary Arab–Palestinian Historiography' [Hebrew], *Hatzionut* 15 (1991), pp. 175–86, and Yehoshua Porat, 'The National Liberation League, Its Advent, Its Essence, and Its Dissolution (1943–1948)', *Hamizrah Hakhadash* 4.14 (1964), 354–66.

11 Kol HaAm [Voice of the People], 11 May 1944. See also Walter Laqueur, *POS, PCP, Maki: The Origins of the Communist Party in Israel* [Hebrew] (Tel Aviv: Am Oved, 1953), p. 195.

12 Quoted by Shmuel Dotan, *Red: The Communist Party in Eretz Israel* [Hebrew] (Kfar Saba: Shevna Hasofer, 1991), p. 471. On the PCP, see also Ran Greenstein, *Zionism and Its Discontents:*

A Century of Radical Dissent in Israel/Palestine (London: Pluto Press, 2014), pp. 50–103.

13 The socialist and anti-Zionist Bund party also decided to advocate a binational solution in Palestine. After the UN resolution on the partition plan, the Bund continued to advocate a single federal state, shared by Jews and Arabs. See 'August Grabski on the Anti-Zionism of the Bund (1947–1972)', *Workers' Liberty*, 10 August 2005.

14 See Avner Ben-Zaken, *Communism as Cultural Imperialism* [Hebrew] (Tel Aviv: Resling, 2006), p. 144.

15 See Henri Curiel, *On the Altar of Peace* [Hebrew] (Jerusalem: Mifras, 1982), p. 28.

16 Remarks by Andrei Gromyko to the UN Special Committee on Palestine, 14 May 1947. https://www.un.org/unispal/document /auto-insert-183337 (also quoted in Leon Zeavi, *Separated or Together* [Hebrew], Tel Aviv: Keter, 2005, p. 419).

17 On this subject, see *Laurent Rucker, Staline, Israël et les Juifs* (Paris: Presses Universitaires de France, 2015).

Notes to Chapter 7

1 [Trans.: see Uri Avnery, 'A Federation in Mideast?', *The Palestine Chronicle*, 26 November 2009: 'On 2 June 1957, my magazine, *HaOlam HaZeh*, published the first detailed plan for an independent Palestinian state that would come into being next to Israel. [. . .] According to the plan, the two states, the Israeli and the Palestinian, would then establish a federation. I thought that its proper name should be "the Jordan Union".' https://www. palestinechronicle.com/a-federation-in-mideast.]

2 [Trans.: Boaz Evron, *Atuna veUtz* [Hebrew] (*Athens and Oz*) (Binyamina: Nahar Press, 2010, n.p.).]

3 After the massacre, Rabbi Binyamin, already elderly but still a member of Ihud, wanted to go and live in the village, but was prevented from doing so by illness.

4 Uri Avnery, *Optimist*, vol. 1 [Hebrew] (Tel Aviv: Editions Yediot Aharonot, 2014), p. 513. As it happens, Avnery is discreet about

his enthusiasm for the military iconography of the Sinai War at the time when it took place. On this point, see Nitza Harel, *Without Fear, without Veils: Uri Avnery and HaOlam HaZeh* [Hebrew] (Jerusalem: Editions Magnes, 2006), pp. 86–7.

5 'Conversation between Etgar and the Founders of Semitic Action' [Hebrew], *Etgar*, 11 January 1962, pp. 4–6; translated here from French.

6 Avreny, *Optimist*, vol. 1, p. 519. In their introduction to the 'Hebrew Manifesto' (September 1958), the founders of Semitic Action emphasised that '[a]ny racial definition is erroneous, stupid and harmful. There is no pure race in the world, and any doctrine claiming that one race is preferable to another is a recipe for disaster. The Semitic family is a linguistic and cultural family – this is how it is treated in the scientific community. Semitic peoples are [. . .] peoples who speak Semitic languages or who are linked to Semitic cultures.'

7 In 1961, a group of conformist intellectuals founded a discussion group called At the Base. It was not until 1967 that the Movement for Peace and Security appeared – a group with a significant number of academics, but without any original ideological background.

8 Avnery says that he learned of this journal in 1941; see Uri Avnery, *The Seventh Day War* [Hebrew] (Tel Aviv: Daf Hadash, 1969), p. 147.

9 See A. G. Horon, *East and West: A History of Canaan and the Land of the Hebrews* [Hebrew] (Tel Aviv: Dvir, 2000), pp. 341–4 (quoted passages translated here from the French). It should be pointed out that, long before the new Israeli archaeologists, Horon was perhaps the first to regard the flight from Egypt as an invented story. See the message dated 23 December 1938 that he received from Jabotinsky: Jabotinsky Institute, Telegram 3896.

10 See the 1970 interview with Yonatan Ratosh in Ehud Ben-Ezer, *Unease in Zion* (ch. 3, n. 20), pp. 232–60.

11 Yonatan Ratosh was an influence on Yair Stern, the leader of the Lehi. Nathan Yalin-Mor admitted that '[a]t the time of Lehi I was

close to Canaanite ideas as regards the separation between the indigenous Hebrews and the Jews from exile, and I advocated the distinction of principle between Hebrew and Jew' (quoted in Yitzhak Paz, *The Legacy of Lehi* [Hebrew], Jerusalem: Herzl Institute, 2021, p. 161). See also Nathan Yalin-Mor, *Israel, Israel ... Histoire du groupe Stern* (Paris: Presses de la Renaissance, 1978).

12 See in particular the article by Benyamin Omri, 'Communication with the Palestinian People', *Etgar*, 29 April 1965.

13 Uri Avnery, 'The Jordan Union' [Hebrew], *HaOlam HaZeh*, 2 June 1957, pp. 3–6. Translated here from French.

14 Ibid.

15 The *Manifesto* was published by Semitic Action in September 1958.

16 Semitic Action, *The Hebrew Manifesto: Principles of Semitic Action*, 2nd edn (Tel Aviv: Central Committee, Semitic Action, 1959).

17 In his political autobiography *Athens and Oz*, Boaz Evron states: 'As the representative of Lehi in the United States [. . .] I came to the decisive conclusion that we and the Jews of the United States are not the same people and do not have the same objectives.' See Evron, *Athens and Oz*, p. 30.

18 'An Always Deceptive Renaissance' [Hebrew], *Haaretz*, 12 March 2010. On the differences between the 'Canaanites' and Semitic Action, see also Boaz Evron, 'The Time for Clarification Has Come' [Hebrew], *Etgar*, 26 November 1964.

19 *Etgar*, 5 October 1964. The fragment quoted is translated from French.

20 Uri Avnery, 'Jacob's Ladder', *Etgar*, 5 October 1964.

Notes to Chapter 8

1 Meron Benvenisti, *The Dream of the White Sabra: Autobiography of a Disillusionment* [Hebrew] (Tel Aviv: Keter, 2012), n.p.

2 [Trans.: Visit https://www.haaretz.com/israel-news/2018-04-19/ty-article-magazine/.premium/time-to-nix-the-two-state-solu

tion-and-stop-israels-apartheid/0000017f-e95b-df5f-a17f-fbdffa
5d0000.]

3 Refugees who tried to return to their homes at night during July
and August 1967 were killed. Those who tried to return during
the day were arrested and driven back to the other side of the
river Jordan. The author of this book, who at the time was posted
to Jericho as a reservist soldier, had to guard prisoners before
they were sent back across the river during the day.

4 *HaOlam HaZeh*, 12 July 1967. See also Uri Avnery, *Optimist*,
vol. 2 [Hebrew] (Tel Aviv: Editions Yediot Aharonot, 2014),
p. 114.

5 On 28 May 1951, during a parliamentary session on emergency
regulations, Menachem Begin declared: 'During the debate, I told
Mr Sharett, acting Head of Government and Foreign Minister,
that according to these emergency decrees, any soldier or police
officer can arrest anyone; they are therefore Nazi laws. In 1945,
when these measures were published, the Haganah broadcast an
announcement to the effect that anyone who dared to impose
them would be considered a criminal. This was an announcement of the 1945 Revolt Movement' (*Human Liberty, according
to the Conception of Menachem Begin* [Hebrew], Jerusalem:
Menachem Begin Heritage Center, 2014, p. 51).

6 Visit https://www.knesset.gov.il/process/docs/autonomy1977
.htm. This was no whim of the moment; at the opening of the
Herout (Freedom) Party Congress on 2 January 1977, Begin had
declared: 'The members of the Arab nation, which we recognise,
will have the free choice of receiving Israeli citizenship or retaining their previous citizenship. If they opt for Israeli citizenship,
they will enjoy the same rights as Jewish citizens, including the
right to vote for parliament. If they do not apply for our citizenship, they will have all the same rights as Jewish residents, except
the right to vote for the Knesset'. See Ziv Rabinovitz and Gerald
Steinberg, 'Menachem Begin's Self-Rule Plan, between Political
Realism and Ideology' [Hebrew], *Hamerhav Hatzibouri* 6 (2012),
p. 82.

7 The sixty-first session of the ninth Knesset, 28 December 1977: the government's announcement of Israel's peace plan; translated here from the French. See also D. Bar-Yossef (ed.), *Nationalism and Homeland in Menachem Begin's Vision* [Hebrew] (Tel Aviv: Begin Heritage Center, 2019), p. 130.

8 See Moshe Arens, 'Who's Afraid of a Binational State?', *Haaretz*, 14 May 2013, and Noam Sheizaf's column 'The Israeli Right's Surprising View of the Israeli–Palestinian Conflict', *Haaretz*, 15 July 2013.

9 One exception on the Israeli radical left was Michel Warschawski, author of *Israël–Palestine: Le défi binational* (Paris: Textuel, 2001).

10 Meron Benvenisti, *Slingshots and Batons: Territory, Jews and Arabs* [Hebrew] (Tel Aviv: Keter, 1988), p. 44.

11 Benvenisti, *The Dream of the White Sabra*, pp. 326–7.

12 Ari Shavit, 'Cry, the Beloved Two-State Solution', *Haaretz*, 6 August 2003; the next four quotations come from this article, which is now archived at https://jfjfp.com/cry-the-beloved-two -state-solution-hanegbi-benvenisti (see also https://www.haare tz.com/2003-08-06/ty-article/cry-the-beloved-two-state-solu tion/0000017f-db2e-d3ff-a7ff-fbae91590000).

13 Tony Judt, 'Israel: The Alternative', *New York Review of Books*, 23 October 2003.

14 Judt responded to his critics in a relatively conciliatory manner, in a new article published in the *New York Review of Books* on 4 December 2023. His criticism of 'his former chosen land' has since become more radical. See e.g. Tony Judt, 'It's Time to Grow Up' [Hebrew], *Haaretz*, 30 April 2006. The influence of Hans Kohn can be detected in his criticism of Jewish nationalism.

15 Gary Sussman, 'The Challenge to the Two-State Solution', *Middle East Report* 231 (2004). Reactions to Judt's text include Joel Kovel, *Overcoming Zionism: Creating a Single Democratic State in Israel/Palestine* (London: Pluto Press, 2007).

16 See e.g. Haim Bresheeth, 'Two States, Too Little, Too Late', *Al-Ahram Weekly*, 15 March 2004; Haim Bresheeth, 'Blueprint

for a One-State Movement: A Troubled History', in Noam Chomsky and Ilan Pappé (eds), *Gaza in Crisis* (London: Penguin, 2010), pp. 125–44.

17 See also Jeff Halper, *Decolonizing Israel, Liberating Palestine: Zionism, Settler Colonialism, and the Case for One Democratic State* (London: Pluto Press, 2019); Jeff Halper, 'The One State Declaration', *Electronic Intifada*, 29 November 2007.

18 Yehouda Shenhav, *Beyond the Two States Solution: A Jewish Political Essay* (London: Polity, 2011).

19 Avraham Burg, 'Toward a Single State for Two Peoples', *Haaretz*, 23 December 2011.

20 Avraham Burg, 'Oslo Is Dead, Where Do We Go from Here?', *Haaretz*, 26 March 2013. See also Avraham Burg, 'Should We Wish for Two States?', *Haaretz*, 28 December 2021.

21 Gideon Levy, 'Come, Binational State', *Haaretz*, 2 February 2014.

22 Gideon Levy, 'Binationalism Is Already Here, and Has Been for a Long Time', *Haaretz*, 5 October 2014; Gideon Levy, 'A Single State', *Haaretz*, 18 October 2015. See also 'Appel / Journée mondiale pour un monde sans mur le 9 novembre 2022', Association France Palestine Solidarité, 9 November 2022. https://www.france-palestine.org/Appel-Journee-mondiale-pour-un-monde-sans-mur-le-9-novembre-2022.

23 All these quotations are from 'A Land for All'. https://www.alandforall.org/english/?d=ltr.

24 Oren Yiftachel, 'Between One and Two: Debating the One-State Solution versus the Idea of an Israel–Palestine Confederation' [Hebrew], *Hamerhav Hatzibouri* 6 (2012), p. 155.

25 Oren Yiftachel, 'A Confederation Now', *Haaretz*, 20 August 2015.

26 Meron Rapoport, 'What Peace Do We Want?', *Haaretz*, 8 November 2017.

27 Uri Avnery, 'Confederation Is the Only Real Solution', *Haaretz*, 30 August 2015.

28 Menachem Mautner and Joel Singer, 'If We Reach a Solution to the Conflict, It Will Look like This', *Haaretz*, 21 October 2021.

29 For a critique of the confederation project, see Haim Bresheeth, 'The Long Con(federation): Understanding the Latest Attempts to Legitimize Israeli Colonization', *Mondoweiss* 32, 30 June 2022.

30 Peter Beinart, 'I No Longer Believe in a Jewish State', *New York Times*, 8 July 2020. See also his interview: Peter Beinart, 'I No Longer Believe in a Jewish State, but I Am Still a Zionist' [Hebrew], *Makor Rishon*, 19 July 2020.

31 Dan Shapiro was not the most Zionist-minded of American ambassadors. David Friedman, ambassador from 2017 to 2021 who openly supported the settlements, surpassed him in this. From 2000 to the present day, the seven American ambassadors to Israel have included five Jews.

32 Ian Lustick, *Paradigm Lost: From Two-State Solution to One-State Reality* (Philadelphia: University of Pennsylvania Press, 2019).

33 Ian Lustick, 'Two-State Illusion', *New York Times*, 14 September 2013.

34 Omri Boehm, *Haifa Republic: A Democratic Future for Israel* (New York: New York Review of Books, 2021). See also Omri Boehm, 'Bauer, Equality Is Not Anti-Semitism', *Haaretz*, 25 September 2021.

35 See Avraham B. Yehoshua, 'Who Is Israeli?', *Haaretz*, 13 September 2013.

36 See Avraham B. Yehoshua, 'Pluriculturalisme: Enclaves ou dialogue', in *Taking the Homeland* [Hebrew] (Tel Aviv: Hakibboutz Hameuchad, 2008), pp. 83–98; Avraham B. Yehoshua, 'Israel to the Israelis', *Haaretz*, 10 June 2009.

37 See Avraham B. Yehoshua, 'Introduction to a Binational State', *Haaretz*, 31 December 2011; Avraham B. Yehoshua, 'The Palestinians Are Also Guilty', *Haaretz*, 23 November 2014.

38 Avraham B. Yehoshua, 'Escape from a Frozen Mind', *Haaretz*, 8 October 2015.

39 Avraham B. Yehoshua, 'Diminishing the Harmfulness of the Israeli Occupation', *Haaretz*, 29 December 2016.

40 Avraham B. Yehoshua, 'The Time Has Come to Abandon the

Two-State Project', *Haaretz*, 12 April 2018. See also Nathalie Hamou, 'Israël–Palestine: L'écrivain Avraham B. Yehoshua réaffirme la piste d'un état binational', *Télérama*, 24 May 18.

41 Avraham B. Yehoshua, 'Plan for Blocking Apartheid', *Haaretz*, 16 April 2018.

Notes to Chapter 9

1 Sari Nusseibeh, as quoted in an interview with Akiva Eldar, 'We Are Running Out of Time for a Two-State Solution', *Haaretz*, 14 August 2008. https://www.haaretz.com/2008-08-14/ty-artic le/we-are-running-out-of-time-for-a-two-state-solution/000001 7f-e157-d38f-a57f-e757e1bb0000.

2 Outside Palestine, certain Arabs with proto-nationalist and Judeophobe tendencies exploited the rise of Zionist colonisation in the second half of the 1940s, using it to denounce Jews and sometimes to incite riots against them.

3 George Antonius, *The Arab Awakening: The Story of the Arab National Movement* (London: Routledge, 2010), pp. 545–6. This text was written after the July 1938 Conference in Evian, which examined the refugee situation and where all western countries refused to increase their admission quotas for Jews who wanted to escape Nazism. Mohamed Hassanein Heikal, a famous Egyptian journalist and politician, also criticised Europe's attitude to the persecution of Jews.

4 Ben-Gurion, *My Talks with Arab Leaders* (ch. 5, n. 19), p. 52.

5 See Elie Osherov, 'Was There an Arab Binationalism? Toward a History of Binationalism Seen from the Other Side' [Hebrew], *Israel* 27–8 (2021), pp. 165–86.

6 See Aharon Cohen, *Israel and the Arab World* [Hebrew], (New York: Funk & Wagnalls, 1970), pp. 351–5; Aharon Cohen, *Why Was Fawzi Al-Husseini Assassinated?* [Hebrew] (Eretz Israel: Hashomer Hatzair, 1947). Aharon Cohen was a signatory to the agreement, along with Ernst Simon and a few others.

7 Quoted in Cohen, *Why Was Fawzi Al-Husseini Assassinated*, p. 331. After the murder Leon Magnes wrote in a letter to the *New*

York Times: 'This is the voice of an Arab brother, the authentic voice of our common Semitic tradition' (Goren, *Dissenter in Zion* (ch. 5, n. 5), p. 455). Sami Taha, a moderate and popular workers' leader in Haifa, had also been assassinated earlier, probably on the orders of Mufti Haj Amin Al-Husseini.

8 'The Palestinian Arabs did not want Jewish settlements in their "state" after the prospective Israeli withdrawal (though, of course, they saw nothing wrong with the existence of dozens of Arab villages and towns in Israel proper)' (Benny Morris, *One State, Two States: Resolving the Israel/Palestine Conflict*, New Haven, CT: Yale University Press, 2009, p. 163). The historian paid his readers the courtesy of not referring to the Arab settlements in Israel as 'colonies', which date back to the Muslim conquest of the seventh century.

9 Interview with Edward Said on the Progressive Radio Network station in 1999. See also Edward Said, 'The One-State Solution', *New York Times*, 10 January 1999. Shortly before this, Jenab Tutunji had suggested the binational idea as an option preferable to the stuttering and prevarication of the Oslo talks; see Jenab Tutunji, 'A Binational State in Palestine', *International Affairs* 73 (1997), pp. 31–58.

10 Lama Abu-Odeh, 'The Case for Binationalism', *Boston Review*, 12 January 2001, and Ghada Karmi, 'A Secular Democratic State in Historical Palestine: An Idea Whose Time Has Come?', *Al Adab*, July 2002. See also Ghada Karmi, 'The One-State Solution: An Alternative Vision for Israeli–Palestinian Peace', *Journal of Palestine Studies* 40.2 (2011), pp. 62–76; Ghada Karmi, *One State: The Only Democratic Future for Palestine-Israel* (London: Pluto Press, 2023).

11 Ahmad Samih Khalidi, 'A One-State Solution', *Guardian*, 29 September 2003.

12 Omar Barghouti, 'Relative Humanity: The Fundamental Obstacle to a One-State Solution in Historic Palestine', *Electronic Intifada*, 6 January 2004.

13 Ali Abunimah, *One Country: A Bold Proposal to End the Israeli–*

Palestinian Impasse (New York: Metropolitan Books, 2006). Alongside these two intellectuals one should mention Leila Farsakh, also the daughter of refugees: she grew up in Jordan and has been appointed professor of political science at Harvard. In March 2007 she published an article in *Le Monde Diplomatique* entitled 'Le Temps est venu d'un état binational' ('The Time Has Come for a Binational State'). More recently she edited the volume *Rethinking Statehood in Palestine: Self-Determination and Decolonization beyond Partition* (Berkeley: University of California Press, 2021).

14 The principle of a single state as the most plausible solution to the conflict has also been advocated by Virginia Tilley, *The One-State Solution* (Ann Arbor: University of Michigan Press, 2005).

15 As'ad Ghanem, 'A Binational Palestine–Israeli State across the Whole Territory of Palestine/Eretz Israel, and the Status of Arabs in Israel within such a Framework', in Sara Ozacky-Lazar, Ilan Pappé, and Assad Ghanem (eds), *Seven Ways: Theoretical Options for the Status of Arabs in Israel* [Hebrew] (Givat Haviva: Institute for Peace Studies, 1999), pp. 271–303. See also As'ad Ghanem, 'The Only Solution: One Egalitarian, Bi-national State', *News from Within* 13.1 (January 1997), pp. 12–15.

16 Ghanem, 'A Binational Palestine–Israeli State', p. 282.

17 See in particular As'ad Ghanem, 'The Binational Idea in Palestine and Israel: Historical Roots and Contemporary Debate', *Journal of Holy Land and Palestine Studies*, 1 September 2002, pp. 61–84; As'ad Ghanem and Dan Bavly, 'Israelis, Palestinians, and the Solution of a National State', in A. Lavi, I. Rone, and E. Fishman (eds), *Twenty-Five Years of the Oslo Process* [Hebrew] (Jerusalem: Carmel, 2019), pp. 591–602.

18 Azmi Bishara, 'The Citizen Azmi', *Haaretz*, 25 November 2002. Bishara's favouring of the binational paradigm can also be seen in an earlier interview, with Graham Usher: Azmi Bishara, 'Bantustanisation or Bi-nationalism? An Interview with Azmi Bishara', *Race & Class* 37.2 (1995). See also Azmi Bishara,

'Bridging the Green Line: The PA, Israeli Arabs, and Final Status: An Interview with Azmi Bishara', *Journal of Palestine Studies* 26.3 (1997), p. 73.

19 The parlament member Jamal Zahalka, Azmi Bishara's successor as leader of Balad, has expressed similar ideas. See Jamal Zahalka, 'Erasing the Idea of Two States', *Maariv*, 8 December 2007.

20 See Mohammad Dahleh, 'Are Palestinians on the Road to Independence?', *IEMed Mediterranean Yearbook*, 2017, pp. 38–43, and Ari Shavit, 'Mohammad and Me', *Haaretz*, 31 December 2002. See also 'Interviews with Supporters of One Democratic State', *Icahd UK*, 10 March 2021. https://icahd.org /2021/03/10/interviews-with-supporters-of-one-democratic-sta te.

21 Michal Sela, 'Nusseibeh: Yes to Annexation', *Koteret Rashit*, 13 November 1985.

22 Ibid.

23 Sari Nusseibeh, *No Trumpets, No Drums: A Two-State Solution of the Israeli-Palestinian Conflict* (New York: Hill & Wang, 1991).

24 See Akiva Eldar, 'We Are Running Out of Time for a Two-State Solution' and 'Palestinians Revive Idea of One-State Solution', *Toronto Star*, 15 September 2008 (both).

Notes to Chapter 10

1 Translated by Linda Zisquit; visit https://kavvanah.blog/2010/07 /20/yehuda-amichai-on-jerusalem.

2 Cecil Hourani, 'The Moment of Truth: Towards a Middle East Dialogue', *Encounter* 29.5 (1967), n.p.

3 He formally expressed his feelings as follows: 'I am one of those who do not want to annex 7.1 million Palestinians as Israeli citizens. [. . .] In the present circumstances, between a bi-national solution and a Jewish state, I prefer a Jewish state. The implementation of sovereignty over the whole of the Eretz Israel of the Mandate means that we will have 7.1 million Palestinians as citizens of the State of Israel. It would perhaps be a Jewish state

in terms of its borders, but it would be binational in its composition, demography, and democracy' (as quoted in Jacques Neriah, *Entre Rabin et Arafat*, Paris: VA Éditions, 2018, n.p.).

4 Much later, when I asked – in an impromptu conversation with Eitan Haber, Yitzhak Rabin's chief of staff at the time – why Rabin had not grasped the opportunity to evict the settlement in order to move the peace negotiations forward, Haber made a gesture of helplessness, then added that they had lacked the courage.

5 [Trans.: e.g. https://www.jwire.com.au/prime-minister-bennett-and-president-isaac-herzog-light-first-candles.]

6 The use of the term 'Mizrahim' to designate Arabic-speaking immigrants may seem rather arbitrary, generalising, and misleading. The differences in political sensitivity between those from Morocco and Iraq and the descendants of Sephardic Jews in Palestine are significant. Unfortunately this is not the place to develop the subject.

7 For a critical analysis of the lobby, see John Mearsheimer and Stephen Walt, *The Israel Lobby and US Foreign Policy* (New York: Farrar, Straus and Giroux, 2007).

8 [Trans: e.g. https://stephensizer.com/2018/03/the-bride-and-the-dowry-israel-jordan-and-the-palestinians-in-the-aftermath-of-the-june-1967-war-avi-raz.]

9 When Rabbis Eliezer Waldman and Moshe Levinger, leaders of the settlers, came to ask for government authorisation to establish a settlement in Hebron in 1967, they were reprimanded by Yigal Allon, the minister of labour at the time: 'Are you crazy? You want government authorization? This is not how Zionism works. We have never asked for authorization from the official institutions, instead, we first established facts on the ground and afterward we asked for authorization. If we had not done it this way, Ginosar and Hanita would not have been established.' As quoted in the interview with Rabbi Eliezer Waldman, 'The First Steps of a Renewed Heaven', *Sovereignty: A Political Journal* 6 (November 2015), pp. 12–13, here 13.

10 The segregation of the indigenous population imposed by European settlers did not begin in 1948; it had existed long before, in various forms. On this subject, see Yehonatan Alsheh, 'The Apartheid Paradigm: History, Politics and Strategy', in I. Saban and R. Zreik (eds), *Law, Minority and National Conflict* [Hebrew] (Tel Aviv: Tel Aviv University Faculty of Law, 2017), pp. 151–83, and also Honaida Ghanim, 'Pas vraiment apartheid: La dynamique entre colonialisme d'implantation et occupation militaire', *L'Espace publique* 6 (2012), pp. 95–112.

11 On 1948 and the Nakba, see Benny Morris, *The Birth of the Palestinian Refugee Problem* (Cambridge: Cambridge University Press, 1989), and also Ilan Pappé, *The Ethnic Cleansing of Palestine* (London: Oneworld, 2007).

12 Theodor Herzl, *Jewish Affairs: Diary*, vol. A [Hebrew] (Jerusalem: Mossad Bialik, 1997), pp. 19–120.

13 Quoted in Benny Morris, *Righteous Victims: A History of the Zionist-Arab Conflict* (New York: Vintage, 2001), p. 144. Reacting a year earlier to the Peel Commission's partition plan, Ben-Gurion wrote to his son: '[A] Jewish state in part [of Palestine] is not an end, but a beginning. [. . .] [It] will serve as a very potent lever in our historical efforts to redeem the whole country' (ibid., p. 138).

14 Ari Shavit, 'Survival of the Fittest: An Interview with Benny Morris' (original Hebrew title 'Waiting for the Barbarians'), *Haaretz Friday Magazine*, 9 January 2004, pp. 4–17.

15 In June 1950, Moshe Dayan, then commander of the southern zone, declared: 'We must consider that the fate of the 170,000 Arabs who remained in the country has not yet been decided. I hope that in the next few years there may still be an opportunity to transfer these Arabs out of Israel' (quoted in Eric Ariel, 'Secret History of the Transfer', *Haaretz*, 27 November 2013). On the events at Kafr Qassim, see Adam Raz, *The Kafr Qassim Massacre: A Political Biography* [Hebrew] (Jerusalem: Carmel, 2018).

16 The Palestinian demand for a full 'right of return' for all 1948 refugees and their descendants (around 5 million people) is

one of the stumbling blocks to any rapprochement. The Israelis consider that this demand would turn them into a minority and would deny their right to an autonomous existence within any future common framework. Criticism of the right of return must, of course, be accompanied by criticism of the Jewish law of return in its current form. Serious proposals for compromise on these issues have made little progress to date. Meanwhile, a third generation of refugee children continues to live in impoverished conditions, particularly in Gaza and Lebanon.

17 By contrast, any Jewish Israeli citizen can marry anyone he or she wishes and the spouse will immediately become a citizen. The 'future vision' documents provide a fascinating testimony to the state of mind of the Palestinian–Israeli intelligentsia at the beginning of the twenty-first century. See S. Ozacky-Lazar and M. Kabha (eds), *Between Vision and Reality: The Vision Papers of Arabs in Israel, 2006–2007* [Hebrew] (Jerusalem: Civic Accord Forum, 2008).

Note to Afterword

1 Quoted in Ronald W. Clark, *Einstein: The Life and Times* (New York: World Publishing Co., 1971), p. 402.

Index

increase of influence in
artistic and literary circles
123
phenomena contributing to
birth of 122–3
popularity of 124
seeking of alliances with
cultural/religious
minorities 123
and Semitic Action 120–4
term and history 120–2
wanting to assimilate Arabs
into Hebrew national
culture 124
Canada 13, 17, 104, 153
cantonisation 149
catastrophes 191
Central and Eastern Europe
13–14, 59
Christians
and Judaism 37, 122, 162
civil nationalism 59
Cohen, Aharon 103
Israel and the Arab World
106
Cohen, Eliza 152
colonisation 1–2, 4, 17, 18–19,
101, 137, 141, 191–2, 197
Buber on 66, 67, 70, 71
expansion of Israeli viii, 20,
141–2, 146, 148, 169, 187
Israeli Jews' view of 188–90
justification of, by Israelis 5, 7,
67, 183
and Orthodox clerics 185–6

view of, by Israeli middle class
189
West Prussian 41–2
Comintern 107
dissolution of (1943) 111
Committee of University
Presidents 186
communism
in Israel *see* Israeli
Communist Party (Maki)
in Palestine *see* PCP
Communist International 121
community federalism 104–5
'concordance democracies' 150
confederation/confederalists
80, 105, 128, 133, 143, 148,
152–5, 197, 198
Conference of American
Zionists (1944) 77
cultural Zionism 53–4
Curiel, Henri 111
Czechoslovakia 13, 59

Dahleh, Mohammad 175
Danziger, Yitzhak 124
Darwish, Mahmoud 1, 168, 170,
177
'Identity Card' 9–10
Dayan, Moshe x, 77, 180
d'Azeglio, Massimo 12–13
Deir Yassin massacre (1948) 79
democracy
concordance 150
and nationalism 11–12
secular 148–9, 197, 198